"...The cover is perhaps the clearest representation of what Roberts' book really is: a clearly-communicated, often satirical, and at some points very stern, no-nonsense account of why home prices soared, fomenting the nation's housing bubble, leaving couples across the nation struggling to stay afloat on their mortgages.

...In a market already flooded with books on the housing crisis, The Great Housing Bubble scores points by focusing on explanation and less on inundating a reader with the sort of heavy-handed quantitative analysis that only a few economists can love. While some figures are necessary, the book's message is never bogged down.

Instead, Roberts presents multiple facets of the real estate market by taking the reader through the fundamentals and broad concepts of real estate economics. He then weaves psychology-based theories with structural factors of the bubble to offer a deeper, more detailed insight into how and why the housing bubble inflated and burst the way it did...."

Paul Jackson – *CEO, Housing Wire Magazine and HousingWire.com*

"A very well-written and thoughtful analysis of what went wrong in the housing world and how we can avoid this problem in the future. Lawrence Roberts has a great understanding of the subject and does an excellent job communicating his ideas to the reader."

Jim Randel – *Best-selling author, Confessions of a Real Estate Entrepreneur*

"The Great Housing Bubble is a fantastic resource for anyone looking to understand why home prices fell. The writing has exceptional depth and detail, and it is presented in an engaging and easy-to-understand manner. It is destined to be the standard by which other books on the subject will be measured. It is the first book written after prices peaked, and it is the first in the genre to detail the psychological factors that are arguably more important for understanding the housing bubble. There have been a number of books written while prices were rising that used measures of price relative to historic norms and sounded the alarm of an impending market crash. Economic statistics and technical, measurable factors show what people did, but they do not explain why they did it. The Great Housing Bubble analyzes not only what happened; it explains why it happened.

Morgan Brown – *The Great Loan Blog*

"The author does an excellent job in showing how various commercial and investment banks sought to create a speculative market for home loans by the process of securitization. The main tool was collateralized debt obligations

(CDO'S).The idea is purely speculative since real estate is a nonliquid durable asset. The bundling and selling of trillions of dollars worth of the subprime backed bonds that were not only highly risky, but of uncertain value, created the bubble that deflated just as every other banker financed, speculative bubble has deflated in world history.

The author does a good job in demonstrating that low interest rates were not the cause of the problem. The main cause of the problem was the loan practices of various financial institutions that threw overboard their own clearly specified creditworthiness criteria and standards for borrowers seeking loans."

Michael Emmett Brady – *PhD Economics*

"...the author has a background in real estate that's far removed from the sales process, he's able to step back and provide the sort of unemotional, macroeconomic overview that seems quite atypical for a guide to investing in real estate.

...Filled with 64 exhibits, 146 footnotes and a nine-page bibliography of source material, "The Great Housing Bubble" is probably not a casual read during a day at the pool or the beach. But for real estate professionals wanting to educate themselves or their clients on how to successfully build wealth through the buying and selling of real property, this author has a lot to teach."

Patrick S. Duffy – *Principal with MetroIntelligence Real Estate Advisors and author of The Housing Chronicles Blog.*

"The author, Larry Roberts, is best known for his daily posts as IrvineRenter on the Irvine Housing Blog. Long before Lehman crashed, Fannie Mae was taken over, and even before home prices were dropping nationally, he was one of the few voices presenting real information on the housing bubble.

The author's background is in new housing development in Southern California. It was a good start to understanding how things worked. Supplemented by knowledge from countless posters at the housing blog, he has been able to show why home prices couldn't stay elevated. Price to income ratios, price to rent ratios, and other factors detailed in the book showed how far out of line prices had become by 2006. A full year before house prices started to crash, he was predicting it, and many of the crash's details. While some people are permanently bullish or bearish on housing, the best are able to understand and explain the mechanisms, tell you what will happen in what sequence.

The Great Housing Bubble is an excellent read, and an important one."

Brian Whitworth – *Principal, FinancialPatents.com*

THE GREAT HOUSING BUBBLE

Why Did House Prices Fall?

Lawrence Roberts

Published by Monterey Cypress Publishing, a division of Monterey Cypress, LLC
5348 Vegas Drive, #44
Las Vegas, NV 89108

MontereyCypressLLC@gmail.com

ISBN: 0-615-22693-0
EAN-13: 978-0-615-22693-4

The author's work can also be found at the Irvine Housing Blog where he has been the primary writer since February of 2007.

www.irvinehousingblog.com

The Irvine Housing Blog has become noted for its unique delivery of real estate market analysis in Slate Magazine, the Washington Post, and Newsweek Magazine. The blog reaches several thousand readers each day.

The author may be contacted at:

IrvineRenter@IrvineHousingBlog.com

To
Michelle and James

ACKNOWLEDGEMENTS

I would like to thank the following people without whom this book would have never been published:

Profette-Anonymous published author, copy editor and support person. Without her encouragement I would not have believed people would be interested in my writing.

Brian Whitworth-Financial researcher and content editor. With his review, challenges to the basic assumptions, and review of the academic literature supporting the thesis, this book was elevated from a series of unsupported opinions to a well-researched and well-documented literary work.

Zovall-Anonymous owner of the Irvine Housing Blog who asked me to write for him in early 2007. If this had not happened, the framework of this book would never have been written.

Sean O'Daniels-Graphic artist whose creative cover design captured the essence of the housing bubble.

Tom Rollinger-Successful hedge fund manager, close friend and great networker who convinced me to finish the book by showing me how it could be marketed effectively.

Sheri Langerman-An early proofreader and editor. Her suggestions and insights helped shape the final text.

Rik Osmer-A tireless supporter, proofreader, and former mortgage broker whose insights into the workings of the mortgage industry greater increased my understanding of the mechanics of the housing bubble.

Cayci Robold-Final proofreader and editor. She caught the mistakes the rest of us missed. Her attention to detail is remarkable.

Richard May-His blog, colored by his irreverent sense of humor, was my inspiration to write about this subject in the public realm.

The Bubble Bloggers-The community of concerned citizens who have been loudly proclaiming the existence of the housing bubble in the noble cause of saving buyers from financial destruction.

The Irvine Housing Blog Community-The regular readers and astute observers on the Irvine Housing Blog have been an ongoing support group with constant encouragement and a feverish desire to see this book in print. This group, more than any other, has acted a crucible burning away the irrelevancies with their feedback and leaving a product which addresses the core of the housing bubble.

TABLE OF CONTENTS

LIST OF EQUATIONS, TABLES AND FIGURES

Preface

I work as a development consultant in the real estate industry in Southern California. My education and experience has acquainted me with a variety of real estate markets, but residential real estate is the one with which I am most familiar. I am not a realtor or a mortgage broker, and my livelihood, though dependent upon the real estate industry, it is not dependent upon facilitating a home-sale transaction. What is presented here is both historical account and unbiased analysis. My observations of the residential real estate market are not tainted by any need or desire to convince anyone they should buy a house. In fact, one of my motivations for writing about the Great Housing Bubble is to convince people *not* to buy a house when prices are inflated and save them from financial ruin. It saddens me to watch homebuyers get caught up in the bubble mythology and enter into a financial transaction that will have a strongly negative impact on their financial lives. People who have already made that decision cannot be helped except at the expense of a naïve buyer. Sellers have the marketing machine of the National Association of Realtors to help them. Buyers have few sources of unbiased information to assist their decision. Part of the purpose of this writing is to educate both buyers and sellers on the realities of the residential real estate market.

One of the difficulties of writing a book on the Great Housing Bubble in 2008 is that the bubble has not played itself out yet. There is a necessary change in tense required when speaking of events prior to 2008 and those projected to occur during and after 2008. Someone reading this in 5 years may look back on it as history, but for those of us living it now, it is a history not yet lived. Much of what is presented here may not come to pass, or it may not happen in the way hypothesized in this book. History will judge whether this is prescient, or if it is "a tale told by an idiot, full of sound and fury, signifying nothing." [1]

Irvine Housing Blog

I discovered Real Estate Bubble Blogs in November of 2006. [2] Many were in existence much earlier, but I was not a big reader of blogs prior to this time. I first discovered the Irvine Housing Blog when my wife found a series of interesting posts on people who were attempting to sell properties for a quick profit (flipping,) and they were getting burned. I was quickly hooked. From the blogroll (links to other blogs) I was able to locate several other bubble blogs, and I quickly became a regular reader and commenter on several blogs in this community.

In February of 2007, I was asked to write for the Irvine Housing Blog. I had a great deal of pent-up energy for writing about the housing bubble. Over the months that followed I wrote a series of analysis posts which became the structure of this book. Daniel Gross, a freelance writer published in Slate Magazine, the Washington Post and Newsweek, characterized the writing as follows (Gross, The Real Morons of Orange County, 2007): "IrvineHousingblog, brilliantly drives home the same point with daily dispatches. The blog is a guide to the seventh circle of real estate hell–people who buy houses on spec with no money down. A typical entry chronicles the purchase price, tracks down the amount of debt on the property, and then calculates how much each party–the buyer, the first mortgage holder, the second mortgage holder–stands to lose assuming the seller receives the asking price."

The Reservoir of Schadenfreude

The readers of the Irvine Housing Blog have a voracious appetite for profiles of losing properties. They are not alone. Why do people get so much pleasure from seeing would-be real estate moguls lose a great deal of money? I can think of no other human endeavor that has engendered so much pleasure in the misfortune of others by otherwise caring, compassionate people. In my opinion, the outpouring of schadenfreude we are seeing as the housing bubble deflates is a mixture of Greek tragedy and bad karma. In short, bubble participants should have seen it coming, and they are getting what they deserve.

Schadenfreude is not a spiritually uplifting emotional response. Most religious traditions would counsel us against it. In Buddhist teaching, people are taught to cultivate feelings of compassion for the misfortune of others–feeling empathy and sadness for the slings and arrows of outrageous fortune when they impact another. [3] The near enemy of compassion is pity: it masquerades as compassion, but it has an element of separateness which detracts from the sense of Oneness with all things. Joy is good: Sympathetic joy, the joy in the happiness of another, is another pillar of a spiritual existence; however, joy in the misfortune of another–schadenfreude–is not a skillful behavior leading to happiness. Even knowing that, many of us feel this joy anyway. Why is that?

I recognized financing terms were creating artificially high prices early on. By 2004, I was telling people I knew that this was a problem which would cause a market crash. Most people looked at me like I was crazy. "Real estate always goes up," I was told. "The government would never allow prices to crash," I was told. "If you do not buy now you will be priced out forever," I was told. This is the intoxicated language of real estate junkies who have overdosed on the real-estate-appreciation kool aid. If these statements had been offered in a defensive manner of someone who is being made to realize they made a serious mistake, I could have felt sympathy for them; I would have been able to disarm their defensiveness and helped them see the light. However, what I generally got was a smug assuredness of someone who truly believed he was right and I was wrong; not just that I was wrong; I was a stupid, cowardly fool who did not have the brains or the bravery to take the free money being given out. This was particularly surprising given my line of work. It was as if a patient after getting a diagnosis of cancer told the doctor that the physician did not understand the tissue growth was a natural, healthy process. The buyers caught up in the Great Housing Bubble did not recognize the financial cancer even when an expert in the field told them how dangerous it was.

During the bubble rally, those of us who chose not to participate were labeled as "bitter renters." It was suggested we were envious of the good fortune of homeowners as their property values rose, as they took on insane amounts of debt, and as they blithely financed a lifestyle well beyond their means. This was undoubtedly true for some, but in my opinion, this is not the primary reason so many derive so much pleasure from the misfortune of those now suffering from declining property values. These same people who chided us for being envious actually wanted us to be envious: they wanted us to know they were the winners in our competitive society; they wanted us to view them as superior. This act of putting themselves above us created a separation which prevented us from feeling sympathetic joy for their good fortune, and it prevented us from feeling compassion for them when they fell.

In our collective unconscious which manifests in our dreams and our mythology, water is often symbolic of our emotions or our emotional state. Have you noticed people are often categorized as deep or shallow? If you are in debt you often feel "underwater." Anger is much like water: if not given an outlet, it will fill a reservoir until it reaches a breaking point and is expressed in a flood of emotional rage. Each encounter with a pathologic, kool-aid-drinking housing bull during the bubble rally has added to this reservoir, and reveling in failed flips is an outlet for this pool of toxic emotional waste.

There is an element of tragedy in every disaster, but financial bubbles are some of the most interesting because they are completely man made. They are created by the accumulation of individual decisions of buyers who are motivated by greed, foolish pride, and a false sense of security. Each of these people should have known better. Many of them were warned of their impending doom by those who saw trouble brewing, and yet, many chose to go down the path to the Dark Side. Newton's Third Law states, "For every action, there is an equal and opposite reaction." The Law of Karma states, "For every event that occurs, there will follow another event whose existence was caused by the first, and this second event will be pleasant or unpleasant according as its cause was skillful or unskillful." It became obvious as the crash began; the behavior of buyers during the bubble rally was not skillful. Whether it is Newton's Third Law, Karma, or a Calvinist form of retributive justice, as this bubble deflates, many of the participants in this bubble are about to experience a great deal of hardship. Like many others, I will enjoy their suffering until my reservoir of schadenfreude is emptied. For the sake of my own personal spiritual well being, I hope this happens soon so I can regain my normal emotional balance and rekindle my feelings of compassion for my fellow human beings.

Introduction

Why did house prices fall? This is the fundamental question to most Americans, and to those who lent them money. Most homeowners did not care why residential real estate prices rose; they assumed prices always rose, and they should simply enjoy their good fortune. It was not until prices began to fall that people were left searching for answers. This book examines the causes of the breathtaking rise in prices and the catastrophic fall that ensued to answer the question on every homeowner's mind: "Why did house prices fall?"

Even though the decline is nowhere near over in 2008, already the Great Housing Bubble witnessed the largest decline in house prices since the Great Depression. The asset bubble for the Great Depression was the stock market while the asset bubble for the Great Housing Bubble was residential real estate. The title of the book, the Great Housing Bubble, is an allusion to the Great Depression of the 1930s. Both of these dramatic events were the result of a wild expansion of credit and a subsequent crash in asset prices that stressed the banking system and led to a dramatic economic slowdown. [4]

The book is arranged into 10 chapters. The first 4 chapters provide background information and are used to define terms and provide a broad conceptual understanding of residential real estate economics, chapters 5 through 8 discuss the structural and psychological factors that inflated and deflated the bubble, and the final two chapters describe methods of coping with the housing bubble. Chapter 1 is a general description of financial bubbles as a psychological phenomenon and the unique beliefs of residential real estate bubbles. Chapter 2 details the financing environment surrounding residential real estate. It defines and categorizes the types of borrowers and the types of loan programs available, and it illustrates how financing impacts the wealth of individual owners and the economy as a whole. Chapter 3 summarizes the mathematics determining the value of residential real estate and examines issues pertaining to the rent-versus-own decision, and chapter 4 delves into the fine points of determining the value of individual lots and raw land. Chapter 5 illuminates the credit bubble (which was largely responsible for the real estate bubble) with rigorous detail on the structure of the secondary mortgage market and how the expansion of credit through this market inflated the housing bubble. Chapter 6 looks at the housing bubble, its various measurements, and explains why the bubble burst. Chapter 7 is a review of the psychology of real estate bubbles. Financial bubbles are primarily psychological phenomenon, and the various aspects of investor psychology are explored to see how they shape the market. Chapter 8 is a projection of future house prices based on the data and conditions as they existed in early 2008. Chapter 9 contains advice for both sellers and buyers who plan to be active while prices are declining. Chapter 10 is a review of the causes of the bubble and proposals for reforms to prevent residential real estate bubbles from happening again.

The examples and data used in the analysis are national in scope, and they are also focused on the local residential real estate market in Irvine, California. The Great Housing Bubble is a national phenomenon; however, the national statistics soften the extremes and make the rise and fall look less remarkable. In some local markets, the price changes are truly extraordinary, and it is through examining these markets that the story of the bubble is best told. A fine exemplar of the Great Housing Bubble is Irvine, California. Irvine is a large, master-planned community of over 200,000 residents. The high incomes of Irvine residents are reflected in the rental rates for properties which are consistently near the highest in the nation. High incomes and rents translate into high real estate prices, even at the bottom of down cycles. When reviewing the properties in Irvine and the price tags attached to them, it is not uncommon for outsiders to believe a decimal point has been misplaced. The lessons learned from the Irvine experience are universal. Though many the examples from this work focus on Irvine, this is a book about the Great Housing Bubble of which Irvine was both a catalyst and one of its biggest participants.

Table 1: Top Subprime Lenders 2006

Rank	Lender	Market Share %
1	Wells Fargo	13.0%
2	HSBC Finance	8.3%
3	New Century	8.1%
4	Countrywide Financial	6.3%
5	CitiMortgage	5.9%
6	WMC Mortgage	5.2%
7	Fremont Investment	5.0%
8	Ameriquest	4.6%
9	Option One	4.5%
10	First Franklin	4.3%
11	Washington Mutual	4.2%
12	Residential Funding	3.4%
13	Aegis Mortgage	2.7%
14	American General	2.4%
15	Accredited Lenders	2.3%
	Top 15 Lenders	80.2%

Source: Inside B&C Lending

INTRODUCTION

The epicenter of the Great Housing Bubble is located in Irvine, California. One of the primary causes of the bubble was the lowering of lending standards and the extension of credit to people who could not handle the responsibility: Subprime borrowers. The word "subprime" has become indelibly linked to the Great Housing Bubble. It is one of the causal factors that make the bubble unique, and the collapse of subprime is widely regarded as the pin-prick which began the bubble's deflation. Irvine, California, is the center of the subprime universe. Three of the top ten subprime lenders, New Century, Ameriquest, and Option One, are (or were) headquartered in Irvine. Most subprime lenders have processing offices in Irvine due to the large number of trained personnel living in the area. Irvine's New Century Financial, formerly the second largest subprime operator, is heralded as the poster child of the bubble. The company name "New Century" implies a new era and a new paradigm. It embodies the fallacious beliefs and ideas that inflated the Great Housing Bubble.

Volatility in real estate prices is not new to California. During the 1970's, real estate prices detached from typical valuations of three-times yearly income seen in the rest of the country. Once residents realized they could push up prices in their real estate markets to dizzying heights, they have been doing it ever since. Greed springs eternal. The Great Housing Bubble is the third such bubble in the last 30 years, and it is the largest of all. The detachment from traditional measures of valuation was so extreme that it is difficult for many to comprehend. Each time the bubble bursts, the crash is incorrectly blamed on some outside force, and each time the rally is thought to be different than the rally in previous cycles. It never is.

What is a Bubble?

A financial bubble is a temporary situation where asset prices become elevated beyond any realistic fundamental valuations because the general public believes current pricing is justified by probable future price increases. If this belief is widespread enough to cause significant numbers of people to purchase the asset at inflated prices, then prices will continue to rise. This will convince even more people that prices will continue to rise. This facilitates even more buying. Once initiated, this reaction is self-sustaining, and the phenomenon is entirely psychological. When the pool of buyers is exhausted and the volume of buying declines, prices stop rising; the belief in future price increases diminishes. When the remaining potential buyers no longer believe in future price increases, the primary motivating factor to purchase is eliminated; prices fall. The temporary rise and fall of asset prices is the defining characteristic of a bubble.

The bubble mentality is summed up in three typical beliefs:
1. The expectation of future price increases.
2. The belief that prices cannot fall.
3. The worry that failure to buy now will result in permanent inability to obtain the asset.

The Great Housing Bubble was characterized by the acceptance of these beliefs by the general public, and the exploitation of these beliefs by the entire real estate industrial complex, particularly the sales mechanism of the National Association of Realtors.

Speculative bubbles are caused by precipitating factors.[5] Like a spark igniting a flame, a precipitating factor serves as a catalyst to begin the initial price increases that change the psychology of market participants and activates the beliefs listed above. There is usually no single factor but rather a combination of factors that stimulates prices to begin a speculative mania. The Great Housing Bubble was precipitated by innovation in structured finance and the expansion of the secondary mortgage market, the lowering of lending standards and the growth of subprime lending, and to a lesser degree the lowering of the Federal Funds Rate. All of these causes are discussed in detail in later sections.

Real Estate Only Goes Up

The mantra of the National Association of Realtors is "real estate only goes up." This economic fallacy fosters the belief in future price increases and the limited risk of buying real estate. In general real estate prices do increase because salaries across the country do tend to increase with the general level of inflation, and it is through wages that people make payments for real estate assets. [6] When the economy is strong and unemployment is low, prices for residential real estate tend to rise. Therefore, the fundamental valuation of real estate does go up most of the time. However, prices can, and often do, rise faster than the fundamental valuation of real estate, and it is in these instances when there is a price bubble.

Greed is a powerful motivating factor for the purchase of assets. It is a natural response for people to desire to make money by doing nothing more than owning an asset. [7] The only counterbalance to greed is fear. However, if a potential buyer believes the asset cannot decline in value, or if it does, it will only be by a small amount for a very short period of time, there is little fear generated to temper their greed. [8] The belief that real estate only goes up has the effect of activating greed and diminishing fear. It is the perfect mantra for creating a price bubble. [9]

Buy Now or Be Priced Out Forever

When prices rise faster than their wages, people can obtain less real estate with their income. The natural fear under these circumstances is to buy whatever is available before there is nothing desirable available in a particular price range. This fear of being priced out causes even more buying which drives prices higher. It becomes a self-fulfilling prophecy. Of course, the National Association of Realtors, the agents of sellers, is keen to exploit this fear to increase transaction volume and increase their own incomes. If empirical evidence of the recent past is confirming the idea that real estate only goes up, the fear of being priced out forever provides added impetus and urgency to the motivation to buy.

Just before the stock market crash signaling the beginning of the Great Depression, Irving Fisher, a noted economist at the time, was quoted as saying "Stock prices have reached what looks like a permanently high plateau." [10] Of course, stock prices dropped significantly after he made this statement. This sentiment is based on the idea that inflated prices can stay inflated indefinitely. However, when valuations cannot be pushed up any higher, prices cannot rise at a fast rate. In residential real estate markets, the rate of price increase would only match inflation because wages and inflation are closely correlated. If the rate of price increase does not exceed ordinary investments, people lose their enthusiasm for residential real estate as an investment, and they begin to look for alternatives: people choose to rent rather than own. Also, when the quality of units available for rent at a given monthly payment far exceeds the quality of those available for sale at the same monthly payment level, people choose not to bid on the property and they rent instead. One sign of a housing bubble is a wide disparity between the quality of rentals and the quality of for-sale houses at a given price point. People choosing to rent curtails the rapid rise in prices and thereby lowers the demand for real estate. This puts downward pressure on prices, which eliminates the primary motivation speculators had for purchasing the asset. Greed created the condition of rapidly rising prices which in turn spawns the fear of being priced out. When greed ceases to motivate buyers, prices fall.

Once prices begin to fall, the fear of being priced "out" forever changes to a fear of being priced "in" forever. A buyer who overpaid and over-borrowed will be in a circumstance where they owe more on their mortgage than the property is worth on the open market. They cannot sell because they cannot pay off the mortgage. They become trapped in their homes until prices increase enough to allow a breakeven sale. This puts the conditions in place to reverse the cycle and causes prices to drop precipitously.

Confirming Fallacies

There are a number of fallacies about residential real estate that either affirm the belief in perpetually rising prices or minimize the fears of a price decline. These fallacies generally revolve around a perceived shortage of housing or a belief that the higher prices are justified by current or future economic conditions. These misperceptions are not the core mechanism of an asset price bubble, but they serve to affirm the core beliefs and perpetuate the price rally.

They Aren't Making Any More Land

All market pricing is a function of supply and demand. One of the reasons many house price bubbles get started is due to a temporary shortage of housing units. [11] This is a particular problem in California because the entitlement process is slow and cumbersome. [12] Supply shortages can become acute, and prices can rise very quickly. In most areas of the country, when prices rise, new supply is quickly brought to the market to meet this demand, and price increases are blunted by the rebalancing of supply and demand. Since supply is slow to the market in California, these temporary shortages can create the conditions necessary to facilitate a price bubble.

The fallacy of running-out-of-land plays on this temporary condition to convince market participants that the shortage is permanent. The idea that all land for residential development can be consumed ignores one obvious fact: people do not live on land, they live in houses, and land can always be redeveloped to increase the number of housing units. Basically, builders can build "up" even if they can't build "out." If running-out-of-land were actually a cause of a permanent shortage of housing units, Japan and many European countries where there is very little raw land available for development would have housing prices beyond the reach of the entire population (Japan tried it once, and their real estate market experienced a 64% decline over a 15 year period until affordability returned). [13] Since prices cannot remain permanently elevated, it becomes obvious that the amount of land available for development does not create a permanent shortage of dwelling units.

Over the long term, rent, income and house prices must come into balance. If rents and house prices become very high relative to incomes, businesses find it difficult to expand because they cannot attract personnel to the area. In this circumstance, one of two things will happen: businesses will be forced to raise wages to attract new hires, or business will stagnate and rents and house prices will decline to match the prevailing wage levels. [14] During the Great Housing Bubble, many businesses in the most inflated markets experienced this phenomenon. The effect is either a dramatic slowing of population growth or net outmigration of population to other areas.

Everyone Wants To Live Here

Everyone believes they live in a very desirable location; after all, they choose to live there. People who make this argument fail to understand that the place they live was just as desirable before the bubble when prices were much lower, in fact, probably more so. What is it about their area that made it two or more times as desirable during the bubble? Of course, nothing did, but that does not stop people from making the argument. [15] There is a certain emotional appeal to believing the place you chose to call home is so desirable that people were willing to pay ridiculous prices to live there. The reality is prices went up because people desired to own an asset that was increasing in price. People motivated by increasing prices do not care where they live as long as prices there are going up.

Prices Are Supported By Fundamentals

In every asset bubble people will claim the prices are supported by funda-mentals even at the peak of the mania. Stock analysts were issuing buy recom-mendations on tech stocks in March of 2000 when valuations were so extreme that the semiconductor index fell 85% over the next 3 years, and many tech companies saw their stock drop to zero as they went out of business. Analysts even invented new valuation techniques to justify market prices. One of the most absurd was the "burn rate" valuation method applied to internet stocks. [16] Rather than value a company based on its income, analysts were valuing the company based on how fast it was spending their investor's money. When losing is winning, something is profoundly wrong with the arguments of fundamental support. The same nonsense becomes apparent in the housing market when one sees rental rates covering less than half the cost of ownership as was common during the peak of the bubble in severely inflated markets. Of course, since housing markets are dominated by amateurs, a robust price analysis is unnecessary. [17] Even a ridiculous analysis, if aggressively promoted by the self-serving real estate community, provides enough emotional support to prompt the general public into buying. There is no real fundamental analysis done by the average homebuyer because so few understand the fundamental valuation of real property. Even simple concepts like comparative rental rates are ignored by bubble buyers, particularly when prices are rising dramatically and such valuation techniques look out-of-touch with the market.

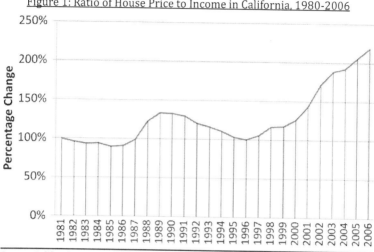

Figure 1: Ratio of House Price to Income in California, 1980-2006

Source: California Association of Realtors; US Census Bureau

When rental cashflow models fail, which they do during the rally of a housing bubble, the arguments justifying prices turn to an owner's ability to make payments. The argument is that everyone is rich, and everyone is making enough money to support current prices. It seems people began believing the contents of their "liar loan" applications during the bubble, or perhaps they counted on the home-equity-line-of-credit spending to come from the inevitable appreciation. [18] Even when confronted with hard data showing the everyone-is-rich argument to be fallacious, people still claim it is true. One unique phenomenon of the Great Housing Bubble was the exotic financing which allowed owners the temporary luxury of financing very large sums of money with small payments. There was some truth to the argument that people could afford the payments. Unfortunately, this was completely dependent upon unstable financing terms, and when these terms were eliminated, so were any reasonable arguments about affordability and sustainable fundamental valuations.

It Is Different This Time

Each time the general public creates an asset bubble, they believe the rally in prices is justifiable by fundamentals. [19] When proven methods of valuation demonstrate otherwise, people invent new ones with the caveat, "it is different this time." It never is. The stock market bubble had its own unique valuation methods as described previously. The Great Housing Bubble had proponents of the financial innovation model. Rather than viewing the unstable loan programs of the bubbles with suspicion, most bubble participants eagerly embraced the new financing methods as a long-overdue advance in the lending industry. Of course, it is easy to ignore potential problems when everyone involved is making large amounts of money and the government regulators are encouraging the activity. Alan Greenspan, FED chairman during the bubble, endorsed the use of adjustable rate mortgages in certain circumstances (Greenspan, Understanding Household Debt Obligations, 2004), and official public policy under the last several presidential administrations was the expansion of home ownership. [20] When everyone involved was saying things were different and when the activity was profitable to everyone involved, it is not surprising events got completely out of control.

The Importance of Financial Bubbles

Why should anyone care about financial bubbles? The first and most obvious reason is that the financial fallout is stressful. People buying into a financial mania too late, particularly in a residential housing market, will probably end up in foreclosure and most likely in a bankruptcy court. In contrast, stock market bubbles will only cause people to lose their initial investment. It may bruise their ego or delay their retirement, but these losses generally do not cause them to lose their homes or declare bankruptcy like a housing market bubble does. In a stock market collapse, a broker will close out positions and close an account before the account goes negative. There is a safety net in the system. In a residential housing market, there is no safety net. If house prices decline, a homeowner can easily have negative equity and no ability to exit the transaction. In a housing market decline, properties become very illiquid as there simply are not enough buyers to absorb the available inventory. A property owner can quickly fall so far into negative territory that it would take a lifetime to pay back the debt. In these circumstances bankruptcy is not just preferable; it is the only realistic course of action. It is better to have credit issues for a few years than to have insurmountable debt lingering for decades.

The real problems for individuals and families come after the bankruptcy and foreclosure. The debt addicted will suddenly find the tools they used to maintain their artificially inflated lifestyles are no longer available. The stress of adjusting to a sustainable, cash-basis lifestyle can lead to divorces, depression and a host of related personal and family problems. One can argue this is in their best interest long-term, but that will be little comfort to these people during the transition. The problems for the market linger as well. Those who lost homes during the decline are no longer potential buyers due to their credit problems. It will take time for this group to repair their credit and become buyers again. The reduction in the size of the buyer pool keeps demand in check and limits the rate of price recovery.

Summary

The Great Housing Bubble, like all asset bubbles, was driven by the belief in permanent, rapid house price appreciation, an unrealistic perception of the risk involved, and the fear that waiting to buy would cause market participants to miss their opportunity to own a house. These erroneous beliefs were supported by groupthink; if everyone else believes it, it must be true. As with any mass delusion, it is difficult to see beyond the comforting fallacies to understand the deeper truth; however, it is essential to do so because the cost in emotional and financial terms of getting caught up in the mania is very high. Foreclosure and bankruptcy are bad for individuals, bad for families, and bad for society.

Conservative House Financing

When people decide they want to buy a house, they figure out how much they can afford, then they search for something they want in their price range. For most people, what they can "afford" depends almost entirely upon how much a lender is willing to loan them. Lenders apply debt-to-income ratios and other affordability criteria to determine how much they are willing to loan. Buyers are generally limited in how much they can borrow because lenders are wise enough not to loan borrowers so much that they default. Borrowers behave much like drug addicts–they will borrow all the money a lender will loan them whether it is good for them or not. Most borrowers are not wise to the differences between the various loan types, and they have limited understanding of the risks they are taking on.

The vast majority of residential home sales have lender financing. The interest rates and various loan terms have evolved over time. After World War II a series of government programs to encourage home ownership spawned a surge in construction and the evolution of private lending terms resulting in the 30-year conventionally amortized mortgage. This mortgage generally required a 20% downpayment, and allowed the borrower to consume no more than 28% of their gross income on housing. These conservative terms became the standard for nearly 50 years. Lending under these terms resulted in low default rates and a high degree of market price stability.

There were experiments with various forms of exotic financing during this period, particularly in markets like California where price volatility required special terms to facilitate buying at inflated pricing. The instability of these loan programs was demonstrated painfully during the deep market correction of the early 90s in California characterized by high default rates and lender losses. Rather than learn a difficult lesson regarding the use of these alternative financing terms from this experience, lenders sought out ways of shifting these risks to others though a complex transaction called a credit default swap. Once lenders and investors in mortgages thought the risk was mitigated, these unstable loan programs were brought back and made widely available to the general public resulting in the Great Housing Bubble.

Mortgage Interest Rates

Mortgage interest rates are the single-most important factor determining the borrowing power of a potential house buyer. When rates are very low, a borrower can service a large amount of debt with a relatively small payment, and when interest rates are very high, a borrower can service a small amount of debt with a relatively large payment. Mortgage interest rates are determined by market forces where investors in mortgages and mortgage-backed securities bid for these assets. The rate of return demanded by these investors determines the interest rate the originating lender will have to charge in order to sell the loan in the secondary market. Some lenders still hold mortgages in their own investment portfolio, but these mortgages and mortgage rates are subject to the same supply and demand pressures generated by the secondary mortgage market.

Figure 2: Components of Mortgage Interest Rates

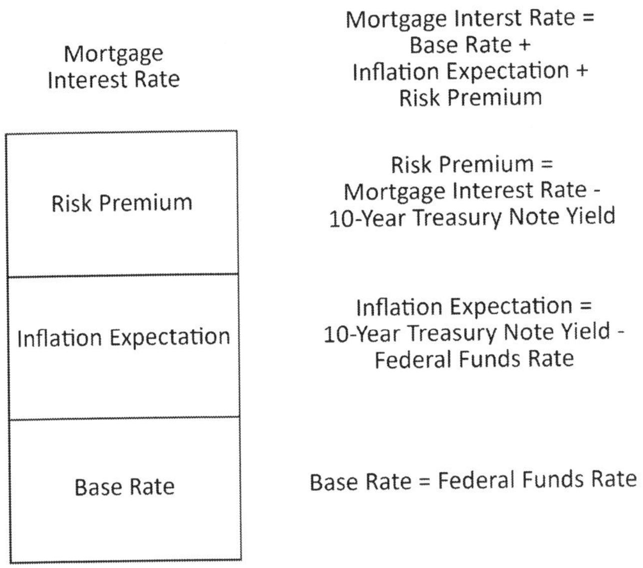

Mortgage
Interest Rate

Mortgage Interst Rate =
Base Rate +
Inflation Expectation +
Risk Premium

Risk Premium	Risk Premium = Mortgage Interest Rate - 10-Year Treasury Note Yield
Inflation Expectation	Inflation Expectation = 10-Year Treasury Note Yield - Federal Funds Rate
Base Rate	Base Rate = Federal Funds Rate

Mortgage interest rates are determined by investor demands for risk adjusted return on their investment. The return investors demand is determined by three primary factors: the riskless rate of return, the inflation premium and the risk premium. The riskless rate of return is the return an investor could obtain in an investment like a short-term Treasury Bill. Treasury Bills range in duration from a few days to as long as 26 weeks. Due to their short duration, Treasury Bills contain little if any allowance for inflation. A close approximation to this rate is the Federal Funds Rate controlled by the Federal Reserve. It is one of the reasons the activities of the Federal Reserve are watched so closely by investors. The closest risk-free approximation to mortgage loans is the 10-year

Treasury Note. Treasury Notes earn a fixed rate of interest every six months until maturity issued in terms of 2, 5, and 10 years. The 10-year Treasury Note is a close approximation to mortgage loans because most fixed-rate mortgages are paid off before the 30 year maturity with 7 years being a typical payoff timeframe.

The difference in yield between a 10-year Treasury Note and a 30-day Treasury Bill is a measure of investor expectation of inflation, and the difference between the yield on a 10-year Treasury Note and the prevailing market mortgage interest rate is a measure of the risk premium. Inflation reduces the buying power of money over time, and if investors must wait a long period of time to be repaid, as is the case in a home mortgage, they will be receiving dollars that have less value than the ones they provided when the loan was originated. Investors demand compensation to offset the corrosive effect of inflation. This is the inflation premium. The risk premium is the added interest investors demand to compensate them for the possibility the investment may not perform as planned. Investors know exactly how much they will get if they invest in Treasury Notes, but they do not know exactly what they will get back if they invest in residential home mortgages or the investment vehicles created from them. This uncertainty of return causes them to ask for a rate higher than that of Treasury Notes. This additional compensation is the risk premium. Mortgage interest rates are a combination of the riskless rate of return, the risk premium and the inflation premium.

The fluctuation in mortgage interest rates has implications for when it is the best time to buy and the best time to refinance a home mortgage. It is a popular misconception that low interest rates make for a good buying opportunity. When interest rates are declining, borrowers can finance larger sums, and this does prompt many people to buy and home prices to rise, but when interest rates are low is also when prices are highest. A buyer in a low-interest-rate environment may obtain an expensive property, but the resale value of that property will decline when interest rates rise because future buyers will not be able to finance such large sums. A low-interest-rate environment is an excellent time to refinance because a conservative borrower can either obtain a lower payment or shorten the amortization schedule and pay the loan off faster. The best time to purchase a house is when interest rates are very high. Again, this is counterintuitive because the interest is so much greater, but this will also mean the amount financed will be much lower and house prices will be relatively low. It is better to buy when interest rates are high and later refinance when interest rates decline. A borrower can refinance into a lower payment, but without additional cash, a borrower cannot refinance into a lower debt.

Types of Borrowers

Borrowers are broadly categorized by the characteristics of their payment history as reflected in their FICO score. FICO risk scores are developed and maintained by the Fair Isaac Corporation utilizing a proprietary predictive model based on an analysis of consumer profiles and credit histories. These models are updated frequently to reflect changes in consumer credit behavior and lending practices. The FICO score is reported by the three major credit reporting agencies, Experian, Equifax and TransUnion. Borrowers with high credit scores have generally demonstrated a high degree of responsibility in paying their debt obligations as promised. Those with low credit scores either have little or no credit history, or they have a demonstrated track record of failing to pay their financial obligations. There are 3 main categories of borrowers: Prime, Alt-A, and Subprime. [21] Prime borrowers are those with high credit scores, and Subprime borrowers are those with low credit scores. The Alt-A borrowers make up the gray area in between. Alt-A tends to be closer to Prime as these are often borrowers with high credit scores which for one or more reasons do not meet the strict standards of Prime borrowers. In recent years one of the most common non-conformities of Alt-A loans has been the lack of verifiable income. In short, "liar loans" are generally Alt-A. As the number of deviations from Prime increases, the credit scores decline and the remainder are considered Subprime.

Types of Loans

There are also 3 main categories of loans: Conventional, Interest-Only, and Negative Amortization. The distinction between these loans is how the amount of principal is impacted by monthly payments. A Conventional mortgage includes some amount of principal in the payment in order to repay the original loan amount. The greater the amount of principal repaid, the quicker the loan is paid off. An Interest-Only loan does just what it describes; it only pays the interest. This loan does not pay back any of the principal, but it at least "treads water" and does not fall behind. The Negative Amortization loan is one in which the full amount of interest is not paid with each payment, and the unpaid interest gets added to the principal balance. Each month, the borrower is increasing the debt. Two of the features of all Interest-Only or Negative Amortization loans are an interest rate reset and a payment recast. All these loans have provisions where the interest rate changes or loan balance comes due either in the form of a balloon payment or an accelerated amortization schedule. In any case, borrowers often must refinance or face a major increase in their monthly loan payment. This increase in payment is what makes these loans such a problem.

Table 2: Loan Type and Borrower Type Matrix

	Conventional	Interest Only	Neg Am
Subprime	Subprime Conventional	Subprime Interest Only	Subprime Neg Am
Alt-A	Alt-A Conventional	Alt-A Interest Only	Alt-A Neg Am
Prime	Prime Conventional	Prime Interest Only	Prime Neg Am

RISK

The category of loan and category of borrower are independent of each other. Starting in the lower left hand corner, there is lowest risk loan for a lender to make, a Prime Conventional mortgage. Up or to the right, the risk increases. The riskiest loan a lender can make is the Negative Amortization loan to a Subprime borrower.

Conventional 30-Year Amortizing Mortgage

A fixed-rate conventionally-amortized mortgage is the least risky kind of mortgage obligation. If borrowers can make their payment–a payment that will not change over time–they can keep their home. A 30-year term is most common, but if bi-weekly payments are made (two extra per year), the loan can be paid off in about 22 years. If borrowers can afford a larger payment in the future, they can increase the payment and amortize over 15 years and pay off the mortgage quickly. The best way to deal with unemployment or other loss of income is to have a house that is paid off. Stabilizing or eliminating a mortgage payment reduces the risk of losing a house or facing bankruptcy. Unfortunately, payments on fixed-rate mortgages are higher than other forms of financing, so borrowers often opt for the riskier alternatives.

The Interest-Only, Adjustable-Rate Mortgage

The interest-only, adjustable-rate mortgage (IO ARM) became popular early in this bubble when fixed-rate mortgage payments were too large for buyers to afford. In the coastal bubble of the late 80s, these mortgages did not become as common, and the bubble did not inflate far beyond people's ability to make fixed-rate conventional mortgage payments. [22] This is also why prices were slow to correct in the deflation of the early 90s. Most sellers did not need to sell, so they just waited out the market. The correction was a market characterized by large inventories, but this inventory was not composed of calamitous numbers of must-sell homes. The few must-sell homes that came on the market in the early 90s drove prices lower, but not catastrophically because the rally in prices did not get too far out of control. The Great Housing Bubble was different.

IO ARMs are risky because they increase the likelihood of borrowers losing their homes. IO ARMs generally have a fixed payment for a short period followed by a rate and payment adjustment. This adjustment is almost always higher; sometimes, it is much higher. At the time of reset, if the borrower is unable to make the new payment (salary does not increase), or if the borrower is unable refinance the loan (home declines in value below the loan amount), the borrower will lose the home. [23] It is that simple.

These risks are real, as many homeowners have already discovered. People try to minimize this risk by extending the time to reset to 7 or even 10 years, but the risk is still present. If a house were purchased in California in 1989 with 100% financing with a 10-year, interest-only loan, at the time of refinance the house would have been worth less than the borrower paid, and they would not have been given a new loan. (Fortunately 100% financing was unheard of in the late 80s). Even a 10 year term is not long enough if purchased at the wrong time. As the term of fixed payments gets shorter, the risk of losing the home becomes even greater.

The most egregious examples of predatory lending occurred when these interest-only loan products were offered to subprime borrowers whose income only qualified them to make the initial minimum payment (assuming the borrower actually had this income). This loan program was commonly known as the two-twenty-eight (2/28). It has a low fixed payment for the first two years, then the interest rate and payment would reset to a much higher value on a fully amortized schedule for the remaining 28 years. Seventy-eight percent of subprime loans in 2006 were two year adjustable rate mortgages. [24] Anecdotal evidence is that most of these borrowers were only qualified based on their ability to make the initial minimum payment (Credit Suisse, 2007). This practice did not fit the traditional definition of predatory lending because the lender was not planning to profit by taking the property in foreclosure. However, the practice was predatory because the lender was still going to profit from making the loan through origination fees at the expense of the borrower who was sure to end up in foreclosure. There were feeble attempts at justifying the practice through increasing home ownership, but when the borrower had no ability to make the fully amortized payment, there was no chance of sustaining those increases.

The advantage of IO ARMs is their lower payments. Or put another way, the same payment can finance a larger loan. This is how IO ARMs were used to drive up prices once the limit of conventional loans was reached (somewhere in 2003 in California). A bubble similar to the last bubble would have reached its zenith in 2003/2004 if IO ARMs had not entered the market and inflated prices further. In any bubble, the system is pushed to its breaking point, and it either implodes, or some new stimulus pushes it higher: the negative amortization mortgage (Option ARM).

Negative Amortization Mortgages

The Negative Amortization mortgage (aka, Option ARM or Neg Am) is the riskiest loan imaginable. It has all the risks of an IO ARM, but with the added risk of an increasing loan balance. Using this loan, there is the risk of not being able to make the payment at reset, and the borrower is much more at risk of being denied for refinancing because the loan balance can easily exceed the house value. In either case, the home will fall into foreclosure. The Option ARM is one of the most complicated loan programs ever developed. It was heralded as an innovation because it allowed people greater control over their monthly payments, and it provided greater affordability in the early years of the mortgage. [25] Twenty-nine percent of purchase originations nationwide in 2005 were interest-only or option ARM (Credit Suisse, 2007). The percentage in California was much higher. The proliferation of this product is largely responsible for the extreme prices at the bubble's peak.

An Option ARM loan provides the borrower with 3 different payment options each month: minimum payment, interest-only payment, and a fully amortizing payment. In theory, this loan would be ideal for those with variable income such as sales people or seasonal workers. This assumes the borrower has months where the income is more than the minimum, the borrower sees a need in good times to make more than the minimum payment and the borrower understands the loan. None of these assumptions proved to be true.

Figure 3: Interest-Only and Negative Amortization Purchases, 2000-2006

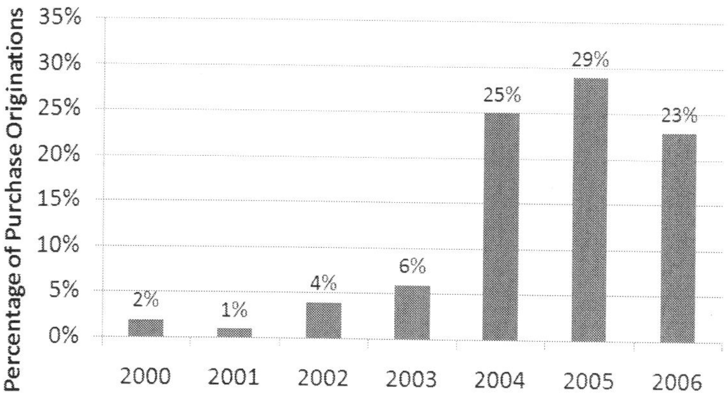

Note: Purchase Originations Only
Source: Loan Performance, Credit Suisse Analysis

When confronted with several different prices for the same asset, people naturally will choose the lowest one. This common-sense idea apparently escaped the innovators who developed the Option ARM. Studies from 2006 showed that 85% of households with an Option ARM only made the minimum payment every month (Credit Suisse, 2007). Many could not afford to pay more, and many more could not see a reason to pay more. Most simply thought they would refinance when the payments got too high.

These loans are also very confusing. The interest rate being charged to the borrower adjusts frequently, and the payment rate (which is not correlated to the actual interest rate being charged) also changes periodically. The separation of the interest rate charged and the interest rate paid is what allows for negative amortization, and it also creates a great deal of confusion. The following is an attempt to explain the mechanics of this loan.

Payment Rate

A negative amortization loan is any loan where the monthly payment does not cover the monthly interest expense. Interest-only or conventionally amortizing loans do not have this feature, and the monthly payments are based on the interest rate charged and/or the duration of the amortization schedule. Since the negative amortization loan breaks down this traditional relationship, there is a completely separate rate calculated for the minimum payment amount. In general, this rate starts out low and increases gradually each year for the first several years. This is to allow the borrower time to adjust to a higher loan payment amount. These yearly increases are usually capped to prevent dramatic phenomenon known as "payment shock." The payment rate is based on an interest rate, but this rate has no relationship to the interest rate the borrower is being charged on the loan balance. The presence of two interest rates is responsible for much of the confusion regarding these loans. The low starting payment rate is often called a "teaser rate" because it is a temporary inducement to take on the mortgage. There was a widespread belief among borrowers that one could simply refinance from one teaser rate to another forever in a process known as serial refinancing. The biggest confusion regarding this loan is when people mistake this payment rate for the actual interest rate they are being charged on the loan. This is a natural mistake to make because historic loan programs did not make this distinction.

Interest Rate Reset

The Option ARM is a hybrid adjustable rate mortgage with payment options. The interest rate being charged to the borrower is subject to periodic fluctuations with changes in market interest rates similar to other adjustable rate mortgages. The timing of adjustment and limits therein are contained in the mortgage contract. The interest rate charged is fixed for certain periods at the end of which there is a change in the interest rate. When the interest rate changes on most adjustable rate mortgages, the payment required of the borrower changes as well. Since the charged interest rate and the payment rate are not the same for Option ARMs, the payment may not be affected and negative amortization can occur. The interest rates on most adjustable-rate mortgages are lower than those for fixed-rate mortgages because the lender is not subject to interest rate risk. If interest rates rise, lenders who have issued fixed-rate mortgages have capital tied up in below-market mortgages. With adjustable rate mortgages, higher interest rates are passed on to the consumer.

Since the low payment option on Negative Amortization loans is so appealing to consumers, the actual interest rate charged on Option ARMs is often higher than interest-only or fixed rate mortgages, which make these loans very attractive to investors. Since the interest rate is higher than the payment rate, negative amortization occurs, and the loan balance grows each month as the deferred interest is added to the loan balance. This capitalized interest is recognized as income on the books of mortgage holders. Generally Accepted Accounting Principles (GAAP) allow this, but the amount of income is supposed to be reduced to reflect the likelihood of actually receiving this money. Since the loan program was new, and default rates were low due to the bubble rally, the reported income was very high making these loans even more appealing to investors. From the investors' perspective, they were buying high-interest loans with great income potential and low default rates. From the borrowers' perspective, they were obtaining a loan at a very low interest rate–a perception rooted in a basic misunderstanding of the loan terms–and a very low payment which allowed them to finance large sums to purchase homes at inflated prices.

This dissonance between the investors who purchased these loans and the borrowers who signed up for them did not become apparent until these loans began to reset to higher rates and recast to higher payments. In short, these loans are time bombs with fuses of varying lengths set to blow up the dreams of investors and borrowers alike.

Payment Recast

Interest-only and negative amortization payments cannot go on forever. At some point, the loan balance must be paid in full. For all adjustable rate mortgages, there is a mandatory recast after a fixed period of time where the loan reverts to a conventionally amortizing loan to be paid over the remaining portion of a 30 year term. This recast eliminates the options for negative amortization and interest-only payments and requires the fully amortized payments on an accelerated schedule for what is often an increased loan balance. For instance, if an interest-only loan is fixed for 5 years, at the end of 5 years, the loan changes to a fully-amortized loan with payments based on the remaining 25 year period. The longer interest-only or negative amortization is allowed to go on, the more severe the payment shock is when the loan is recast to fully amortizing status. Also, in the case of negative amortization loans, the total loan balance is capped at a certain percentage of the original loan amount, typically 110% but sometimes higher. If this threshold is reached before the mandatory time limit, the loan is also recast as a conventionally amortizing loan. Since many borrowers were qualified based on their ability to make the minimum payment at the teaser rate, when the loan recasts and the payment significantly increases (double or triples or more,) the borrower is left unable to make the payment, and the loan quickly goes into default.

The natural question to ask is, "Why would lenders do this?" There is no easy answer. Most simply did not care. The lender made large fees through the origination of the loan and subsequent servicing, and the loan itself was sold to an investor. The investor bought insurance against default, and many of these loans were packaged into asset backed securities which were highly rated by ratings agencies due to their low historic default rates. Nobody cared to examine the systemic risk likely to result in extremely high future default rates because the business was so profitable at the time of origination. Most assumed this would go on forever as house prices continued to appreciate. It was envisioned that most borrowers would either increase their incomes enough to afford these payments or simply refinance into another highly profitable Option ARM loan. In hindsight, the folly is easy to identify, but for those involved in the game, there was little incentive to question the workings of the system, particularly since it was so profitable to everyone involved.

Stated Income Loans

One unique phenomenon of the Great Housing Bubble was the utilization of stated-income loans, also known as "liar loans" because most people were not truthful when stating their income. Loan documentation is usually a routine part of obtaining financing. Lenders ordinarily require a borrower to provide documentation proving income, assets and debt. However, during the final stages of the Great Housing Bubble, loan documentation was seen as an unnecessary barrier to completing more transactions, and loan programs which circumvented normal documentation procedures flourished. The fact that these programs existed at all is remarkable proof of the risk lenders were taking through the relaxing or outright elimination of lending standards. Eighty-one percent of Alt-A purchase originations in 2006 were stated-income, and 50% of subprime originations in 2005 and 2006 were stated income (Credit Suisse, 2007). Stated income loans increased from 18% of originations in 2001 to 49% in 2006 according to Loan Performance. In a related study by the Mortgage Asset Research Institute, 60% of stated-income borrowers had exaggerated their incomes by more than 50%.[26, 27] Obviously, lying about one's income to obtain a loan is not a conservative method of financing a property purchase.

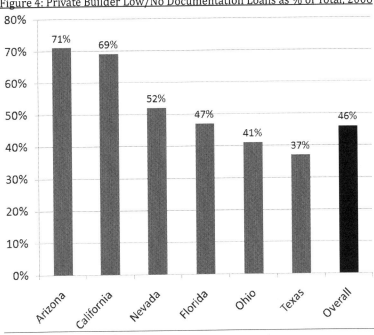

Figure 4: Private Builder Low/No Documentation Loans as % of Total, 2006

Source: Credit Suisse Analysis

The stated-income loan was originally provided to borrowers such as the self-employed who most often do not have W-2s to verify income. When these loan programs were first started, they were not made available to borrowers with W-2s as the transparency of the lie would have been obvious to all parties. During the bubble rally, this loan was made available to anyone, and lying was not only encouraged, borrowers were often assisted in fabricating paperwork by aggressive loan officers and mortgage brokers. [28] Since the loan could be packaged and sold to investors who had no idea what they were buying, there was a complete lack of concern for whether or not the borrower actually made the money stated in the loan application and thereby could actually make the payments on the loan. Everyone involved was raking in large fees, the borrower was obtaining the real estate they desired, and for a time, the investor was receiving payments from the borrower. [29] As long as prices were rising, everyone benefited from the arrangement. Of course, once prices started to fall, borrowers did not want to continue making payments they could not afford, and the whole system collapsed in a massive credit crunch.

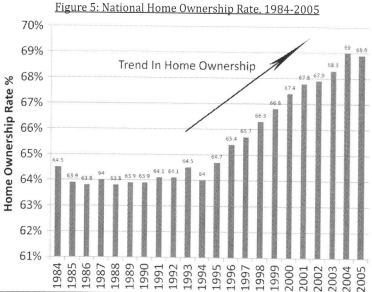

Figure 5: National Home Ownership Rate, 1984-2005

Source: US Census Bureau

Downpayments

The risk management measure not related to the mortgage terms is the downpayment. Most people do not think of downpayments as a way of managing risk, but lenders do. Downpayments reduce risk in two ways: first, they lower the monthly payment, and second, they provide a cushion ensuring the borrower can refinance (if necessary) should the house value decline. The problem with downpayments is obvious: few people save enough money to have one.

Eliminating downpayments through the use of 80/20 combo loans was another massive stimulus to the housing market. Subprime loan originations in 2006 had an average loan-to-value ratio of 94%. That is an average downpayment of just 6%. Also, 46% of home purchases in 2006 had combined loan-to-value ratios of 95% or higher (Credit Suisse, 2007). Lenders used to require

19

downpayments because they demonstrated the borrower's ability to save. At one time, having the financial discipline to be able to save for a downpayment was considered a reliable indicator as to a borrower's ability to make timely mortgage payments. Once downpayments became optional, a whole group of potential buyers who used to be excluded from the market suddenly had access to money to buy homes. Home ownership rates increased about 5% nationally due in part to the elimination of the downpayment barrier and the expansion of subprime lending.

Equity Components

In simple accounting terms, equity is the difference between how much something is worth and how much money is owed on it (Equity = Assets–Liabilities). [30] People who purchase real estate use the phrase "building equity" to describe the overall increase in equity over time. However, it is important to look at the factors which either create or destroy equity to see how market conditions and financing terms impact this all-important feature of real estate.

Figure 6: Types of Equity

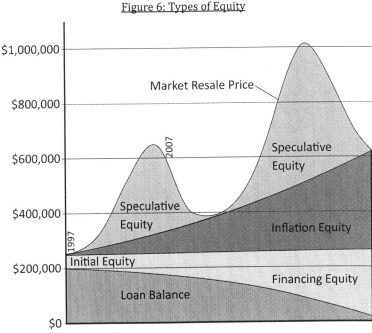

For purposes of illustration, equity can be broken down into several component parts: Initial Equity, Financing Equity, Inflation Equity, and Speculative Equity. Initial Equity is the amount of money a purchaser puts down to acquire the property. Financing Equity is the gain or loss of total equity based on the decrease or increase in loan balance over time. Inflation Equity is the increase in resale value due to the effect of inflation. This kind of appreciation is the "inflation hedge" that provides the primary financial benefit to home owner-ship. Finally, there is Speculative Equity. This is the fluctuation in equity caused by speculative activities in a real estate market. This can cause wild swings in equity both up and down. If life's circumstances or careful analysis and timing cause a sale at the peak of a speculative mania, the windfall can be dramatic. Of course, it can go the other way as well. If a house is purchased at its fundamen-tal valuation where the cost of ownership is equal to the cost of rental using a conventionally amortized mortgage with a downpayment, the amount of owner's equity is the combination of the above factors.

Initial Equity

The initial equity is equal to a purchaser's downpayment. If a buyer pays cash for a home, all equity is initial equity. Since most home purchases are financed, this initial equity is usually a small percentage of the purchase price, generally 20%. A downpayment is the borrower's money acquired through careful financial planning and saving, gifts from family members, or from the profits gained at the sale of a previous home. Downpayment money is not "free." This money generally is accumulated in a savings account, or if a buyer chooses to rent instead, downpayment money could be put in a high-yield savings account or other investments. There is an opportunity cost to taking this money out of another investment and putting it into a house. This cost and its impact on home ownership costs are detailed in later sections.

Financing Equity

Financing equity is determined by the terms of the loan. With a conven-tionally amortizing mortgage, a portion of the payment each month goes toward paying down the loan balance. As this loan balance decreases, the owner's equity increases. This is a substantial long-term benefit of home ownership. With an interest-only mortgage, the loan balance does not decrease because only the interest is paid with each payment. With this kind of loan, there is no financing equity. One of the major drawbacks of using an interest-only loan does not become apparent until the house is sold and the seller wants to take the equity to the next home in a move-up. Since no financing equity has accumulated, the seller obtains less equity in the transaction. This means the move-up buyer will be able to afford less. Over the short-term, financing equity is not significant because the loan balance is not paid down by a large amount, but if the house has been held for 10 years or more, or if the loan was amor-tized over a shorter term, the financing equity can be a large amount. This can make a real difference when the total equity amount is to be put toward a larger, more expensive home. Also, financing equity is a great reservoir for retirement savings. In fact, it is the primary mechanism for retirement savings of most Americans outside of social security. [31]

The worst possible loan is the negative amortization loan because of its impact on equity. As noted in the figure on the next page, if a negative amortiza-tion loan is utilized, it will consume all equity in its path. It is a form of cash-out financing that reduces equity. This loan relies on inflation and speculative equity to have any equity at all. The negative amortization loan will only begin to build financing equity after the loan recasts and becomes a fully-amortized loan and the payments skyrocket–assuming the borrower does not default. Most people cannot afford the fully-amortized payment, or they probably would not have used this form of financing initially. Even after the recast and the dramatic increase in payments, the loan does not get back to the original balance for many years.

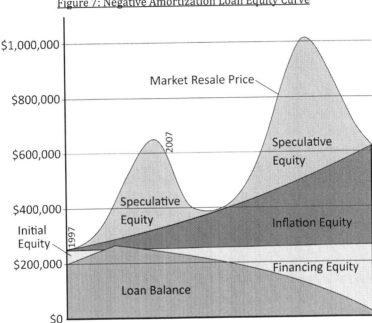

Figure 7: Negative Amortization Loan Equity Curve

Inflation Equity

House prices historically have outpaced inflation by 0.7% nationally. [32] In a normal market, this is the only appreciation homeowners obtain. This appreciation is caused by wage inflation translating into higher housing payments and the ability of borrowers to obtain larger loan amounts to bid up prices. In areas like Irvine, California, where wage growth has outpaced the general rate of inflation, the fundamental valuation of houses has increased faster than inflation. The related benefit to home ownership obtained through utilizing a fixed-rate, conventionally-amortizing mortgage is mortgage payments are frozen and the cost of housing does not increase with inflation. Renters must contend with ever-increasing rents while homeowners with the proper financing do not face escalating housing costs. Over the short term this is not significant, but over the long term, the monthly savings accruing to owners can be very sizable, and if the owner owns long enough or downsizes later in life, housing costs can be nearly eliminated when a mortgage is paid off (except for taxes, insurance and upkeep). Although this benefit is attractive, it is not worth paying much of a premium to obtain. The long-term benefit is quickly negated if there is a short-term additional cost associated with obtaining it. For instance, if a property can be rented for a certain amount today, and this amount will increase by 3% over 30 years, the total cost of ownership–even when fixed–cannot exceed this figure by more than 10% to break even over 30 years. The shorter the holding time, the less this premium is worth. In short, capturing the benefit of inflation equity requires a long holding period and a minimal ownership premium.

Speculative Equity

Speculative Equity is purely a function of irrational exuberance. [33] It has become a common element in certain markets, and capturing it is the dream of every would-be speculator who buys residential real estate. It is a loser's game, but it does not stop people from chasing after it. Will the markets bubble again? Who knows? Human nature being what it is, the delusive beliefs of irrational exuberance may take root and the cycle may continue. In the aftermath of the Great Housing Bubble legislators may pass laws from preventing it from happening again. Of course, such laws require enforcement, and when greed takes hold, enforcement may simply not occur. For those that purchased at the peak of the bubble, they need another bubble or they may not get back to breakeven in the next 20 to 30 years. [34] If however, there is another bubble, those who purchased at rental equivalent value after the crash will have an opportunity to reap a huge windfall at the expense of those who purchase at inflated prices in the future. As PT Barnum is credited with saying, "There is a sucker born every minute." [35]

The speculators who purchased at the peak of the Great Housing Bubble who put no money down (no Initial Equity) and utilized negative amortization loans–and there were a great many of these people–will have a painful future. The loan balance will be increasing at a time when resale home prices are falling. They will be so far underwater; they will need scuba equipment to survive. Plus, during the worst of their nightmare, their loan will recast, and they will be asked to make a huge payment on a property worth roughly half their loan balance. What default rates will these loans see? Realistically, they will all default. The only reason they purchased was to capture speculative profits which did not materialize. Even if some of these people hold on, and there is another speculative bubble similar to the last one, it will take 10 years or more for them to get back to breakeven, not including their carry costs. If there is no ensuing bubble, it will be 20 years. If you factor in their holding costs, they may never get back to breakeven.

Equity is made up of several component parts: Initial Equity, Financing Equity, Inflation Equity, and Speculative Equity. Each of these components has different characteristics and different forces that govern how they rise and fall. It is important to understand these components to make wise decisions on when to buy, how much to buy, and how to finance it. Failing to understand the dynamics involved can lead to an equity graph like the one for the peak buyer who purchased at the wrong time and utilized the wrong terms. Nobody wants to suffer that fate.

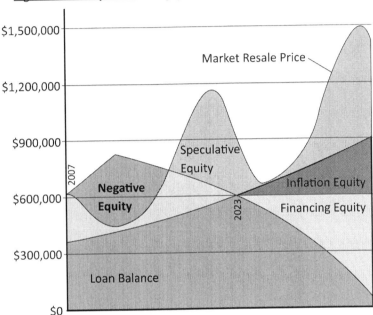

Figure 8: Peak Buyer, No Downpayment, Negative Amortization Loan

Mortgage Equity Withdrawal

Mortgage Equity Withdrawal or MEW is the process of obtaining cash through refinancing residential real estate using the accumulated equity as collateral for the loan. Before MEW homeowners would have to wait until the property was sold to get their equity converted to cash. Apparently, this was deemed an inefficient use of capital, so lenders found ways to "liberate" this equity with home equity lines of credit or cash-out mortgage refinancing. Home equity lines of credit are popular with lenders despite the additional risk of being in the second or third lien position because borrowers are less likely to default or prepay than non-cash-out refinancing. [36] The impact of MEW on equity is obvious; it reduces equity by increasing the loan balance. It has been noted that equity is a fantasy and debt is real, and MEW is the process of living the fantasy with the addition of very real debt. MEW has been utilized by homeowners for home improvement for decades, but the widespread use of this money for consumer spending was largely an innovation of the Great Housing Bubble. [37] Since consumer spending is almost 70% of the US economy, mortgage equity withdrawal was the primary mechanism of economic growth after the recession of 2001–a recession caused by the deflation of another asset bubble, the NASDAQ technology stock bubble.

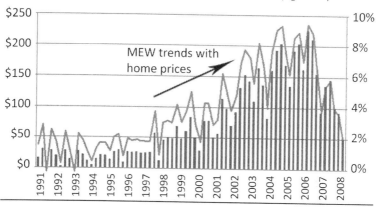

Figure 9: Mortgage Equity Withdrawal, 1991-2006

Source: Divisions of Research & Statistics and Monetary Affairs, Federal Reserve Board
Real Estate and Finance Blog - Calculated Risk

Many people who extracted their home equity lost their homes for lack of ability to refinance or make their new payments. After so many people lost their homes due to their own reckless borrowing, it is natural to wonder why these people did it. Why did they risk their home for a little spending money? First, it was not just a little money. Many markets saw home values increase at a rate equal to the local median income. It was as if their home was another breadwinner. The lure of this easy money was too much for many to resist. The rampant, in-your-face, marketing of these loans in every available media outlet touting the glossy "lifestyle" of over-the-top consumerism was a drug to many spending addicts. Also, during the bubble rally people really believed their house values would go up forever, and they would always have the ability to refinance enormous debts at low interest rates and maintain very low debt service costs. Most people did not think it possible they would end up in circumstances where they would lose their homes; however, they were mistaken. Given these beliefs, the equity accumulating in their house was "free money" they just needed to access in order to live and to spend like rich people. Even though they were consuming their net worth, and making themselves poor, they believed they were rich, and they wanted to spend accordingly.

Most homeowners do not save money for major improvements and re-quired maintenance, and these homeowners often take out home equity lines of credit as a method of mortgage equity withdrawal to fund home improve-ment projects. The logic here is that renovations improve the property so an increase in property value offsets the additional debt. In reality, home im-provement projects rarely adds value on a dollar-for-dollar basis, particularly with exterior enhancements which often only return 50 cents on the dollar in value. [38] The home-improvement craze was so common that the term "pergra-niteel" was coined to describe the Pergo fake wood floors, granite countertops, and steel appliances that defined the Great Housing Bubble era in much the same way as shag carpeting and wood wall paneling defined the interior decorating of the 1970s.

Much of the money homeowners borrowed fueled consumer spending and reinforced poor financial management techniques. It was common during the bubble rally for people to run up enormous credit card bills then refinance every year and pay them off. [39] It is foolish enough to finance consumer spending, but it is even more foolish to pay for this spending over the 30-year term of a typical mortgage. The consumptive value fades quickly, but the debt endures for a very long time. Many people responded to the "free money" their house was earning by liberating their equity as soon as they could so they could buy cars, take vacations, and generally live the good life. This borrow-and-spend mentality was actually encouraged by lenders who were eager to make these loans and even the government which was benefiting by economic expansion and higher tax receipts.

The recession of 2001 was caused by the collapse of stock prices and the resulting diminishment of corporate investment. The recession was shallow, but the economy had difficulty recovering mostly due to continued erosion of manufacturing jobs. [40] The Federal Reserve under Alan Greenspan was despe-rate to reignite economic growth, so the FED funds rate was lowered to 1% and kept there for more than a year. It was hoped this increased liquidity would go into business investment to restart the troubled economy; instead, it went into mortgage loans and consumers' pockets through mortgage equity withdrawal. Basically, the economic recovery from 2001 through 2005 was an illusion created by excessive borrowing and rampant spending by homeowners. The economy did not grow through production; it grew through consumption.

There are many theories as to the decline and fall of the Roman Empire. [41] One of the more intriguing is the idea that Rome fell because it was weakened by the parasitic nature of Rome itself. Rome existed to consume the resources of the empire. Boats would come to the city loaded with goods and leave the city empty. Consumption kept the masses happy and thereby quelled civil unrest. The Roman Empire was the world's only superpower with an unsur-passed military might. Equally unsurpassed was its ability to consume re-sources. Does any of this sound like the United States? The United States has clearly become a consumer nation, and the government continues to borrow huge sums of money to keep the economic engine of consumption going. In early 2008, Congress passed a "stimulus" package where many people would receive direct gifts of money in the hope they would spend it and keep the economy going. Since the Federal Government was already running a deficit, this money was borrowed from future tax receipts. In other words, this handout was obtained from future generations. With house prices crashing, direct handouts of borrowed government money were necessary to make up for the loss of borrowed private sector money that used to be available through mortgage equity withdrawal.

The Fallacy of Financial Innovation

The cutting edge is sharp. Innovators often pay a heavy price for attempts at advancement. Sometimes these advances lead to quantum leaps in human knowledge and understanding. Sometimes the time, effort, and money are merely thrown into the abyss. The financial innovations of the Great Housing Bubble are of the latter category. When the lending industry developed exotic loan products, they touted them as "innovation," and they sold these toxins far and wide. [42] Since these loans achieved the highest default rates ever recorded, it is apparent the "innovations" of the bubble rally were not entirely successful. It is amazing that a group of assumingly intelligent bankers came up with these loans and expected a positive outcome. [43] The "innovation" meme is nothing more than a public relations effort to convince brokers the products were safe to sell and borrowers the products were safe to use. It is hard to fathom the widespread acceptance of this nonsense, but that is the nature of the pathological beliefs of a financial mania.

Many in the lending industry think their work is like science that continually advances. It is not. It is far more akin to assembly line work where the same widgets are pumped out year after year. When lenders start to innovate, trouble is brewing. The last significant advancement in lending was the widespread use of 30-year amortizing loans that came into favor after World War II. Prior to that time, home loans were interest-only, short-term loans with very high equity requirements (50% was most common). This proved problematic in the Great Depression as many out-of-work owners defaulted on their loans. A mechanism had to be found to get new buyers into the markets and allow them to pay off the loan. The answer was the 30-year, fixed-rate amortizing loan. To say this was an innovation is a stretch as this loan has been around as long as banking has existed, but it did not become widely used until equity requirements were lowered. The lenders were willing to lower the equity requirements as long as the loan was amortizing because their risk would decline as time went by and the loan balance was paid off.

Over the last 60 years since World War II ended, a number of experimental loan programs have been attempted. These include interest-only loans, adjustable rate loans, and negative amortization loans among others. It is this group of loans that has consistently failed in the past for one simple reason: if payments can adjust higher, people will default. The Option ARM is certainly the most sophisticated loan ever developed. It is also a dismal failure, not because it lacks sophistication, but because it has embedded within it the possibility (near certainty) of an increasing payment. Any loan program that has the possibility of a higher future payment will fail because there will be a certain number of people who cannot afford the higher payment.

Here is where the lenders delude themselves and deceive the general public after a financial debacle like the Savings and Loan problems of the 1980s or the Great Housing Bubble. They blame the collapse and the high default rates on some outside factor rather than the terms and conditions the lenders created all on their own. There are still many out there who believe the high default rates and problems in the housing market in the 90s in California were caused by a weak economy. This is rubbish. House prices declined for 6 years. The decline started before the economy went soft, and it continued well after it had recovered. People defaulted because they overextended themselves on loans to buy overpriced housing, and toward the end of the mania, many were using interest-only loans. Whenever lenders start loaning people money with total debt-to-income ratios over 36% people will default. Whenever lenders start loaning more than 80% of the purchase price, people can sink underwater and when they do, they will default. This is not new. It happened in the early 90s; it happened during the Great Housing Bubble, and it happened for the same reasons: lax lending standards.

Someday the lending community may actually innovate and come up with some financial product that has low default rates which most people can qualify to obtain–or not. Unless you change human nature, there are always going to be people who are too irresponsible to make consistent payments. People either do or do not make their payments. This is the key to any loan program. New terms and schedules can be reinvented over and over again, and it will always boil down to people making payments. When complicated loan programs contain provisions that make it difficult for people to make pay-ments–like increasing payment amounts–they will default, and the loan program will fail. This is certain.

Whenever lenders create new, "sophisticated" loan programs that require advanced financial management on the part of the borrower, both the lenders and the borrowers fall victim to the Lake Wobegon effect. [44] Everyone thinks they have above average abilities when it comes to managing their finances. In reality, perhaps 2% of borrowers have the financial discipline to handle an Option ARM loan. Unfortunately, 80% of borrowers think they are in this 2%. The reason for this comes from the inherent conflict between emotions and intellect. Eighty percent of borrowers may understand the Option ARM loan (or think they do,) but when the pressures of daily life create emotional demands for spending money on one's lifestyle, the intellectual knowledge that this money should go toward a housing payment is conveniently set aside. It is this 2% of the most disciplined borrowers who will cut back on discretionary spending to make their full housing payment. Everyone else will make the minimum payment, fall behind on their mortgage, and end up in foreclosure.

It seems lenders forget basic facts about lending every so often and create a new financial bubble. Perhaps they succumb to the pressure of the investment community or their own shareholders, or perhaps they just start believing their own "innovation" marketing pitch and forget the basics of sound lending practices. This is why there are recessions at the end of a business cycle. These pathologic lending practices must be purged from the system or else they will survive to build an even bigger and costlier bubble. Although it is difficult to imagine a bubble bigger than the Great Housing Bubble, it is still possible.

In the aftermath of a financial fiasco, lenders return to the practices that did not fail them in the past. The only program lenders know empirically to be stable is a 30-year, fixed-rate, conventionally amortizing loan based on 80% of appraised value taking no more than 28% of a borrower's gross income (36% maximum total debt). The credit crunch facilitated the decline in housing prices after the Great Housing Bubble. Large downpayments came back, and government assisted financing became widely used by first-time homebuyers to overcome the high equity requirements. The credit crunch was not caused by some unexpected or unknown factor; it was caused by the failure of lenders. Credit continued to tighten until lenders stopped making bad loans. The bad loans did not disappear until lenders returned to the stable loan programs with a proven track record. That is how the credit cycle works. [45]

Summary

To be financially conservative is to accumulate wealth and to be risk adverse. It requires managing equity, paying down a mortgage loan, and allowing net worth to accumulate rather than depleting it via consumer spending through mortgage equity withdrawal. Many people do not realize the risk they take on when they use some of the innovative loan programs developed during the bubble. Exotic financing terms are not exotic anymore. Interest-only, adjustable rates and negative amortization have become so ubiquitous that nobody seems to remember why 30-year fixed-rate mortgages are used. A home should be financed with a fixed-rate conventionally-amortized mortgage and a sizable downpayment. The reason for this is simple stress management: nobody wants to spend the next several years worried about a loan reset or the need for increasing house values or future salary increases. People should not buy with the desire to make a fortune in real estate. Instead, they should purchase with the intent to have a stable housing payment, and a stress-free life.

Fundamental Valuation of Houses

The fundamental value of all housing prices is equivalent rents. Rents define the fundamental value of real estate because rental is a direct proxy for ownership; both rental and ownership provide for possession of property. Equivalent rents are a major component of the United States Government's Consumer Price Index (CPI). [46] According to the US Department of Labor, "This approach measures the change in the price of the shelter services provided by owner-occupied housing. Rental equivalence measures the change in the implicit rent, which is the amount a homeowner would pay to rent, or would earn from renting, his or her home in a competitive market. Clearly, the rental value of owned homes is not an easily determined dollar amount, and Housing survey analysts must spend considerable time and effort in estimating this value." Prior to the first California housing bubble in the late 1970s, the housing cost component of the CPI was measured using actual price changes in the asset. When this bubble created an enormous distortion in this index, the rental equivalence model was constructed. It has been used to smooth out the psychologically-induced housing price bubbles ever since.

An argument can be made for the real cost of construction as the fundamental valuation of houses. If house prices in a market fall below the cost of new construction, no new houses will be built because a builder cannot make a profit. If there is continuing demand for housing, the lack of supply will create an imbalance which will cause prices to increase. When new construction becomes profitable again, new product will be brought to market bringing supply and demand back into balance. If demand continues to be strong, builders will increase production to meet this demand keeping prices near the real cost of construction.

Based on a theory of rational market participants, one would expect that when prices go up and the cost of ownership exceeds the cost of rental, people choose to rent rather than own, and the resulting drop in demand would depress home prices: The inverse would also be true. Therefore, the proxy relationship between rental and ownership would keep home prices tethered to rental rates. However, this is not the case. [47] If there were only a consumptive value to real estate, the cost of ownership and the cost of rental probably would stay closely aligned; however, since there is an opportunity to profit from speculative excesses in the market, rising prices can lead to irrational exuberance as buyers chase speculative gains.

Rental rates tend to keep pace with wages because people normally pay rent out of current income. As people make more money, they compete for the available rentals and drive prices up at a rate about 1% greater than the overall rate of inflation. [48] There are times when supply and demand issues in local markets create fluctuations in this relationship, but as a rule, rents track wages pretty closely. Since house prices are tied to rents, and rents are tied to wages, house prices are indirectly tied to wages. When house prices increase faster than wage growth, the price levels become unsustainable, and if the differential is too great, a bubble is inflated. [49]

Figure 10: National Rent-to-Income Ratio, 1988-2006

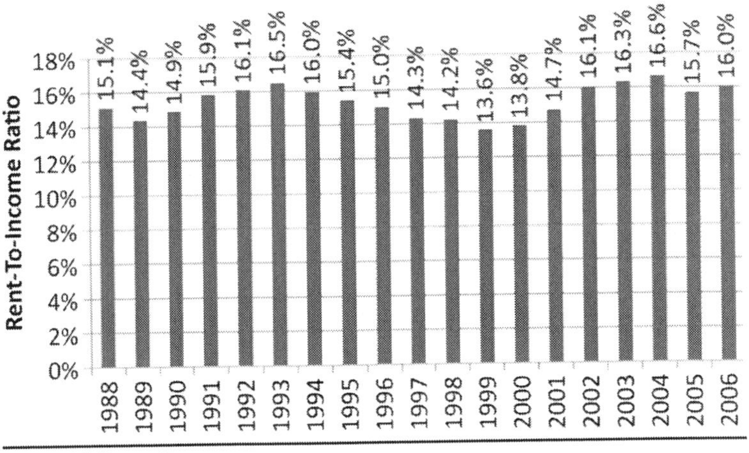

Source: US Census Bureau

Ownership Cost Math

A useful way to look at the cost of housing is to evaluate the total monthly cost of ownership. There are 7 costs to owning a house. Although some of these costs are not paid on a monthly basis, they can be evaluated on a monthly basis with simple math. These costs are:

1. Mortgage Payment
2. Property Taxes
3. Homeowners Insurance
4. Private Mortgage Insurance
5. Special Taxes and Levies
6. Homeowners Association Dues or Fees
7. Maintenance and Replacement Reserves

Mortgage Payment

The mortgage payment is the first and most obvious payment because it is the largest. It is also an area where people take risks to reduce the cost of housing. It was the manipulation of mortgage payments that was the focus of the lending industry "innovation" that inflated the housing bubble. The relationship between payment and loan amount is the most important determinant of housing prices. This relationship changes with loan terms such as the interest rate, but it is also strongly influenced by the type of amortization, if any. Amortizing loans, loans that require principal repayment in each monthly payment, finance the smallest amount. Interest-only loan terms finance a larger amount than amortizing loans because none of the payment is going toward principal. Negatively amortizing loans finance the largest amount because the monthly payment does not cover the actual interest expense.

Property Taxes

Property taxes have long been a source of local government tax revenues. Real property cannot be moved out of a government's jurisdiction, and values can be estimated by an appraisal, so it is a convenient item to tax. In most states, local governments add up the cost of running the government and divide by the total property value in the jurisdiction to establish a millage tax rate. California is forced to do things differently by Proposition 13 which effectively limits the appraised value and total tax revenue from real property. [50] Local governments are forced to find revenue from other sources. Proposition 13 limits the tax rate to 1% of purchase price with a small inflation multiplier allowing yearly increases. [51] The assessed value can only increase 2% a year regardless of actual market appreciation. The assessed value is set to market value when the property is sold. Often the lender will compel the borrower to include extra money in the monthly payment to cover property taxes, homeowners insurance, and private mortgage insurance, and these bills will be paid by the lender when they come due. If these payments are not escrowed by the lender, then the borrower will need to make these payments. The total yearly property tax bill can be divided by 12 to obtain the monthly cost.

Homeowners Insurance

Homeowners insurance is almost always required by a lender to insure the collateral for the loan. Even if there is no lender involved, it is always a good idea to carry homeowners insurance. The risk of loss from damage to the house can be a financial catastrophe without the proper insurance. A standard policy insures the home itself and its contents. Homeowners insurance is a package policy which covers both damage to property and liability or legal responsibility for any injuries and property damage by the policy holder. Damage caused by most disasters is covered with some exceptions. The most significant exceptions are damage caused by floods, earthquakes and poor maintenance.

Private Mortgage Insurance

Mortgages against real property take priority on a first recorded, first paid basis. This is known as their lien position. This becomes very important in instances of foreclosure. The first mortgage holders get paid in full before the second mortgage holder get paid and so on through the chain of mortgages on a property. In a foreclosure situation, subordinate loans are often completely wiped out, and if the loss is great enough, the first mortgage may be imperiled. Because of this fact, if the purchase money mortgage (first lien position) exceeds 80% of the value of the home, the lender will require the borrower to purchase an insurance policy to protect the lender in event of loss. This policy is of no use or benefit to the borrower as it insures the lender against loss. It is simply an added cost of ownership. Many of the purchase transactions during the bubble rally had an 80% purchase money mortgage and a "piggy back" loan of up to 20% to cover the remaining cost. These loan pairs are often referred to as 80/20 loans, and they were used primarily to avoid private mortgage insurance. There were very common during the bubble.

Special Taxes and Levies

Several areas have special taxing districts that increase the tax burden beyond the normal property tax bill. Many states have provisions which allow supplemental property tax situations. The State of California has Mello Roos fees. A Community Facilities District is an area where a special tax is imposed on those real property owners within the district. This district is established to obtain public financing through the sale of bonds for the purpose of financing certain public improvements and services. These services may include streets, water, sewage and drainage, electricity, infrastructure, schools, parks and police protection to newly developing areas. The taxes paid are used to make the payments of principal and interest on the bonds.

Homeowner Association Dues and Fees

Many modern planned communities have homeowners associations formed to maintain privately owned facilities held for the exclusive use of community residents. These HOAs bill the owners monthly to provide these services. They have foreclosure powers if the bills are not paid. It is given the authority to enforce the covenants, conditions, and restrictions (CC&Rs) and to manage the common amenities of the development. It allows the developer to legally exit responsibility of the community typically by transferring ownership of the association to the homeowners after selling off a predetermined number of lots. Most homeowners' associations are non-profit corporations, and are subject to state statutes that govern non-profit corporations and homeowners' associations. In cases where a large number of houses are unsold, in foreclosure, or are owned by lenders, remaining homeowners may encounter large increases in assessments. In some cases, the additional cost can become unaffordable to remaining homeowners pushing more of them to sell or be foreclosed on by their own homeowners association.

Maintenance and Replacement Reserves

An often overlooked cost of ownership is the cost of routine maintenance and the funding of reserves for major repairs. For example, a composite shingle roof must be replaced every 20-25 years. It may take $100 a month set aside for 20 years to fund this replacement cost. Also, condominium associations often levy special assessments to undertake required work for which the reserves are insufficient. In the real world, most people do not set aside money for these items. Most will attempt to obtain a Home Equity Line of Credit (HELOC) to fund the repairs when they are necessary. Of course, this assumes a property has appreciated and that such financing will be made available.

Tax Savings

There are two other variables people often consider when evaluating the cost of ownership that is not included in the prior list: income tax savings and lost downpayment interest. When a borrower takes out a home loan, the interest is tax deductible up to a certain amount. For borrowers in the highest marginal tax bracket, the savings can be significant, and this can make a dramatic difference in the true cost of ownership. However, this benefit diminishes over time as the loan is paid off and the interest decreases. Plus, contrary to popular belief, it is never good financial planning to spend $100 to save $25 in taxes. Also, these benefits are almost universally overestimated by people considering a home purchase. Renters considering home ownership will need to remember that they will be giving up the standard deduction when they itemize to obtain the Home Mortgage Interest Deduction (HMID). [52] A "married filing jointly" taxpayer will forgo a $10,700 deduction in 2007. This reduces the net impact of the HMID. Anecdotally, even those in the highest tax brackets usually do not get more than a 25% tax savings.

Hidden Savings

This is the forgotten benefit of a conventionally amortizing loan: forced savings. Most people are not good at saving. The government recognized this years ago when they started taking money out of people's salaries to pay income taxes because they knew people would not do it on their own. People who become homeowners during their lifetimes often have the equity in their home as their only source of retirement savings other than social security. To accurately calculate the cost of ownership, this hidden savings amount needs to be deducted from the total cost of ownership because this money will generally come back to the borrower at the time of sale. Since taxpayers in the United States get a capital gains exemption up to $250,000 per person or $500,000 per couple, this savings amount does not need to be adjusted for capital gains taxes in most circumstances.

Lost Downpayment Interest

Unless 100% financing is utilized, a cash downpayment will generally be withdrawn from an interest bearing account to purchase a house. The monthly interest that would have accrued if the downpayment money was still in the bank is a cost of ownership. This is perhaps the most overlooked ownership cost. For instance, if you are putting 20% down on a $244,900 property, you will be taking $48,980 from a bank account where it would have earned 5% in 2007. This $2,449 in interest comes to $204 in lost interest the moment this money gets tied up in real property. If someone chooses to rent rather than buy, this interest income would be earned. Of course, this earned income is also taxed, so 75% of this number is the net opportunity cost of a downpayment.

To establish the cost of ownership, each of these costs, if applicable, must be quantified. When the total monthly cost of ownership is equal to the rental rate, the market is considered to be at fair value for owner-occupants. In fact, this is the equilibrium in most real estate markets across the nation. In a strange way, the bubble did not upset this equilibrium. The use of negative amortization loans with artificially low teaser rates allowed borrowers to obtain double the loan amount with the same monthly payment: double the loan; double the purchase price. This is how prices were bid up so high so fast without a commensurate increase in wages. The elimination of these loans is also the reason prices collapse.

Running the Numbers

Below is a typical cost of ownership for a $244,900 Median property in the US (2006):

Equation 1: Cost of Ownership for 2006 Median Property in United States

$ 244,900	Purchase Price
$ 48,980	Downpayment @20%
$ 195,920	Mortgage @ 80%
$ 1,238.35	Mortgage Payment @ 6.5%
$ 204.08	Property Taxes @ 1%
$ 51.02	Homeowners Insurance @ 0.25%
$ 51.02	Special Taxes and Levies @ 0.25%
$ 100.00	Homeowners Associate Dues or Fees @ $100
$ 306.13	Maintenance and Replacement Reserves @1.5%
$1,950.60	Monthly Cash Cost
$ (278.06)	Tax Savings @ 25% of mortgage interest and property taxes
$ (177.11)	Equity hidden in payment
$ 153.06	Lost Downpayment Income @ 5% of Downpayment
$ 1,648	Total Cost of Ownership

Notes:

- The mortgage payment assumes a 30-year fixed-rate conventionally amortized mortgage at 6.5% interest.

- The property taxes are set at the 1% limit imposed by Proposition 13.

- The homeowners insurance is estimated at one-quarter of one percent per year.

- Private Mortgage Insurance is estimated at one-half of one percent per year. It is not included in the calculation above because this example utilized 80% financing. If the financing amount required PMI, the costs would have been over $100 a month higher.

- Special Taxes or Levies (Mello Roos) is estimated at one-quarter of one percent per year. Some neighborhoods do not have Mello Roos as the bonds have been paid off. Some Mello Roos fees are as high at 1%.

- HOA dues are estimated at $100: some are lower, and some are much higher.

- Maintenance and replacement reserves are estimated at 1.5%. This may be the most contentious estimate of the group because most people assume they will simply borrow their way around these costs when they are incurred. This certainly has been the pattern during the bubble years when credit was free flowing. This method of home improvement and maintenance may be significantly more difficult as the credit crunch and declining values make financing much more difficult to obtain. In any case, these costs are real, and failing to acknowledge them denies the realities of home ownership.

- The sum of the above costs is the monthly cash cost of ownership. A homeowner may not write a check for each of these costs every month, but the costs are still incurred, and renters do not pay them.

- The tax savings are based on the maximum interest payment at the beginning of a loan amortization schedule. This tax savings will decline each month as the mortgage is paid off. Contrary to popular belief, this is not a bad thing. Also, the property taxes are also deductible, but Mello Roos are not fully deductible (even though most people mistakenly deduct it).

- The opportunity cost of lost interest assumes a 5% interest rate on the downpayment reduced by 25% for taxes on this earned income.

The actual cost of ownership on a typical $244,900 property would be approximately $1,648 per month. Some will be higher and some will be lower, but the calculation above, when adjusted for the specific property details being examined, yields the cost of property ownership.

Price-to-Rent Ratio

So what general relationships can be inferred from the ownership cost breakdown provided above? First, notice the relationship between monthly cost and price. This property is worth 154 times the monthly cost when you fully examine the cost of ownership. Also, notice the relationship between monthly payment and price. This property is worth 198 times the monthly payment. Common mistake homebuyers make when considering a home purchase is to look at only the payment and ignore the other costs of owner-ship. Most assume, or have been told by realtors and mortgage brokers trying to make a commission that the tax benefits offset the other costs of ownership. Clearly, this is not the case. The true cost of ownership is about 30% higher than the monthly payment.

The price-to-cost and price-to-payment relationships become important when one wants to evaluate the relative value of the property compared to market rents. Since housing is a consumer good that can be obtained through either renting or owning, it is rational to compare the costs of each method of possessing property to see which provides a better value to the consumer. Just as stocks have price-to-earnings ratios (PE Ratios) used to establish relative value, houses have a price-to-rent ratio to establish relative value. [53] When a property can be rented for an amount equaling its monthly cost of ownership, it is at rental parity. This is the breakeven point where a consumer would be indifferent in financial terms to own or to rent. Of course there are reasons to own or to rent which are not financial, but from a strictly financial standpoint, this is where the fundamental value lies.

The price-to-rent ratio is very sensitive to changes in interest rates. When interest rates are low, the cost of money is low, so larger sums can be borrowed and vice-versa. Nationally, the price-to-rent ratio increased steadily from 1988 through 2004 in a range from 157 to 199 while mortgage interest rates declined from 10.34% in 1988 to 5.84% in 2004. This increase in price was mostly the result of lowered interest rates as the out-of-pocket expense remained relatively constant. The dramatic increase in prices after 2004 was not supported by incomes or rents, and it is part of the evidence of a real estate bubble. [54]

The price-to-rent ratio is also the basis for a commonly used valuation measure used in the property management business, the Gross Rent Multiplier (GRM). The GRM is a convenient way to evaluate whether or not a rental rate will cover the monthly cost of a particular property. It was developed by landlords seeking a method to quickly evaluate the purchase price of a proper-ty to see if it would be a profitable investment. When performing such an evaluation, a cashflow investor will typically look for a GRM near 100 to find a property with positive cashflow. This method can also be easily adapted to calculate the breakeven point where an owner/occupant would break even compared to renting. Considering the full cost of ownership–including those costs often ignored–the price-to-rent ratio and Gross Rent Multiplier is lower than most think. The GRM is a convenient measure of value because it spares you the toil of performing the above, detailed calculation to evaluate a large number of properties.

Figure 11: National Price-to-Rent Ratio, 1988-2007

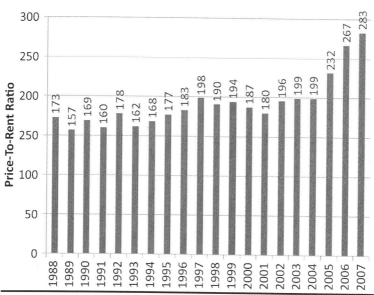

Source: US Census Bureau

Investment Value

The United States Department of Labor Bureau of Labor Statistics measures the Rent of primary residence (rent) and Owners' equivalent rent of primary residence (rental equivalence). They make this distinction because a house has both a consumptive purpose and an investment purpose. The consumptive value is measured by rent or rental equivalence. There is legitimate financial reason to pay more than the rental equivalence price. The normal rate of house appreciation–not the unsustainable kind witnessed during the Great Housing Bubble–can provide a return on investment. The source of this added value is the leverage of mortgage financing and the hedge against inflation obtained through a fixed-rate mortgage. The investment premium, which is about 10%, is less than most people think.

The rental equivalence value is the fundamental value of real estate, and it is also its consumptive value. This value can be easily measured as demonstrated in the previous section. There is an independent investment value that can also be measured and added to the consumptive value to arrive at the maximum resale value of the property. Investment value is derived from two sources: the increase in property value through appreciation and the long-term savings over renting caused by inflation. These two components are measured separately to demonstrate how they function and how much each of them is worth.

Since the return on investment generated from residential real estate occurs in the future, a discounted cashflow analysis is required to determine the net present value of the future returns. Calculating net present value sounds complex, and manually going through the calculations is quite cumbersome, but electronic spreadsheets make this an easy task. The concept is simple: how much money would investors put in an investment today if they knew the rate of growth and the cash value to be realized in the future. For instance, if investors put $100 in a bank earning 5% interest, they would have $105 at the end of the year. Net present value looks at the situation in reverse. If investors knew they would receive $105 at the end of the year and the market interest rate was 5%, they would be willing to pay $100 for it today. Similarly, the investment value of residential real estate is the value today of an amount of money to be received in the future either through sale or savings on rent.

Discount Rates

The investment value of a property can only be measured against other investment opportunities available to an investor. If investors can earn 4.5% by investing in government treasuries, they will demand a higher return to invest in an asset as volatile and as illiquid as residential real estate. The rate of return an investor demands is called a "discount rate." The discount rate is different for each investor as each will have different tolerances for risk. During the Great Housing Bubble discount rates on most asset classes were at historic lows due to excess liquidity in capital markets. The discount rate used in the analysis is the variable with the greatest impact on the investment value. Because of the risks of investing in residential real estate, a strong argument can be made that a low discount rate is unwarranted and investors would typically demand higher rates of return for assuming the inherent risks. A low discount rate exaggerates the investment premium and makes an investment appear more valuable, and a high discount rate underestimates the investment premium and makes an investment appear less valuable.

The US Department of the Treasury sells a product called Treasury Inflation-Protected Securities (TIPS). The principal of a TIPS increases with inflation, and it pays a semi-annual interest payment providing a return on the investment. When a TIPS matures, they buyer is paid the adjusted principal or original principal, whichever is greater. This is a risk-free investment guaranteed to grow with the rate of inflation. The rate of interest is very low, but since the principal grows with inflation, it provides a return just over the rate of inflation. Houses have historically appreciated at just over the rate of inflation as well; therefore a risk-free investment in TIPS provides a similar rate of asset appreciation as residential real estate (approximately 4.5%). Despite their similarities, TIPS are a much more desirable investment because the value is not very volatile, and TIPS are much easier and less expensive to buy and sell. Residential real estate values are notoriously volatile, particularly in coastal regions. Houses have high transaction costs, and they can be very difficult to sell in a bear market. It is not appropriate to use a 4.5% rate similar to the yield on TIPS or the rate of appreciation of residential real estate as the discount rate in a proper value analysis.

Another convenient discount rate to use when assessing the value of residential real estate is the interest rate on the loan used to acquire the property. Borrowed money costs money in the form of interest payments. A homebuyer can pay down the loan on the property and earn a return on that money equal to the interest on the loan as money not spent. Eliminating interest expense provides a return on investment equal to the interest rate. Interest rates during the Great Housing Bubble on 30-year fixed-rate mortgages dropped below 6%. An argument can be made that 6% is an appropriate discount rate; however, 6% interest rates are near historic lows, and interest rates are likely to be higher in the future. Interest rates stabilized in the mid 80s after the spike of the early 80s to quell inflation. The average contract mortgage interest rate from 1986 to 2007 was 8.0%. If a discount rate matching the loan interest rate is used in a value analysis, it is more appropriate to use 8% than 6%.

Investors in residential real estate (those who invest in rental property to obtain cashflow) typically ignore any resale value appreciation. These investors want to receive cash from rental in excess of the costs of ownership to provide a return on their investment. Despite their different emphasis for achieving a return, the discount rates these investors use may be the most appropriate because it is for the same asset class. Cashflow investors in rental real estate have already discounted for the risks of price volatility and illiquidity. Historically, investors in cashflow producing real estate have demanded returns of near 12%. During the Great Housing bubble, these rates declined to as low as 6% for class "A" apartments in certain California markets. [55] It is likely that discount rates will rise back to their historic norms in the aftermath of the bubble. If a discount rate is used matching that of cashflow investors in residential real estate, a rate of 12% should be used.

Once money is sunk into residential real estate, it can only be extracted through borrowing–which has its own costs–or sale. Money put into residential real estate is money taken away from a competing investment. When buyers are facing a rent versus own decision, they may choose to rent and put their downpayment and investment premium into a completely different asset class with even higher returns. This money could go into high yield bonds, market index funds or mutual funds, commodities, or any of a variety of high-risk, high-return investment vehicles. An argument can be made that the discount rate should approximate the long-term return on high yield alternative investments, perhaps as high as 15% or 18%. Although an individual investor may forego these investment opportunities to purchase residential real estate, it is not appropriate to use discount rates this high because many of these investments are riskier and more volatile than residential real estate.

The discount rate is the most important variable in evaluating the investment value of residential real estate. Arguments can be made for rates as low as 4.5% and as high as 18%. Low discount rates translate to high values, and high rates make for low values. The extremes of this range are not appropriate for use because they represent alternative investments with different risk parameters that are not comparable to residential real estate. The most appropriate discount rates are between 8% and 12% because these represent either credit costs (interest rates) or the rate used by professional real estate investors. The examples in this section will use these two rates to illustrate the range of values rational investors in residential real estate would use to value an investment premium.

Appreciation and Transaction Fees

The portion of investment value caused by appreciation can only be evaluated by an accurate estimate of appreciation during the ownership period. The general public grossly overestimates the rate of home price appreciation. [56] Historically, houses have appreciated at a rate 0.7% over the long-term level of inflation. From 1983 to 1998, a period of low inflation and declining mortgage interest rates before the Great Housing Bubble, the rate of house price appreciation was 4.5% nationally which was 1.4% over the rate of inflation. [57] Appreciation rates are tied to income and rents because this is the fundamental value of residential real estate.

Profiting from house price appreciation requires getting more money from the sale of a property than was originally paid for it and not having that profit cancelled out by moving costs, transaction fees, and a large spreads between the cost of ownership and the cost of rental during the ownership period. Buying and selling residential real estate incurs significant transaction costs that are not reflected in the price. It is quite common for properties to sell for more than their purchase price and still be a loss for the seller. When people purchase residential real estate they pay numerous closing costs including title insurance, recording fees, document stamps and taxes, mortgage application fees, survey fees, inspection fees, appraisal fees, et cetera. These fees often total between 2% and 4% of the purchase price not including any prepaid interest points on the mortgage. When people go to sell residential real estate they generally go to real estate broker who will charge them a 6% commission. There has been an increasing popularity in the use of discount brokers, but the National Association of Realtors has done a remarkable job of keeping brokerage commissions at 6% despite market pressures to lower them. These transaction costs are part of every residential real estate transaction, and they take a substantial portion of the profit on properties with short holding periods, and if the holding period is not long enough, transaction fees create losses.

The negotiating abilities of buyers and sellers and the overall market environment greatly impact the profits from real estate. Sellers almost universally believe their properties are worth more than the market will bear. People become emotionally attached to their houses, and because it is very valuable to them, they assume it is just as valuable to a person who is not attached to the property. Sellers always hope to find the buyer who will appreciate their home as much as they do and thereby pay top dollar for it. The vast majority of homeowners have unrealistic expectations of appreciation. The combination of emotional attachment and unrealistic appreciation expectations cause sellers to believe their house is more valuable than it is, and when it comes time to sell, they price it accordingly.

Sellers usually are forced to discount a property from their perceived value in order to sell it, except in raging bull markets when sellers can sometimes get more than their asking price. In bear markets, they may have to discount the property significantly in order to sell it. Bear markets are the most difficult because sellers have difficulty lowering their prices, particularly if they must sell at a loss. [58] Sometimes the difficulty in lowering price is caused by the amount of debt on the property, and sometimes it is caused by seller's emotional issues. No matter the cause, the seller's aversion to lowering asking price often results in a failure to sell the property. Since this process of discounting to sell is already reflected in the historic appreciation rate, no further adjustment is required to account for it.

The key variables for the calculation of the portion of investment value due to appreciation are the rate of appreciation, the investment discount rate and the transaction fees. In the calculations that follow the rate of appreciation is 4.5%, the discount rate is 8%, and transaction costs are 2% for the purchase and 6% for the sale. There is a 20% downpayment, and the loan is assumed to be an interest only to avoid the complications of a decreasing loan balance in the calculation and isolate the appreciation premium.

Due to the high transaction costs, the property does not reach breakeven until two full years of ownership. In a discounted cashflow basis, the property does not break even until after 4 full years of ownership. It is these high transaction costs that compel many with short-term housing needs to rent rather than own. Assuming an 8% discount rate and a term of ownership of 10 years or more, there is a premium for ownership of approximately 10%. This means the owner could pay up to 10% over the rental equivalent value and still obtain an 8% return on their money–assuming they can sell it for 10% over rental equivalent as well.

There is a tendency in the general public to assume the leverage of real estate provides excessive returns. It does magnify the appreciation, but since the historic and sustainable rate of appreciation is a low 4.5%, the leverage is applied to a small growth rate resulting in less than stellar investment returns. In the previous examples, if the downpayment is lowered to 10%, the investment premium at an 8% discount rate rises to 15%, and with a 12% discount rate, there are some ownership periods justifying a premium. If the downpayment is dropped to 1%, the ownership premium rises as high at 20%. At its most extreme with 100% financing, any positive return becomes infinite because the investor has no cash investment. Ownership premiums of 10% to 20% sound large, but in coastal markets during the Great Housing Bubble, buyers were paying ownership premiums in excess of 100%. There is no fundamental valuation justification for these price premiums, only rationalizations and hopes that a greater fool will appear and pay continually higher prices, or in the case of 100% financing speculation, that losses can be passed on to a lender if market prices decline.

Table 3: Appreciation Premium and Holding Period using an 8% Discount Rate

$200.00	House Price
$40.000	Downpayment
$4.000	Closing Costs at 2%
4.5%	Rate of Appreciation
8.0%	Discount Rate

Year	Resale Value	Selling Fees at 6%	Revenue From Sale	Seller Cash at Closing	Profit or (Loss)	Net Present Value	% of Home Value
0	$200,000	$12,000	$188,000	$28,000	($16,000)	($16,000)	-8.0%
1	$209.000	$12.540	$196.460	$36.460	($7.540)	($9.482)	-4.7%
2	$218.405	$13.104	$205.301	$45.301	$1.301	($4.780)	-2.4%
3	$228.233	$13.694	$214.539	$54.539	$10.539	($653)	-0.3%
4	$238.504	$14.310	$224.193	$64.193	$20.193	$2.948	1.5%
5	$249.236	$14.954	$234.282	$74.282	$30.282	$6.070	3.0%
6	$260.452	$15.627	$244.825	$84.825	$40.825	$8.754	4.4%
7	$272.172	$16.330	$255.842	$95.842	$51.842	$11.040	5.5%
8	$284.420	$17.065	$267.355	$107.355	$63.355	$12.963	6.5%
9	$297.219	$17.833	$279.386	$119.386	$75.386	$14.558	7.3%
10	$310.594	$18.636	$291.958	$131.958	$87.958	$15.854	7.9%
11	$324.571	$19.474	$305.096	$145.096	$101.096	$16.879	8.4%
12	$339.176	$20.351	$318.826	$158.826	$114.826	$17.659	8.8%
13	$354.439	$21.266	$333.173	$173.173	$129.173	$18.218	9.1%
14	$370.389	$22.223	$348.166	$188.166	$144.166	$18.577	9.3%
15	$387.056	$23.223	$363.833	$203.833	$159.833	$18.756	9.4%
16	$404.474	$24.268	$380.206	$220.206	$176.206	$18.774	9.4%
17	$422.675	$25.361	$397.315	$237.315	$193.315	$18.647	9.3%
18	$441.696	$26.502	$415.194	$255.194	$211.194	$18.391	9.2%
19	$461.572	$27.694	$433.878	$273.878	$229.878	$18.019	9.0%
20	$482.343	$28.941	$453.402	$293.402	$249.402	$17.545	8.8%
21	$504.048	$30.243	$473.805	$313.805	$269.805	$16.981	8.5%
22	$526.730	$31.604	$495.127	$335.127	$291.127	$16.336	8.2%
23	$550.433	$33.026	$517.407	$357.407	$313.407	$15.622	7.8%
24	$575.203	$34.512	$540.691	$380.691	$336.691	$14.847	7.4%
25	$601.087	$36.065	$565.022	$405.022	$361.022	$14.019	7.0%
26	$628.136	$37.688	$590.448	$430.448	$386.448	$13.146	6.6%
27	$656.402	$39.384	$617.018	$457.018	$413.018	$12.234	6.1%
28	$685.940	$41.156	$644.784	$484.784	$440.784	$11.290	5.6%
29	$716.807	$43.008	$673.799	$513.799	$469.799	$10.319	5.2%
30	$749.064	$44.944	$704.120	$544.120	$500.120	$9.327	4.7%

Larger discount rates eliminate the appreciation premium on residential real estate. The money tied up in a 20% downpayment on residential real estate appreciating at 4.5% provides a rate of return less than 12%; therefore when the gains from appreciation are discounted at 12%, the net present value never goes positive. When investors demand returns equal to or greater than 12%, there is no investment value from appreciation in residential real estate.

Table 4: Appreciation Premium and Holding Period using a 12% Discount Rate

$200.000	House Price
$40.000	Downpayment
$4.000	Closing Costs at 2%
4.5%	Rate of Appreciation
12.0%	Discount Rate

Year	Resale Value	Sales Fees at 6%	Revenue From Sale	Cash Back at Closing	Profit or (Loss)	Net Present Value	% of Home Value
0	$200,000	$12,000	$188,000	$28,000	($16,000)	($16,000)	-8.0%
1	$209.00	$12.54	$196.46	$36.460	($7.540)	($10.220	-5.1%
2	$218.40	$13.10	$205.30	$45.301	$1.301	($7.042)	-3.5%
3	$228.23	$13.69	$214.53	$54.539	$10.539	($4.625)	-2.3%
4	$238.50	$14.31	$224.19	$64.193	$20.193	($2.861)	-1.4%
5	$249.23	$14.95	$234.28	$74.282	$30.282	($1.652)	-0.8%
6	$260.45	$15.62	$244.82	$84.825	$40.825	($915)	-0.5%
7	$272.17	$16.33	$255.84	$95.842	$51.842	($577)	-0.3%
8	$284.42	$17.06	$267.35	$107.355	$63.355	($572)	-0.3%
9	$297.21	$17.83	$279.38	$119.386	$75.386	($847)	-0.4%
10	$310.59	$18.63	$291.95	$131.958	$87.958	($1.351)	-0.7%
11	$324.57	$19.47	$305.09	$145.096	$101.096	($2.043)	-1.0%
12	$339.17	$20.35	$318.82	$158.826	$114.826	($2.887)	-1.4%
13	$354.43	$21.26	$333.17	$173.173	$129.173	($3.851)	-1.9%
14	$370.38	$22.22	$348.16	$188.166	$144.166	($4.909)	-2.5%
15	$387.05	$23.22	$363.83	$203.833	$159.833	($6.036)	-3.0%
16	$404.47	$24.26	$380.20	$220.206	$176.206	($7.214)	-3.6%
17	$422.67	$25.36	$397.31	$237.315	$193.315	($8.425)	-4.2%
18	$441.69	$26.50	$415.19	$255.194	$211.194	($9.656)	-4.8%
19	$461.57	$27.69	$433.87	$273.878	$229.878	($10.894	-5.4%
20	$482.34	$28.94	$453.40	$293.402	$249.402	($12.129	-6.1%
21	$504.04	$30.24	$473.80	$313.805	$269.805	($13.352	-6.7%
22	$526.73	$31.60	$495.12	$335.127	$291.127	($14.557	-7.3%
23	$550.43	$33.02	$517.40	$357.407	$313.407	($15.739	-7.9%
24	$575.20	$34.51	$540.69	$380.691	$336.691	($16.892	-8.4%
25	$601.08	$36.06	$565.02	$405.022	$361.022	($18.014	-9.0%
26	$628.13	$37.68	$590.44	$430.448	$386.448	($19.100	-9.6%
27	$656.40	$39.38	$617.01	$457.018	$413.018	($20.151	-10.1%
28	$685.94	$41.15	$644.78	$484.784	$440.784	($21.163	-10.6%
29	$716.80	$43.00	$673.79	$513.799	$469.799	($22.136	-11.1%
30	$749.06	$44.94	$704.12	$544.120	$500.120	($23.070	-11.5%

Inflation Premium

Table 5: Inflation Premium from Rental Savings

$200.000	House Price	
160	Price to Rent Ratio	
3.5%	Rate of Rent Increase	
8.0%	Discount Rate	

Year	Annual Rent	Annual Ownership Cost	Rent Savings	Net Present Value	Percent of Home Value
0	$15,000	$15.000	$0	$0	0.0%
1	$15.525	$15.000	$525	$450	0.2%
2	$16.068	$15.000	$1.068	$1.298	0.6%
3	$16.631	$15.000	$1.631	$2.497	1.2%
4	$17.213	$15.000	$2.213	$4.003	2.0%
5	$17.815	$15.000	$2.815	$5.777	2.9%
6	$18.439	$15.000	$3.439	$7.784	3.9%
7	$19.084	$15.000	$4.084	$9.990	5.0%
8	$19.752	$15.000	$4.752	$12.367	6.2%
9	$20.443	$15.000	$5.443	$14.889	7.4%
10	$21.159	$15.000	$6.159	$17.530	8.8%
11	$21.900	$15.000	$6.900	$20.270	10.1%
12	$22.666	$15.000	$7.666	$23.089	11.5%
13	$23.459	$15.000	$8.459	$25.969	13.0%
14	$24.280	$15.000	$9.280	$28.895	14.4%
15	$25.130	$15.000	$10.130	$31.851	15.9%
16	$26.010	$15.000	$11.010	$34.827	17.4%
17	$26.920	$15.000	$11.920	$37.810	18.9%
18	$27.862	$15.000	$12.862	$40.790	20.4%
19	$28.838	$15.000	$13.838	$43.759	21.9%
20	$29.847	$15.000	$14.847	$46.709	23.4%
21	$30.891	$15.000	$15.891	$49.632	24.8%
22	$31.973	$15.000	$16.973	$52.522	26.3%
23	$33.092	$15.000	$18.092	$55.375	27.7%
24	$34.250	$15.000	$19.250	$58.186	29.1%
25	$35.449	$15.000	$20.449	$60.951	30.5%
26	$36.689	$15.000	$21.689	$63.666	31.8%
27	$37.974	$15.000	$22.974	$66.329	33.2%
28	$39.303	$15.000	$24.303	$68.938	34.5%
29	$40.678	$15.000	$25.678	$71.489	35.7%
30	$42.102	$15.000	$27.102	$73.983	37.0%

Residential housing does have a cash-saving value, if financed with a fixed rate mortgage. Over time, the growth in income and rents increases the cost of housing for renters. The inflation of housing costs for renters is greatly lessened for homeowners using a fixed-rate mortgage because their housing costs are effectively frozen at the rate of their ongoing mortgage payment. Other costs, such as property taxes, insurance and maintenance do still rise with inflation, but since the mortgage payment is about two-thirds of the cost of ownership, fixing this amount provides a large benefit. Over time, the savings accruing to homeowners from a level housing payment can be quite substantial. Applying the same technique of discounted cashflow analysis, this savings over time can be evaluated.

Since the savings grow every year, the value of the inflation premium grows as the term of ownership is extended, and this premium is not as sensitive to changes in the discount rate as is the appreciation premium. The premium accruing from the savings on rent can be substantial, but ownership periods vary, and the national average is less than 7 years; therefore, if a buyer pays this premium up front by paying more than the rental equivalent value, they do not reach breakeven for several years. In the early years of the mortgage, the owner who paid in excess of the rental equivalent value actually falls behind the renter in terms of out-of-pocket cash outlays for housing. Over time, as the renter faces yearly increases in rents, the homeowners will eventually be paying less, and the savings will make up for the earlier period of deficit.

Table 6: Inflation Premium from Rental Savings with 7 year Ownership Period

$200.000	House Price
160	Price to Rent Ratio
3.5%	Rate of Rent Increase
8.0%	Discount Rate
11.6%	Ownership Premium

Year	Annual Rent	Annual Ownership Cost	Rent Savings	Net Present Value	Percent of Home Value
0	$15,000	$16.738	($1,738)	($1,610)	
1	$15.525	$16.738	($1.213)	($2.650)	-1.3%
2	$16.068	$16.738	($670)	($3.182)	-1.6%
3	$16.631	$16.738	($108)	($3.261)	-1.6%
4	$17.213	$16.738	$474	($2.938)	-1.5%
5	$17.815	$16.738	$1.077	($2.260)	-1.1%
6	$18.439	$16.738	$1.700	($1.267)	-0.6%
7	$19.084	$16.738	$2.346	($0)	0.0%
8	$19.752	$16.738	$3.014	$1.508	0.8%
9	$20.443	$16.738	$3.705	$3.224	1.6%
10	$21.159	$16.738	$4.421	$5.120	2.6%

The above analysis assumes renters face the full brunt of increasing rental rates. For many apartment dwellers, this is true as landlords will raise rents every year knowing that if a renter moves out, there will be another to replace them at market rates. The circumstance is a bit different for private landlords. Most private individuals that rent out investment properties are far more concerned with the loss of cashflow resulting from the property sitting vacant than they are about maximizing income through raising rents each year. Most long-term landlords have conventional, fixed-rate financing on their properties, and because their costs are not increasing, and because they do not want to endure vacancy loss, they seldom raise rents. When they do, they do not tend to raise them to market for fear of the tenant moving out. The result of this is that housing costs are somewhat fixed for long-term renters who rent from private individuals. These renters get to enjoy almost the same benefits of fixed housing costs as homeowners. The implication of this landlord behavior is that homeowners do not necessarily see the dramatic savings over renting suggested in the calculation of the inflation premium.

The investment value for home ownership is a combination of the appreciation value and the inflation value. Both accrue to homeowners for different reasons. The appreciation value is caused by the general tendency of house prices to increase over time with the inflation of income and rents. The inflation value is a cashflow savings accruing to owners as rental rates increase while their cost of ownership is fixed. There are many variables that influence the investment value, and much depends on the assumptions behind the variables selected. Based on a typical ownership period of 7 years, and an investment environment adhering to historic norms, residential real estate has an investment value of approximately 10% of the fundamental value of the property. Buyers who pay this 10% premium will see a return on their investment if they stay in the property long enough. Buyers who pay premiums in excess of this amount or who own the property for shorter timeframes do not see a return on their investment. Buyers in the Great Housing Bubble paid well in excess of the fundamental and investment value of real estate primarily due to unrealistic expectations for appreciation. If a buyer believes properties are going to appreciate at a 15% rate every year forever, paying a 100% premium over fundamental value is justified; however, since house prices cannot rise at that rate in a sustained manner, such premiums are ill advised.

Renting Versus Owning

Renting versus owning is both an intellectual, financial decision and an emotional decision. The financial decision is first and foremost an analysis of the comparative cost of renting versus owning. The cost of a rental can be determined fairly easily as there are usually a number of comparable properties on the market to establish a realistic rental rate for any given property. Of course, it is easy to justify in one's mind a comparative rent that is higher than the market will bear. A person who is "in love" with a house will almost certainly imagine it will command a rent amount that exceeds the reality of the market. It is probably a good idea to take 5% to 10% off comparable rental rates on properties offered on the market. Once a realistic comparative rental rate is established, and a realistic evaluation of the true costs of ownership as outlined above is complete, a simple comparison of the two figures will reveal if a property is overvalued, undervalued or at parity.

Some people expend a great deal of effort evaluating the costs of ownership to determine if it is a correct decision, but many people do not. Some people make the decision to purchase the most expensive asset they will ever own with no analysis at all. The decision to buy a house is primarily an emotional one. Even those who go through all the analysis generally only do so to provide rationalizations for their emotional decision. During price rallies, greed becomes a powerful emotion motivating people to fudge any financial analysis performed. Another factor often called the "nesting instinct" causes both men and women to want a place to call their own, particularly when there are children in the family or on the way. There is nothing wrong with making decisions that are heavily influenced by emotions. Most people pick a spouse this way. The real challenge is to have the emotions and the intellect working together to make a decision that is both fiscally sound and emotionally satisfying. Of course, this is easier said than done.

Summary

The fundamental value of all housing prices is equivalent rents because rental is a direct proxy for ownership. Unfortunately, during the Great Housing Bubble, appraisers used comparative-sales prices to establish value rather than an approach using rental income. This allowed prices to detach from fundamental valuations due to irrational exuberance. To determine the value of a property, one must evaluate the local rental market to establish comparable rental rates, and one must carefully evaluate the true, total cost of ownership. A potential buyer can determine the maximum amount that should be paid for a property by manipulating the loan and downpayment amounts so the monthly cost of ownership matches the cost of a rental. Of course, in the real world most people do not bother with this type of analysis, but then, in the real world, many people mistakenly overpay for residential real estate.

Valuation of Lots and Raw Land

The valuation of land used for residential housing is mysterious and often misunderstood. [59] The valuation of lots and raw land requires a detailed knowledge of construction and marketing costs as well as a good estimate of the sales price of the final product: a residential housing unit. In short, the value of a lot is the total revenue (sales price of the home) minus the costs of production and the necessary profit. Land value is a residual calculation.

Irvine, California, has been almost entirely developed by a single land owner, The Irvine Company, as a large, master-planned community. The development has been wildly successful. The median income of buyers on The Ranch is 30% above the Orange County median. This translates into higher home prices and higher land values. The Irvine Company makes a profit by selling its land to builders who build and sell houses in the community. Once the forces governing land value are understood, it becomes obvious why the Irvine Company is protective of house prices in Irvine, and why The Irvine Company wants to maximize salable density on its land holdings like any other developer would.

Land Price as a Residual Value

The value of a piece of land is whatever is "left over" after all the other costs of production and profits are subtracted from revenue. This is a key point. Land for residential home use has no intrinsic value. It is a commodity useful for the production of houses just like lumber or concrete. A finished lot is a manufactured product, and it is subject to many of the same market forces as commodity markets. If land or lots become scarce, the price increases; if this commodity is plentiful, the price decreases. If the sales price of the final product increases revenue–like in a bubble–the value of land increases; however, if revenue decreases–like after a bubble–the value of land decreases. For a given price level, if the cost of house construction increases, the value of land decreases; if the cost of house construction decreases, the value of land increases. This last point is often confusing as the inverse relationship between building cost and land value does not seem intuitive, but since land value is a residual calculation, this relationship is the reality of the marketplace. The value of a piece of land used for residential housing is directly tied to the revenues and costs of house construction.

Individual Lots

The equations which govern the valuations of large parcels are very similar those which determine the value of an individual lot; therefore, to better understand the valuation of large parcels, one should fully understand how to evaluate an individual lot. The market value of an individual lot is equal to the revenue it could generate when a residential housing unit is built on it minus the cost of creating that revenue (construction cost, marketing, profit, and other costs). Sales revenue will largely be determined by what can be built on the lot and how much that unit would sell for in the market. The dimensions of the lot, building codes, and the local zoning ordinances create constraints on what can be built. Most often there is some variety in choices available to construct on a given lot. Each of these options has a revenue potential and an estimated cost. Builders produce the combination which yields the greatest profit.

Imagine a 6,000 Square Foot (SF) lot that is 60' wide by 100' deep. A typical lot such as this would have a front setback of 20', side setbacks of 5', and a rear setback of 30' leaving a 50' wide by 50' deep building envelope for the house foundation. This site could comfortably accommodate a 2,000 SF single-story house (some area is lost by not making the house a perfect rectangle). For the sake of making the calculations easy to follow, assume this house could sell for $1,000,000 (peak prices in Irvine were around $500 / SF).

An individual speculator would be paying retail prices for house construction. This would be upwards of $150 SF. The cost of construction would be around $300,000 (2000 * 150 = $300,000). There would be a 6% sales commission (1,000,000 * 0.06 = $60,000), plus financing costs, overhead costs, and other miscellaneous costs which will add up to about 10% of the project cost (1,000,000 * 0.1 = $100,000). Therefore, your revenue minus expenses would be $1,000,000 - $60,000 - $100,000 - $300,000 = $540,000. This is how much money would be available to pay for a lot at the breakeven point. Since a speculator would want to make a profit, the lot is discounted from $540,000 until an amount is reached to compensate for the risk and the headaches that go along with the project. Perhaps the speculator would want to make $120,000 (approximately 12% of sales price) in order to do this work? If so, the speculator would be able to offer $420,000 ($540,000 - $120,000 = $420,000) for the lot. If they are the highest bidder, they get the lot, and the project is theirs. (This same basic calculation also works for tear-down projects known as "scrapers").

Multiple Lots

Production homebuilders control the price of larger parcels with multiple lots because they have the larger sums required to complete the purchase, and they can bid higher than individuals and still make a healthy profit. Production builders have a much lower construction cost than any individual because they are geared up for mass production. They have the buying power to squeeze costs down far lower than any individual working on their own or with a custom home builder. Production builders' costs in the California market in 2007 averaged around $85 per square foot (SF). [60]

A note about the numbers: part of the process of selling a large parcel to a production homebuilder is coming to an agreement as to the costs to complete the infrastructure of the project. In order to facilitate this negotiation, both parties often turn to a neutral third party to establish costs. Specialized consulting firms meet this need. These firms provide cost estimates with much more detail than what is presented here, but the numbers are reflective of a typical situation.

The following exercise is an example of how a production builder would analyze a 100-lot subdivision in which it believes homes could be sold for an average of $1,000,000 per unit.

<u>Equation 2: Value of Hypothetical 100-Lot Subdivision</u>

Revenue
$ 1.000.000   Sales Price

Costs
  Fixed Costs

	2.000	Average House Square Footage
	$ 85	Average Cost per Square Foot
$ 170,000		Average Cost of Physical Structure
$ 40.000		Average Per-Lot Cost of Infrastructure
$ 210,000		Total Average Fixed Construction Costs

  Variable Costs

$ 120.000	12%	Profit Margin
$ 50,000	5%	Marketing
$ 30.000	3%	Overhead
$ 50.000	5%	Finance
$ 30.000	3%	Other
$ 280,000	28%	Total Variable Costs

$ 490.000   Total Costs (Fixed plus Variable)

Residual Lot Value
$ 510.000   (Revenue minus Costs)
     100   Number of Lots
$ 51.000.000   Finished Lot Land Value

The production builder can pay more for each lot because of its advantage in construction costs. Notice the very large dollar amount builders were paying for finished lots during the peak of the bubble. After the bubble peaked, the value of the land began to drop quickly. The builders were forced to take "impairment" write-offs because they overpaid for land, and the asset on their books was no longer worth what they paid for it. [61] Land prices are particularly sensitive to changes in housing prices.

Density and the Value of Land

A builder bids for land based on the potential number of units to be built. The size and configuration is not as important as the unit count: builders pay for lots, not land. Therefore, sellers of land (like The Irvine Company) want to maximize salable density. Developers and builders want to get the highest number of units per acre they can possibly sell. Density is a multiplying factor. For instance, if the million dollar home in the production builder example required a full acre of land, the land value would be $510,000 per acre; however, if the builder can fit 5 homes on the acre of land and still obtain the $1,000,000 sales price, the value of the land would be $2,550,000 or 5 times as much. For obvious reasons, landowners like high densities. The Irvine Company is widely known in the industry for creating innovative high-density product. This is born from the necessity to increase unit yield to maximize land value.

House Price and the Value of Land

The Irvine Company, or any land developer, is very motivated to see home prices increase rather than decrease because land prices are extremely sensitive to changes in house prices. The residual land value calculation reveals that only 28% of the costs vary with the sales price of the final product. The other 72% pays for the fixed costs of construction and provides residual land value. Assuming the final sales price covers the fixed costs (residual land values for residential construction can go negative,) of each additional dollar, $0.72 falls to land value. In other words, owners and developers of land make $7,200 per unit for each $10,000 increase in house sales price. If a piece of land is being developed at 5 units per acre, the land developer would make $36,000 per acre for each $10,000 increase in house sales price. From 2000 to 2006, the median sales price in Irvine increased over $400,000. This added $1,440,000 in land value to every acre of land the Irvine Company could develop at 5 units per acre. With the thousands of acres of developable land in their portfolio, this added up to a great deal of money.

Irvine's Woodbury

Woodbury is an Irvine Company Village of 4,270 units started in 2004. [62] As this Village is constructed on a 1 mile square, it sits on 640 acres for a density of 6.67 dwelling units per acre (DU/AC). Based on the discussion above, the total land value of the residential portion of the Woodbury Village can be estimated:

Equation 3: Valuation of Woodbury Community at Peak House Pricing

Revenue
$	722.928	Sales Price at 2006 Median

Costs
Fixed Costs

		2.000	Average House Square Footage
		$ 85	Average Cost per Square Foot
$	170,000		Average Cost of Physical Structure
$	40.000		Average Per-Lot Cost of Infrastructure
$	210,000		Total Average Fixed Construction Costs

Variable Costs

$	86.751	12%	Profit Margin
$	36,146	5%	Marketing
$	21.688	3%	Overhead
$	36.146	5%	Finance
$	21.688	3%	Other
$	202,420	28%	Total Variable Costs
$	412.420		Total Costs (Fixed plus Variable)

Residual Lot Value

$	310.509	(Revenue minus Costs)
	4.270	Number of Lots
$ 1,325,871,379		Finished Lot Land Value

Woodbury is worth $1.3 Billion dollars–that is Billion with a "B." If the Irvine Company could have built out this village for an average home sales price of $722,928 (the median at the end of 2006,) that is how much they would have made (the land was purchased so long ago that their land cost basis is nearly zero). If prices crash 50% from the peak, Woodbury is worth $214 Million dollars–that is million with an "M." A 50% reduction in house price means an 85% reduction in land value.

Why is land value so sensitive to home prices? As discussed previously, variable costs are only 28% of the home sales price, and land value is a residual calculation. Everything that is not a cost falls to land value; therefore, 72% of any increase or decrease in the price of a home flows directly to land value. In essence, this makes land an extremely leveraged commodity. If the value of a house changes by $10,000, the value of the lot it sits on changes $7,200. Multiply that times the 6.67 units per acre, and you can see how each $10,000 change in the value of a house changes the value of an acre of land in Woodbury by $48,024. Since Woodbury sits on 640 acres, the total value of Woodbury changes by $30,735,360 for each $10,000 change in the sales price of a home.

Equation 4: Valuation of Woodbury Community after 50% House Price Decline

Revenue		
$	361.464	Sales Price

Costs
Fixed Costs

	2.000	Average House Square Footage
	$ 85	Average Cost per Square Foot
$	170,000	Average Cost of Physical Structure
$	40.000	Average Per-Lot Cost of Infrastructure
$	210,000	Total Average Fixed Construction Costs

Variable Costs

$	43.376	12%	Profit Margin
$	18,073	5%	Marketing
$	10.844	3%	Overhead
$	18.073	5%	Finance
$	10.844	3%	Other
$	101,210	28%	Total Variable Costs

$	311.210	Total Costs (Fixed plus Variable)

Residual Lot Value

$	50.254	(Revenue minus Costs)
	4.270	Number of Lots
$	214,585,689	Finished Lot Land Value

Landowners Capitulate

Sellers and land developers do not control the market; they only control the "ask." Potential buyers determine the "bid." If bids do not reach the ask, there is no sale (which is why volumes decline dramatically after the peak). If this were not true, sellers and developers could just decide all houses must sell for $10,000,000. In 300 years when those prices may be reasonable, they will start selling homes again. Sellers cannot hold to peak prices forever. Holding to the peak prices of yesterday is a fool's game many homeowners play. If these properties are heavily leveraged, the debt service consumes their cash reserves, and the property ends up in foreclosure. It is no different for owners and developers of raw land and lots. What is true for the Irvine Company is true for all owners of raw land. The Irvine Company example provides a glimpse into the economics of land development everywhere.

Summary

The people who were actively investing in land development during the bubble made more money than most of us can imagine. The extreme sensitivity of these investments to changes in home sales price resulted in properties obtaining sales multiples of 10 times or greater in just a few years. [63] Many homeowners who either accidentally or by design timed the market well made huge windfalls during the bubble; however, the real action was in land development.

The Credit Bubble

The Great Housing Bubble was not really about housing; it was about credit. Most financial bubbles are the result of an expansion of credit, and the Great Housing Bubble was no exception. Housing just happened to be the asset class into which this capital flowed. It could have been stocks or commodities just as easily, and if the government gets too aggressive in its actions to prevent a collapse in housing prices, the liquidity intended to prop up real estate prices will likely flow into some other asset class creating yet another asset price bubble.

The root causes of the Great Housing Bubble can be traced back to four interrelated factors:

1. Separation of origination, servicing, and portfolio holding in the lending industry.
2. Innovation in structured finance and the expansion of the secondary mortgage market.
3. The lowering of lending standards and the growth of subprime lending.
4. Lower FED funds rates as an indirect and minor force. [64]

The Federal Home Loan Mortgage Corporation, also known as Freddie Mac, was created by Congress in 1970 to make possible a secondary mortgage market to provide greater liquidity to banks and other lending institutions to facilitate home mortgage lending. The Federal National Mortgage Corporation, also known as Fannie Mae, was originally created by the Federal Housing Authority (FHA) in 1938. In the beginning, Fannie Mae would securitize FHA loans, and it was the first to create a secondary mortgage market. In 1968, the company was privatized to remove its debt from the balance sheet of the Federal Government. Fannie Mae's role in purchasing FHA loans was replaced by the Government National Mortgage Association, also known as Ginnie Mae. Both Freddie Mac and Fannie Mae are private corporations that have the implied backing of the Federal Government even though their activities are explicitly not guaranteed (until they were taken into conservatorship in September 2008). Collectively Freddie Mac, Fannie Mae and Ginnie Mae are known as Government Sponsored Entities or GSEs, and they are responsible for maintaining a secondary market for mortgage backed securities.

Fannie Mae and Freddie Mac buy and sell mortgage loans to create a secondary market. [65] Mortgage originators bring groups of loans to the two companies which will either buy the loans to hold in their own portfolios, or they will bundle these loans together into securities in a process known as a "swap." In a swap program, the originator provides the group of loans, and Fannie Mae and Freddie Mac promise the originator they will receive payments from the pool–whether Fannie Mae and Freddie Mac receive said payments or not. This guarantee is tantamount to insurance as the two companies are taking on all risk of default for a small annual "guarantee fee," usually equal to 20 basis points (0.2% of the guarantee amount). Fannie Mae and Freddie Mac have strict loan origination guidelines because of the insurance they are providing. In the terms of the mortgage industry, "conforming" loans are those loans that meet the underwriting standards of Fannie Mae and Freddie Mac. In the later stages of the rally in the Great Housing Bubble, more and more mortgage loans were being originated that did not conform to Fannie Mae's and Freddie Mac's standards. The asset-backed securities (ABS) market packages these non-conforming loans into collateralized debt obligations and garnered significant market share. Despite their more conservative lending standards, Fannie Mae and Freddie Mac guaranteed many loans that performed poorly in the fallout of the Great Housing Bubble. They guaranteed many exotic loan types with inflated appraisals and committed many of the same errors as asset-backed securities (ABS) issuers during the bubble.

Figure 12: Percentage Held of Household Mortgage Debt, 1971-2006

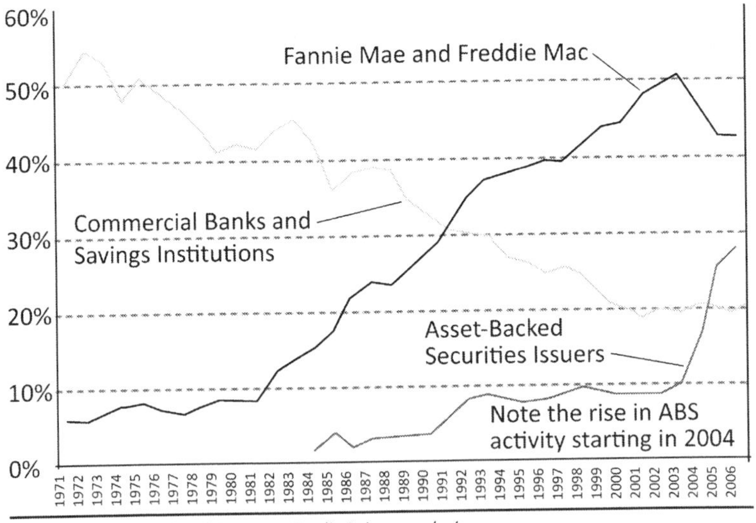

Source: OFHEO, Federal Reserve, Credit Suisse analysis

As the secondary mortgage market continued to grow, lending institutions began to sell the loans they originated rather than keeping them in their own portfolios. The banks began to make money by originating and servicing loans rather than by keeping them and earning interest. This was a radical change in lending practices and incentives; lending institutions stopped being concerned with the quality of the loans because they did not keep them, and instead they became very concerned with the volume of loans originated and the fees these generated. The originators were only concerned with meeting the parameters set forth by buyers of mortgage backed securities in the secondary market. When the parties purchasing these loans reduced standards to the point where everyone qualified, loan originators gave everyone loans. Lower lending standards opened the door for lenders to provide loans to those with low FICO scores in great volume: subprime borrowers. When combined with the widespread belief that home prices would never go down, the combination inflated the Great Housing Bubble.

Figure 13: Subprime Originations, 1994-2006

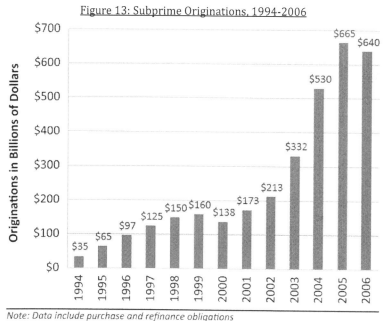

Note: Data include purchase and refinance obligations
Source: Inside Mortgage Finance Statistical Annual, 2007 Edition; Credit Suisse analysis

Subprime lending as an industry barely existed prior to 1994. There were few lenders willing to loan to people with poor credit, and there was no secondary market to purchase these loans if they were originated. The growth of subprime was the direct result of the lowering of lending standards created by the change of incentives brought about by the creation of the secondary market. These factors alone were not enough to create the Great Housing Bubble, but they provided the basic infrastructure to allow the delivery of capital that caused house prices to take flight. The catalyst or precipitating factor for the price rally was the Federal Reserve's lowering of interest rates in 2001-2004.

Many mistakenly believe the lower interest rates themselves were responsible by directly lowering mortgage interest rates. This is not accurate. Mortgage interest rates declined during this period, and this did allow borrowers to finance somewhat larger sums with the same monthly loan payment, but this was not sufficient to inflate the housing bubble. The lower Federal Funds rate caused an expansion of the money supply, and it lowered bank savings rates to such low levels that investors sought other investments with higher yields. It was this increased liquidity and quest for yield that drove huge sums of money into mortgage loans.

Structured Finance

Structured finance is an innovation of the finance industry on Wall Street. It is a method of redistributing risk based on complex legal and corporate entities such as corporations, limited liability companies or some other kind of legal entity capable of entering into contracts. The shares or other interests in structured financial entities are derivatives that obtain their value from an underlying asset. Any asset that has a regular cashflow can be pooled through structured finance to create an asset-backed security. This cashflow can be split among various parties and valued based on the risk of repayment. For instance, the most common form of structured finance utilized to inflate the Great Housing Bubble was the collateralized debt obligation or CDO. A CDO derives its value from the underlying, asset-backed securities which in the Great Housing Bubble were generally bundles of mortgage loans. Mortgage loans generate a steady cashflow stream as individual homeowners pay their mortgage obligations, and these loans are collateralized by residential real estate. In the event of default on the mortgage held by a CDO, a house can be put through foreclosure to satisfy the mortgage debt and thereby return capital to the CDO.

In any asset-backed security, assets are bundled together to reduce risk and make the asset more attractive to investors. In contrast, if an individual buys a mortgage loan from a lender in order to receive the interest payments, this investor assumes all the risk of default. The default loss risk might be low, but if one party must bear this risk, the investor significantly discounts the security to compensate. However, if this individual investor buys a small share of a large pool of mortgage loans, the investor reduces risk exposure significantly and thereby the discount for purchasing it. The value of the security is increased by pooling and thereby lowering the risk. Also, for an individual investor to purchase a mortgage loan requires a significant equity investment as mortgage loans are often in the hundreds of thousands of dollars. If a number of mortgage loans are pooled and sold off to many investors as shares or interests in a financial intermediary like a CDO, the equity requirement can be lowered considerably thus opening this type of investment to a broader investment community. It is the spreading of risk and the lowering of equity thresholds that makes structured finance such an appealing investment tool.

Figure 14: Structure of a Collateralized Debt Obligation

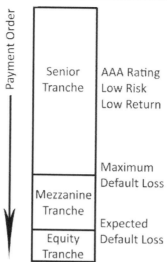

Collateralized debt obligations, like other asset-backed securities, are divided in segments known as tranches (rhymes with launches). These tranches are typically titled: senior, mezzanine and equity based on their risk exposure. There is no single structure or formula for a CDO, and many contain numerous subdivisions resulting in more segments than the three described. Similar to the lien order of mortgage obligations, these tranches are paid in order of priority. The senior tranche is paid first, the mezzanine tranche is paid next, and finally the equity tranche is paid any remainder. Since these obligations are paid in order, the senior tranche has the least risk exposure and lowest returns, and the equity tranche has the highest risk and greatest potential for return. To further lessen risk (and make the transaction even more complicated) insurance policies are often issued to insure the buyer of a senior tranche against loss. These policies known as credit default swaps were a very lucrative business during the Great Housing Bubble. It was such good business that many insurers took excessive risks and lost a great deal of money when house prices declined. [66]

The real magic of structured finance is its ability to take assets of low investment quality and turn it into something viable. George Soros aptly titled his book, "The Alchemy of Finance." [67] Like the alchemists of medieval Europe, modern investment bankers try to turn lead into gold. The syndicators who create and manage collateralized debt obligations assess the risk of loss on the underlying asset and break it down into three categories corresponding to the three tranches. The equity tranche in a CDO assumes the expected risk of loss. For example, if subprime loans expect an 8% loss from defaults, then the equity tranche will be 8% of the CDO. The syndicator typically keeps this equity tranche as part of their incentive fee, but practically speaking, the discount would be so steep it is hardly worth selling. If defaults losses are less than 8%, they see tremendous profits, and if it is over 8%, they see nothing. The Mezzanine tranche assumes the risk beyond the expected risk. If the average default loss is around 8%, and the highest default loss ever recorded is 24%, the mezzanine tranche exists to take on this risk. There is a very good chance they will see most or all of their money because the average default loss is being absorbed by the equity tranche. The senior tranche is supposed to have no risk from default loss. The line between mezzanine and senior is at or beyond the highest default loss rate ever recorded. This is not to say there is no risk, but it would take an unprecedented event to see any losses in this tranche–something like the collapse of the Great Housing Bubble.

Syndicators of collateralized debt obligations go to the open market to raise sufficient capital to buy the necessary securities and cover their fees. Since there is very little risk to the senior tranche holders, they require a lesser return on their investment. Although they own 76% of the CDO and receive 76% of the cashflow, they will pay more than 76% of the capital costs of the syndication (close to 85%) and still receive their required rate of return because the underlying subprime loan pool is paying in excess of the return required by senior tranche holders. The mezzanine tranche has more risk, and they will require a higher rate of return more closely approximating the interest rate on the underlying subprime mortgage. The remaining cost of the syndication is raised by the mezzanine tranche. The equity tranche raises no additional capital, and it is generally kept on the books of the syndicator as a bonus.

One can argue that structured finance creates greater efficiency in our financial system because capital is freed to pursue other objectives. Although, it can also be argued, as Warren Buffet has, that derivatives, the product of structured finance, are "financial weapons of mass destruction." (Buffet, 2002) Both arguments stem from the same characteristic of these securities: excessive debt. When the loan that became part of the collateralized debt obligation was originated, this money was created out of nothing by the originating lender. This is how all money is created in a fractional reserve banking system (Heffernan, 2005). As long as there is sufficient cashflow, debt creation is normal; however, when excessive debt is created and available cashflow cannot service this debt, the system experiences the very serious problem of insolvency which can lead to monetary deflation–the disappearance of lender-created money into the ether from which it was created.

If an individual investor wanted to buy a mortgage loan, the purchase would proceed with equity rather than lender-created money. However, once packaged into a CDO, the senior tranche is often purchased by an investment banker or another lender which also created this money from nothing. Since the equity tranche raises no capital, the mezzanine tranche may be the only money in the structure not created by a lender out of the ether. With so little "real" money in the deal, there is very little buffer between what would be a loss of invested capital and a banking loss of created capital. There is a tipping point where the debt service exceeds the cashflow, and when this tipping point is reached, the entire debt structure may collapse in a deflationary spiral. [68] The structured finance products such as collateralized debt obligations and their derivatives are highly leveraged instruments with a very sensitive tipping point. These instruments are also highly sensitive to short term credit availability and lending rates. The long-term CDOs were often financed by continually rolling over short term debt. Rising cost of short-term debt would take a while to cause problems, but a sudden withdrawal of credit availability, as was witnessed during the credit crunch, meant desperate sales for those who owned these instruments. Monetary deflation was a major concern to the Federal Reserve as the Great Housing Bubble began to deflate.

The use of structured finance techniques in the syndication of collateral debt obligations was not by itself a problem causing the Great Housing Bubble. This was part of the infrastructure for delivering capital to the mortgage market which began with the creation of the secondary mortgage market. In the aftermath of the crash of house prices, collateralized debt obligations received a bad reputation as dangerous securities unworthy of the safe, "AAA" ratings they received from the companies that evaluate the creditworthiness of financial instruments. The advantages of structured finance did not disappear because of problems with the market or the ill-advised ratings these securities received. Collateralized Debt Obligations as syndicators of mortgage-backed securities nearly disappeared in 2008. However, they did not go away, and they will continue to be an integral part of the capital delivery system providing money for buyers to purchase residential real estate.

Systemic Risk in the Housing Market

Credit rating and analysis of collateralized debt obligations and all structured finance products are integral to the smooth function of the secondary market for mortgage loans. A credit rating agency is a company that analyzes issuers of debt and debt-like securities and gives them an overall credit rating which measures the issuer's ability to satisfy its debt obligations. There are more than 100 major rating agencies around the world, and three of the largest and most important ones in the United States are Fitch Ratings, Moody's and Standard & Poor's. A debt issuer's credit rating is very similar to the FICO score of an individual rated by the Fair Isaac Corporation widely used in the United States by institutional lenders. Of greater importance to the housing market, the credit rating agencies also analyze and rate the creditworthiness of the various tranches of collateralized debt obligations traded in the secondary mortgage market.

Credit ratings are widely used by investors because they provide a convenient tool for comparing the credit risk among various investment alternatives. The analysis of risk is crucial in determining the interest rate a syndicator will need to offer to attract sufficient investment capital. From the other side of the transaction, it is important to the investor who is comparing the interest rates being offered by various investments. The ratings agencies provide this critical, third-party analysis both sides of the transaction can rely upon for unbiased, accurate information. When the ratings agencies are doing their job well, there is greater efficiency in capital markets as syndicators of securities are obtaining maximum market values, and investors are minimizing their risks. This efficiency in the capital markets leads to better resource utilization and stronger economic growth.

Unfortunately for many investors in collateralized debt obligations during the Great Housing Bubble, the ratings agencies did not provide an accurate or credible rating of many CDO tranches. When the housing market pricing declined, many CDO tranches were subsequently downgraded. In defense of the agencies, they were providing an analysis of risk based on existing market conditions. Their reports contained caveats concerning downside risks in the event market conditions changed, but this list of risks is standard in any analysis and widely ignored by investors who are counting on the rating to be a market forecasting tool rather than the market reporting tool it really is. Credit rating agencies are not in the business of market forecasting or evaluating systemic risks.

There is a deeper problem with the ratings agencies that began to surface in the Great Housing Bubble. Ratings agencies used to charge investors for their risk analysis, but there was a transition to charging the issuers instead. As one might imagine, there are reports that ratings agencies were concerned if they gave CDOs poor ratings, their primary source of income would go elsewhere. This put pressure on the agencies to overlook certain problems or merely list them as footnotes to their reports rather than lower a rating due to a foreseeable contingency such as a decline in house prices.

Mortgage Default Losses

There is risk of loss in any investment, and losses in collateralized debt obligations arise from the difference in the book value of the underlying mortgage note and the actual resale value of the collateral on the open market, if this collateral is subject to foreclosure. There is an important distinction that must be made between the default rate on a mortgage loan and the resultant loss incurred when a default occurs. High mortgage default rates do not necessarily translate into high mortgage default losses and vice-versa.

Subprime loans have had comparatively high default rates since their introduction. When subprime mortgages began to capture broader market share starting in 1994, the rate of home ownership in the United States began to rise. The increasing use of subprime loans and the subsequent increase in home ownership rates put upward pressures on house prices. As house prices began their upward march, the default losses from subprime defaults began to fall because the collateral was obtaining more resale value, or was being sold by the subprime borrower before foreclosure. This made subprime lending, and its associated high default rates, look less risky to investors because these default rates were not translating into default losses. As time went on and prices continued to rise, subprime lending established a track record of investor safety which drew more capital into the industry. However, since the relative safety of subprime lending was entirely predicated upon rising prices, it was an industry doomed to fail once prices stopped rising.

Take this phenomenon to its extreme and its instability becomes readily apparent. Imagine a time when prices are rising, perhaps even due purchases by subprime borrowers, and imagine what would happen if 100% of the subprime borrowers defaulted without making a single payment. It would take approximately one year for the foreclosure and relisting process to move forward, and during that year, the prices of resale houses would have increased. When the lender would go to the open market to sell the property, it would obtain enough money to pay back the loan and the lost interest so there would be no default loss. What just happened? Lenders became de facto real estate speculators profiting from the buying and selling of homes in the secondary market rather than lenders profiting from making loans and collecting interest payments. This profiting from speculation is the core mechanism that disguised the riskiness of subprime lending. When these speculative profits evaporated when prices began declining, the subprime industry imploded and its implosion exacerbated the decline of home prices.

Risk Synergy

One of the major failings of the credit markets in the Great Housing Bubble was the failure to take a holistic view and evaluate the systemic risks involved. A standard credit analysis reviews various risk parameters and attempts to rate the impact of each. The implicit assumption is that the total risk is equal to the sum of the parts; however this is not necessarily the case. Synergy is when the whole is greater than the sum of its parts, and there is a strong synergy in default loss risk in collateralized debt obligations that became apparent during the Great Housing Bubble. The credit rating agencies failed to identify this risk synergy until after the fact.

The risk of default loss in a tranche of a collateralized debt obligation is directly related to the default loss risk in the underlying mortgage notes. There are six general areas of credit default loss risk that may be evaluated independently, but their interactions are often synergistic in nature: creditworthiness risk, high combined-loan-to-value default risk, high debt-to-income ratio risk, fraud and misrepresentation risk, investment perception risk, and resale value risk. Of these general areas of risk, market valuation is most responsible for creating synergistic effects and amplifying default losses. Since many of the more "innovative" loan programs entered the market during a time of rising prices, there was no history of performance of these securities in other market conditions making it very difficult to assess the impact a down market would have on default rates. As it turns out, exotic loan programs do not perform well in any conditions other than a raging bull market.

Creditworthiness Risk

Every mortgage loan that is originated contains an evaluation of the creditworthiness of the borrower who is responsible for making timely mortgage note payments. The most common evaluation tool is the FICO score. Prime borrowers have the highest FICO scores, they are considered the lowest default risk, and they receive the lowest interest rates as a result. Subprime borrowers have the lowest FICO scores, they are considered the highest default risk, and they receive the highest interest rates. This is the best documented and most carefully evaluated risk parameter. Before many of the loan programs were introduced during the Great Housing Bubble, FICO scores strongly correlated with default rates. This correspondence broke down in the price decline when the bubble popped because the other risk factors proved to have a greater influence than expected.

High CLTV Defaults

The combined-loan-to-value (CLTV) is the total debt of all mortgage obligations as a percentage of the appraised value of a particular property. A high CLTV generally corresponds to a low downpayment, but as resale values fell in the market crash, the CLTV rose for many borrowers as a consequence of falling prices. Although all borrowers with high CLTV loan balances show high default rates, it is important to distinguish between those borrowers who had a high CLTV because of a low downpayment and those who had a high CLTV because of falling values. Even though downpayments are a sunk cost and irrelevant to the market value of a house, they do have a strong psychological impact on the behavior of homeowners. [69] People who put little or no money of their own money into the purchase of real estate exhibit greater default rates because they are not losing much of *their* money. Most people really do not care if the lender loses money, particularly if they will not have to repay the lender for the loss or incur tax penalties on the forgiven debt. When borrowers have less of their money in a transaction they are less likely to sacrifice to stay current on their mortgage note obligations, and they are more likely to default if resale values decline, particularly if their payments are greater than the cost of a comparable rental.

Fraud and Misrepresentation Risk

Most purchasers of collateralized debt obligations did not realize there was a huge amount of fraud and misrepresentation in the underlying loans they were purchasing. High CLTV financing, particularly the widely offered 100% financing, became the ideal tool for fraud. Fraudulent transactions require "straw buyers" willing to sacrifice their credit for a fee (or identity theft,) appraisers willing to inflate the houses value, and realtors and mortgage brokers either willing to go along with the transaction for cash or too ignorant to see the truth. In a transaction, the straw buyer purchased a house for greater than its true market value, and the excess payment was used to pay off the corrupted parties. Fraud was much easier to commit with 100% financing because the bank loaned the full amount of an inflated appraisal. It is much harder to commit fraud when the bank only loans 80% of a property's value. Most often the seller was in on the scam and was using the transaction to get out of a bad deal, but sometimes sellers were also innocent victims. The straw buyer had no intention of repaying the loan from the start, and the property quickly went into foreclosure.

A more common problem was misrepresentation of income. Stated-income loans, also known as "liar loans," were very common during the bubble rally. People would simply make up a number that qualified them for a loan and state it on their mortgage application. One of the assumptions purchasers of CDOs made was that the originators of the underlying loans made sure the borrowers in reality made enough money to pay back the loan. Often times the extent of the loan originators' due diligence was examining the borrower's signature on the loan application and trusting in the veracity of the signatory. This was a very serious problem for valuing an interest in a CDO because there was no way to accurately determine the viability of the income stream when the income of those responsible for paying the underlying mortgage notes was in doubt.

High DTI Defaults

The debt-to-income ratio is the total amount of payments compared to gross income expressed as a percentage. A lender evaluates the DTI of the mortgage loan as well as the total DTI of all borrower indebtedness when making a determination of creditworthiness. Historically, a borrower could not have a mortgage DTI in excess of 28% and a total DTI greater than 36% to qualify for a loan because debt burdens in excess of these figures proved to have high default rates. Despite this historical knowledge, lenders widely ignored these standards in the Great Housing Bubble in the quest for more customers. During the rally, few of these people defaulted because they were offered even more debt through home equity lines of credit from which they could make mortgage payments, and the few who did get into financial problems simply sold their house to pay off the mortgage. During the rally, people were keen to take on mortgage debt because interest rates were low, and it was a necessary tool for obtaining real estate and its commensurate appreciation benefits. It did not matter to buyers if 50% of more of their gross income was going toward debt service if the property itself was providing the additional income necessary to sustain their lifestyle. Of course, this only works when prices are increasing rapidly. Once prices stopped rising, the property could no longer provide additional income, and the borrowers had to make the crushing payments out of their true income. Without the benefits of appreciation, borrowers quickly found the burden of a high debt-to-income ratio overwhelming, and many borrowers defaulted because the payments were too much to handle–just as the lessons from history said they would be.

Investment Perception Risk

One of the biggest fallacies pushed on the general public is the notion that residential real estate is a great investment. This idea caused people to view houses as an investment and treat them accordingly. [70] When the participants in a housing market perceive houses as an investment, they will more easily default on the loan than if they viewed the house solely as a home for their family. People develop emotional attachments to their family homes, and they will sacrifice much in order to keep it. People behave in a more businesslike manner when they view a house as an investment, and they are willing to give up the house if the investment does not perform as planned. When faced with the reality that house prices were not going to continue to go up and payments were in fact going to continue to cause losses, many people decided to stop making payments and allow their investment go into foreclosure. Financially, it was the logical decision given the alternative of continuing to make payments on a losing investment. When the "Great American Dream" of home ownership was tainted by investment motives, it became a nightmare for speculators and CDO investors alike.

Resale Value Risk

The biggest risk faced by buyers of collateralized debt obligations is the default loss risk of the underlying mortgage when the collateral for the mortgage (the house) is overvalued in markets characterized by low affordability. The greatest risk of default is based on changes in the resale value of homes. All other default loss risk factors are masked when prices are increasing, and they are amplified when prices decline. Valuation risk is the ultimate synergistic factor.

There are three methods of appraising the resale value of residential real estate: the comparative-sales approach, the cost approach, and the income approach. The comparative-sales approach uses recent sales of similar properties in the market because comparable sales reflect the behavior of typical buyers in the marketplace. The cost approach determines market value by calculating the replacement cost of an identical structure plus the cost of the land or lot upon which the house would sit. The income approach determines market value by analyzing market rents of comparable properties and applies the gross rent multiplier of expected rents. Most lenders give the greatest weight to the comparable sales approach when establishing market value before applying any loan-to-value limitations to the loan amount. The income approach is generally only considered for non-owner occupied homes. [71] The three-test approach to appraising market value as used during the Great Housing Bubble is fraught with risk and is seriously flawed.

The comparative-sales approach reinforces the delusive behavior and irrational exuberance of a financial mania. If everyone is overpaying for real estate, the comparative-sales approach simply enables greater fools to continue overpaying for real estate. Since market prices for houses which serve as loan collateral fall to fundamental valuations based on income after the financial mania runs its course, mortgages originated based on the comparative-sales approach have a great deal of market risk not reflected in the pricing of collateralized debt obligations based on the underlying mortgage loans.

The cost approach has an even greater level of market risk. The cost of a structure may represent a relatively small percentage of the market value of real estate in high-value markets. In some of the most overvalued markets during the bubble, the replacement cost of the structure may have been $250,000 while the value of the underling land was $450,000; however, since the market value of land is a residual calculation based on the market value of the property, the value of the land cannot be determined independently of the house situated on it. Either the comparative-sales approach or the income approach must first be applied to establish the market value of the property before any calculation of the market value of the land can be determined. In short, since the cost approach is dependent upon another valuation method, it is not useful as an independent method of property valuation. Also, since the valuation of land is extremely sensitive to small changes in the valuation of the property, the cost approach is misleading with respect to the valuation of residential real estate.

The only reliable method for the valuation of residential real estate is the income approach, and it is the only approach that is widely ignored by the lending community. It has been demonstrated in previous residential market bubbles in California and in major metropolitan areas in other states that once a price decline begins, prices fall to fundamental valuations based on income and rent. [72] The reason for this is that once the speculative investment incentive is removed from the market, buyers do not support prices until there is a new reason for them to buy: they can save money versus renting. Comparative rents are the fundamental valuation of residential real estate. Mortgage default loss risk is low only when market prices are in line with comparative rents or when market prices are increasing. Default loss risk is low when prices are in line with rents because a property can be converted from owner-occupied to a rental unit and the payment can still be covered. Default loss risk is low when prices are rising because a borrower experiencing financial difficulty can always sell the property to repay the loan. Unfortunately, once market prices increase above the level of comparative rents, they endure a period of decline back to comparative rent levels; therefore, if lenders continue to use the comparative-sales approach, they will enjoy a temporary period of low market risk while prices increase and another painful period of losses when prices decrease. As was demonstrated in the aftermath of the Great Housing Bubble, these periods of lender losses can imperil the entire banking and financial system. The only way to prevent the pain of loss is to recognize the end-game risks when prices are increasing and choose not to participate in that lending environment. Many lenders did not participate in the crazy lending of the Great Housing Bubble, and they were not significantly damaged in the aftermath; however, the hunger for mortgage loans from the CDO market compelled many lenders to participate or get buried by their competitors. The only real market-based solution to the problem of originating bad loans must come from the CDO market.

The CDO Market Solution

The solution to preventing future bubbles in the residential real estate market lies in the market for collateralized debt obligations and conforming loans insured by the government sponsored entities (GSEs). The GSEs created the secondary mortgage market in the 1970s, and the CDO market is the extension of this market bringing large amounts of investment capital to residential real estate. During the Great Housing Bubble the CDO market did not properly evaluate the risk of default on the underlying mortgage notes they pooled.

If the CDO market were to evaluate mortgage default loss risk based on the income approach rather than the comparative-sales approach, the performance of CDOs would be greatly improved, and investor confidence would return to the market. It is only after the risks are properly evaluated that capital would return to this market. If the CDO market evaluates risk based on the income approach, the lenders that originate loans hoping to sell them to CDOs would be forced to do the same. If lenders originate loans based on the income approach, the irrational exuberance that creates financial bubbles would not be enabled. People would still be free to overpay for houses with their own money, but the scope and scale of financial bubbles would be limited to the funds of buyers, and the banking system would not be imperiled by the foolishness of the market masses when prices fall to fundamental valuations based on rent and income.

Visualizing the Bubble

With a huge influx of capital into the secondary mortgage market when the Federal Reserve lowered interest rates in 2001-2004, the industry was under tremendous pressure to deliver more loans to hungry investors seeking higher yields. This caused the already-low loan standards to be all but eliminated. All of the worst "innovations" in the lending industry occurred during this period: Negative Amortization loans, Stated-Income loans (Liar Loans,) NINJA loans (no income, no job, no assets,) 100% financing, FICO scores under 500, and one-day-out-of-bankruptcy loans among others. The joke was if borrowers could "fog a mirror" or if they "had a pulse," they could get a loan for as much as they wanted to buy a house. It is not hard to envision the impact this had on house prices.

Imagine a room with 100 people representing the pool of subprime borrowers. These are new entrants to the market. They were previously unable to buy due to bad credit, lack of savings, and other reasons. All of them are told they are going to bid on an asset that never goes down in value, and they will be given the ability to borrow unlimited funds (stated-income "liar loans") The only caveat is the borrowed money must be paid back when the asset is sold (not that they care, they already have bad credit). Imagine what happens?

People start to buy the asset, and prices rise. Others in the room seeing the rising prices come to believe that the value of the asset never declines, and they join in the bidding. As the bidding drives prices even higher, a manic quality takes over the bidding and people compete with each other, often bidding higher than the asking prices. Nobody wants to be left out. There are fortunes to be made. Greed drives prices upward at a staggering rate. As the last of the 100 people buy, prices are very high, everyone has made money, and it looks as if prices will continue to rise forever . . .

Then something strange happens: there is nobody left to make a purchase. (A key indication of the end of a speculative mania is a huge decline in sales, as was witnessed over 2006 and 2007). Transaction volume drops off dramatically, and prices stop their dizzying ascent. Nobody is particularly alarmed at first, but a few of the more cautious sell their assets to pay off their loans. Since there are no more new buyers, the first selling actually causes prices to drop. This is unprecedented: prices have never declined! Most ignore the problem and comfort themselves with the history of rising prices; however, a few are spooked by this unprecedented drop and sell the asset. This selling drives prices even lower. Now those who still own the asset become worried, some continue to deny that there is a problem, and some get angry about the price declines. Some of the late buyers actually owe more than they paid for the asset. They sell the asset at a loss. The lenders now lose some money and refuse to loan any more money to be secured against the asset. Now there are even fewer buyers and a large group of owners who all want to sell before prices drop any lower. Panic selling ensues. Everyone wants to sell at the same time, and there are no buyers to purchase the asset. Prices fall dramatically. This asset which was sought after at any price is now for sale at any price, and there are few takers. People in the market rightfully believe the asset will continue to decline. Owners of the asset have accepted the new reality; they are depressed and despondent.

In any group of people, there are always a few who do not believe the "prices always rise" narrative. Some recognize that asset prices cannot rise indefinitely and cannot stay detached from their fundamental valuations. These people witness the rally and the resulting crash without participating. They wait patiently for prices to drop back to fundamental values, and then these people buy. As these new buyers enter the market, prices stop their steep descent and market participants start to hope again. It takes a while to work off the inventory for sale in the market, so prices tend to flatten at the bottom for an extended period of time; however, just as spring follows winter, appreciation returns to the market in time, and the cycle begins all over again.

What is written above is true of any asset whether it be stocks, bonds, houses or tulips. [73] In this case, it is the local housing market, and the room of new buyers represents subprime borrowers, but the concepts are universal. One phenomenon somewhat unique to the housing market is the forced sale due to foreclosure (stocks have margin calls). Even if the psychological factors at work during the panic could somehow be quelled, the forced sales from foreclosures would drive down prices anyway. True panic is not required to crash a housing market, only dropping prices and an inability to make payments. Subprime lending was one of the leading causes of the Great Housing Bubble, and its implosion exacerbated the market decline.

Responsibility for the Bubble

Who is responsible for the Great Housing Bubble? It is one thing to identify who or what caused the bubble, but it is another to assign responsibility and blame. Borrowers, lenders, investors, and the FED are all responsible; it is only a matter of degree. Irresponsible borrowers are like children, if you offer them something they want, no matter the terms, they will take it. The federal government realized this basic fact years ago when they passed predatory lending laws. This does not make the borrower any less responsible, but by definition, subprime borrowers are irresponsible. If they took responsibility for their debts, they would not be subprime. [74] So if a large amount of money is lent to the most irresponsible among us, it is reasonable to expect them to spend it irresponsibly and not worry about paying it back. In this case, past performance *is* an indicator of future performance. It should come as no surprise that the subprime experiment ended badly.

Despite the low expectation of subprime performance, people need to be held accountable for their actions. It seems our entire culture is based on having victim status and being irresponsible. Borrowers should not be bailed out by any government program as it would just create more dependence and greater risk taking. The people who paid too much and cannot pay it back have to be allowed to lose their homes. That is life. The responsible should not pay to subsidize the irresponsible. This is one of those instances where irresponsible will be made to take responsibility.

Lenders are also responsible in this matter. Mortgage lenders provide a service because without them most people would be dead by the time they had saved enough money to buy a home for cash. However, when lenders start handing out home equity lines of credit for consumption, they are as bad as the credit card issuers preying on people's reckless irresponsibility. Once mortgage lenders crossed that line, they ceased to be serving the needs of homebuyers and instead began serving the wants of the credit addicted: shame on them.

Of course, none of this would have happened without the contributions of the enablers at the Federal Reserve and on Wall Street. The Federal Reserve lowered rates and then Alan Greenspan told borrowers to take out adjustable rate mortgages under certain circumstances. As one might suspect, he did this so his fellow bankers would not be stuck with low-interest loans for 30 years, but he gave the world of homebuyers the "green light" for taking on high risk loans. Then Wall Street investors flooded with liquidity from cheap money from home and overseas started chasing returns. High-interest, subprime loans looked attractive, and as long as house prices went up and nobody defaulted, everything was fine. Who is to blame for that situation? The Bank of Japan for creating the carry trade? The Federal Reserve for lowering rates to avoid a recession? The financial wizards who invented collateralized debt obligations? The ratings agencies who labeled these investments "AAA?" The investors who were chasing high yields? Or all of them?

The borrowers are certainly at fault; if for no other reason than they signed the papers and took the money. The lenders are also at fault because they should have known better than to give borrowers loans they could not afford, provide loans with no income documentation, and ignore proven guidelines for loan-to-value and debt-to-income. Lenders simply cannot abdicate responsibility in this matter for financial, legal and moral reasons. The Federal Reserve and Wall Street investors are also at fault for creating the situation and enabling this to occur. In the end, all the responsible parties were ruined: borrowers lost their houses and went bankrupt, lenders like New Century went out of business and/or lost billions, Wall Street investors shared in the losses with the lenders, and Alan Greenspan is remembered by history as the architect of the largest, most painful financial bubble in history.

In assigning blame, it is also important to recognize that many innocent people were victims of the housing bust: children of the overleveraged and dishonest, neighbors of homes with dead lawns and graffiti, taxpayers whose money might be used in a bailout, responsible depositors who have to endure returns less than the rate of inflation, condo owners who have to pay the gap left in condo dues on foreclosed units, government employees who were hired in the optimism of rising budgets who are now laid off when tax revenues decline, and bubble buyers who were not motivated by speculative gains but merely looking to shelter their family. The decline of house prices punishes sinners and saints alike.

Summary

The Great Housing Bubble was a credit bubble. It was enabled by the widespread use of structured finance and collateralized debt obligations, and it was inflated by the irrational exuberance of buyers. The infrastructure for delivering capital to inflate the bubble was put in place years prior with the development and evolution of the secondary mortgage market. The system for delivering capital was greatly enhanced by the creation of collateralized debt obligations. Errors in the evaluation of risk to mortgage capital caused money to flow into this market that should have been diverted elsewhere. This free-flow of capital inflated the Great Housing Bubble.

The Housing Bubble

Prices went up a large amount during the Great Housing Bubble, but what makes this price increase a bubble? To answer this question it is necessary to accurately measure price levels and review historic measures of affordability to establish these price levels are not sustainable. [75] Measuring house prices is not a simple task, and there are many methods market watchers use to evaluate market prices. These include the median, the average cost per square foot, and the S&P/Case-Shiller indices. Price levels in financial markets represent the collective result of individual actions. There are techniques to measure the actions of the individual market participants and their impact on house prices. These measures are debt-to-income ratios and price-to-income ratios. The amount of debt people are willing to take on compared to the income they have available is their debt-to-income ratio. The amount of money people are able to put toward the purchase of residential real estate compared to their income is their price-to-income ratio. These ratios are important because they show how much people are borrowing and spending from their earnings to acquire real estate. When these ratios break with historic patterns, they signify a housing bubble.

There is a point where people are not able to bid up prices any higher because they do not have the savings or the borrowing power to pay more. This affordability limit determines where bubble rallies end; however, this limit is not predetermined or in a fixed location. The purpose of exotic financing programs is to expand this limit and bring more customers to the market and generate fees for the lenders. Unfortunately, these products have continually proven to be unstable, and the high default rates and lender losses inevitably lead to a contraction of credit known as a credit crunch. Interest-only and negative amortization loans created the housing rally and their elimination due to borrower default created the housing crash. As mentioned previously, the housing bubble was a credit bubble.

Price Measurements

There is no perfect measure for any broad financial market activity. Markets for stocks, bonds and other securities are the most widely reported and measured financial markets. It is relatively easy to measure activity in these markets because all sales are recorded at a few central exchanges and the "products" are uniform (one share of stock is equal to another). In contrast, real estate markets are much more difficult to evaluate. [76] Real estate transactions are recorded into the public record in thousands of locations across the country. Keeping an organized database of these records is such a daunting task that the title insurance industry has taken this responsibility as part of its business model, and many people are devoted to the arduous task of obtaining and organizing these records on a daily basis. Real estate does not have the uniformity of stocks or other financial instruments. Each property has unique qualities that differentiate it from all other properties making like-kind comparisons very difficult. Geographical location is a major influence on the value of real estate. Even if two properties could be found with identical physical characteristics, the values of these properties could vary considerably based on where they are located. Ideally, a market measure would record the changes in sales prices of identical assets or in the case of an index, a group of similar assets. The unique nature of real estate assets makes it difficult to use standard measures of reporting utilized in other financial markets.

Due to the problems of asset uniformity and variability based on location, real estate markets are typically measured using some form of median pricing over a specified geographic area. The median is a statistical measure of central tendency where half the data points are above and half the data points are below. For instance, in a list of 5 numbers sorted by size ($100,000, $200,000, $300,000, $500,000, $900,000,) the third number in the list ($300,000) would be the median because it has two numbers that are larger and two numbers that are smaller. The median ($300,000) is used rather than an average ($400,000) because a few very expensive properties can increase the average significantly, and the resulting number does not represent the bulk of the price activity in the market.

One of the problems with a median as a measure of house prices is a lag between when a top or a bottom actually occurs and when this top or bottom is reflected in the index. During the beginning of a market decline, the lower end of the market has a more dramatic drop in volume than the top of the market. This causes the median to stay at artificially high levels not reflective of pricing of individual properties in the market. In other words, for a time things look better than they are. At the beginning of a market rally, transaction volume picks up at the bottom of the market at first restarting the chain of move ups. During this time, the prices of individual properties can be moving higher, but since the heavy transaction volume is at the low end, the median will actually move lower.

The median is a good measure of general price activity in the market, but it does have a significant weakness: it does not indicate the value buyers are obtaining in the market. The houses or structures built on the land compose the most significant portion of real estate value in most markets. These structures deteriorate over time and require routine maintenance that is often deferred. During times of prosperity, many people renovate homes to add value and improve their living conditions. The impact of deterioration and renovation of individual properties is not reflected in the median resale value. Also, at the time of sale, there are often buyer incentives which inflate the recorded sales price relative to the actual cost to the buyer. These buyer incentives also distort the median sales price as a measure of value.

Many data reporting services measure, record, and report the average sales cost on a per-square-foot basis to address the problem of evaluating what buyers are getting for their money. For instance, in a declining market if people start buying much larger homes at the limit of affordability, the generic median sales price would remain unchanged, but since buyers are getting much larger homes for the same money, the average cost per-square-foot would decline accordingly. This makes the average cost per-square-foot a superior measure for capturing qualitative changes in house prices; however, this method of measurement does not capture the relative quality of the square footage purchased, only the price paid for it. High quality finishes may justify a higher price per square foot. There is no way to objectively evaluate the impact finish quality has on home prices. The main problems with using the average cost per-square-foot to measure price is that it does not provide a number comparable to sales prices since it has been divided by square feet, and it is not widely measured and reported.

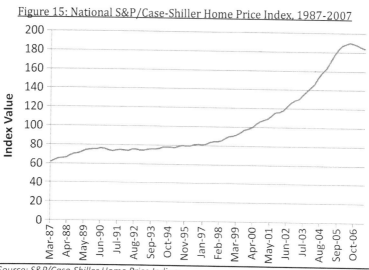

Figure 15: National S&P/Case-Shiller Home Price Index, 1987-2007

Source: S&P/Case-Shiller Home Price Indices

To address some of the weaknesses of the generic median sales price as a measure of market value, Karl Case and Robert Shiller developed the Case-Shiller indices for measuring market trends. [77] This index measures the change in price of repeat sales. It solves the dilemma of pricing like-kind properties–almost. Although these indices capture the price movements of individual properties far better than the generic median sales price, it does not take into account value added through renovation and improvement. To address this issue, the index gives less weight to extreme price changes assuming the outlier is a significant renovation. However, if there is a market-wide renovation of properties, as was the case in many markets during the Great Housing Bubble; this will cause a distortion in the index. The other weaknesses of the Case Shiller indices concern how and where it is reported. Since it is an index of relative price change rather than a direct measure of price, the index is reported as an arbitrary number based on a baseline date; therefore, the numbers are not useful for evaluating current pricing. The index is also confined to 20 large metropolitan areas around the United States. The large geographical coverage areas are required to obtain enough repeat sales to construct a smooth index. The broad yet limited geographical coverage fails to capture price changes in smaller markets. Also, since the Case-Shiller index is a measure of changes in prices of sales of the same home, it does not include any newly constructed homes. No measure is perfect, but the Case-Shiller index is the best at measuring historic movements in pricing because its methodology is focused on repeat sales of the same property.

Figure 16: Los Angeles S&P/Case-Shiller Index, 1987-2007

Source: S&P/Case-Shiller Home Price Indices

The examples from this work will use the median sales price, not because it is the best method, but because it is the most widely used and best understood of the common measures. Also, since it gives a number reflective of sales values in the marketplace, it is the easiest to understand and interpret. This measure has weaknesses, but over time it does a reasonable job of documenting overall prices and trends in the marketplace.

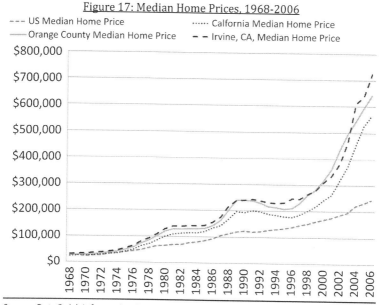

Figure 17: Median Home Prices, 1968-2006

Source: DataQuick Information Systems; National Association of Realtors; US Department of Labor

The Great Housing Bubble was an asset bubble of unprecedented proportions. Between 2000 and 2006, home prices increased 45% nationally, and in California home prices increased 135%. [78] Had this amazing price increase coincided with a period of high inflation, it may not have been indicative of a price bubble, merely the general increase in prices of all goods and services; however, inflation was low during this period. The inflation adjusted price increases nationwide were 23% and in California it was 100%. There was no great improvement in the quality of houses justifying the higher prices. Although some homeowners made cosmetic improvements, the vast majority of homes were unchanged during this period, and many deteriorated with age. Resale homes did not undergo any form of manufacturing process where value was added to the final product. There was little real wealth created during the bubble, just a temporary exaggeration of value.

Price-To-Income Ratios

Price-to-income ratios represent the amount borrowed relative to the incomes of the borrower. There are many variables that impact house prices, and some of the variability in prices over time can be attributed to changes in these variables; however, since most houses are purchased with lender financing, and since lender financing is linked to income, the price-to-income ratio is the best metric for evaluating long-term housing price trends. The price-to-income ratio does not need to be adjusted for inflation as both prices and income will rise with the general level of inflation. Most of the fluctuations in the ratio are based on changes in financing terms, in particular interest rates, and of course, irrational exuberance.

The Great Housing Bubble saw unprecedented price-to-income ratios because interest rates were at historic lows and the use of exotic financing including negative amortization loans were at historic highs. When measured against historic norms of house price to income, the degree of price inflation was staggering. [79] In markets where bubble behavior is not prevalent, price to income ratios hover between 2.3 and 2.8. In bubble markets there is a tendency to maintain higher ratios, and the range over time is much greater. Any ratio less than 3 is generally considered affordable.

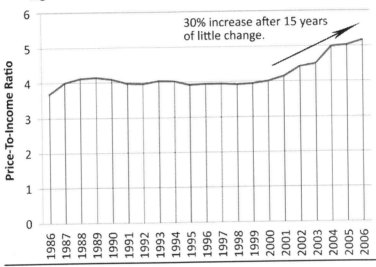

Figure 18: National Ratio of House Price to Income, 1986-2006

Source: U.S. Census Bureau

In bubble markets ratios of 3 to 4 are as affordable as they get. Anything greater than 4 is a strain on family budgets and generally a sign of an inflated market. Ratios greater than 5 are considered very unaffordable and prone to high rates of default because they tend to be characterized by exotic financing. Price-to-income ratios in the bubble of the early 90s in California did not exceed 6 because interest rates were higher and because negative amortization loans were not widely available. During the Great Housing Bubble, the national ratio of house price to income increased 30% from 4.0 to 5.2. This means 30% more debt is serviced by the same income. Some of this increased ability to service debt is explained by lower interest rates and exotic loan terms, and some of this increase came from people choosing to take on larger debt loads due to the irrational expectation of ever increasing house prices coupled with loose lending standards which enabled the populace to take on these debts.

The national trends were small compared to the frenzied activities of bubble markets in California where most markets saw their house price to income ratio double.

Figure 19: Price-To-Income Ratio in California, OC and Irvine, 1986-2006

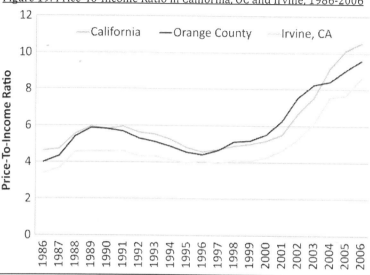

Source: US Census Bureau; California Association of Realtors; DataQuick Information Systems

Buyers were never forced to buy; it was always a choice. During the market rally, greedy buyers motivated by rising prices and fueled by loose lending standards were able to bid prices up to ridiculous levels. The exotic financing was not a *result* of high prices; it was the *cause* of high prices. Lenders were keen to offer these products because they were not taking on the risk, and it allowed them to keep transaction volumes high. The lenders profits came from transaction volume. By late 2007, the market balance had shifted from favoring sellers to favoring buyers. The once greedy buyers were becoming desperate sellers: their dreams of riches from perpetual appreciation were in tatters. Many were forced to sell due to their inability to make their mortgage payments. Those that hung on were homeowners with 50% or more of their income going toward paying off an asset which was declining in value. It was not a set of circumstances to be envied.

Price-To-Rent Ratios

Price-to-rent ratios represent the cost of a dwelling unit relative to the cost of a comparable dwelling unit. This ratio is also subject to the same variability exhibited by the price to income ratio. [80] This is not surprising considering rent is generally paid out of current income, so incomes and rents tend to track one another fairly closely. The ratio of rent to income has stayed within a range from 13.6% to 16.5% from 1988 to 2006. This demonstrates renters have been putting roughly the same percentage of their incomes toward housing for the 18 years period of data examined. The evidence from the sudden and dramatic changes in the price-to-income ratio and the price-to-rent ratio points to a housing bubble. [81] If these two measures of value had been supported by a rise in the rent-to-income ratio, the increase in prices might have been explainable by a shortage in dwelling units causing all consumers of housing to see an increase in the percentage of their income going toward housing. Evidence from the rent-to-income ratio is to the contrary.

Figure 20: National Price-to-Rent Ratio, 1988-2007

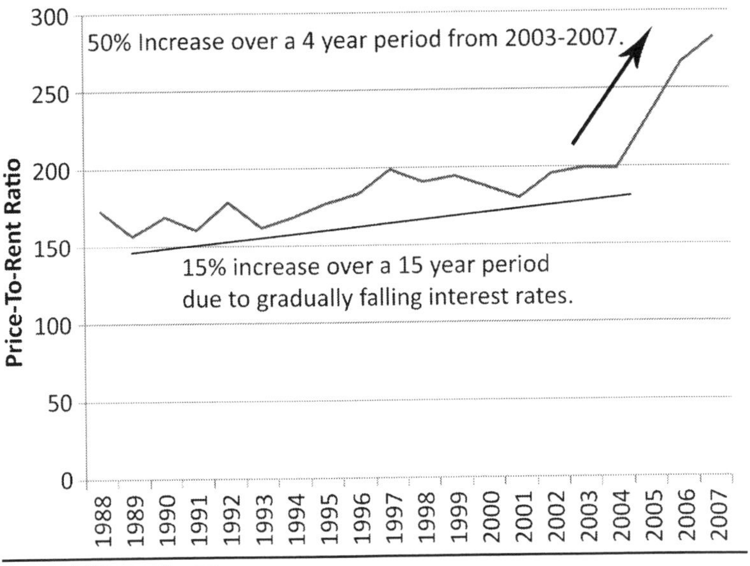

Source: US Census Bureau

Debt-To-Income Ratios

There was a significant price bubble in residential real estate in the late 1980s crashing in the early 1990s. This coastal bubble was concentrated in California and in some major metropolitan areas in other states, and it did not spread to housing markets nationwide. When comparing this previous bubble to the Great Housing Bubble, the macroeconomic circumstances were different: prices and wages were lower in the last bubble, interest rates were higher, the economies were different, and other factors were also unique; however, the evaluation of personal circumstances each buyer goes through when contemplating a purchase is constant. The cumulative impact of the decisions of buyers is represented in the debt-to-income ratios–how much each household pays to borrow versus how much they make. Comparing the trends in debt-to-income ratios provides a great tool for elucidating the behavior of buyers.

Typically debt-to-income ratios track interest rates. As interest rates decline, it becomes less expensive to borrow money so borrowers have to put less of their income toward debt service. The inverse is also true. On a national level from 1997 to 2006 interest rates trended lower due to low inflation and a low federal funds rate. During this same period people were increasing the amount of money they were putting toward home mortgage debt service. If the cost of money is declining and the amount of money people are putting toward debt service is increasing, the total amount borrowed increases dramatically. Since most residential real estate is financed, this increased borrowing drove prices up and helped inflate the Great Housing Bubble.

Figure 21: Debt-To-Income Ratio and Mortgage Interest Rates, 1997-2006

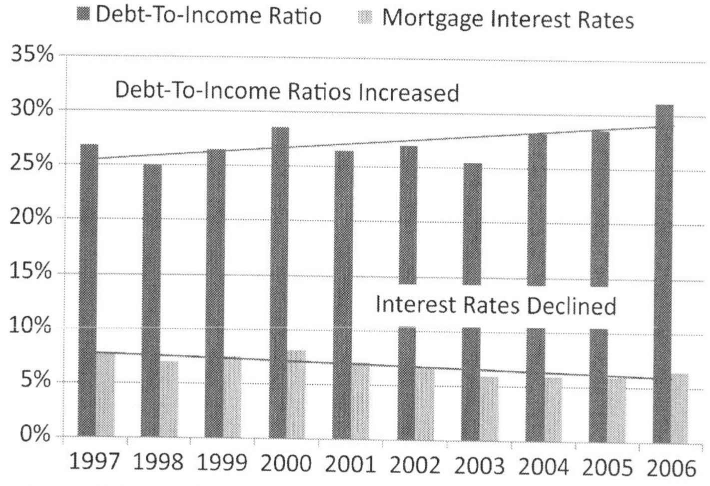

Note: Assumes a Fixed-Rate 30-year conventionally amortized mortgage with 20% down.
Source: US Census Bureau, DataQuick Information Systems, Freddie Mac

The figure on the following page shows the historic debt-to-income ratios for California, Orange County and Irvine from 1986 to 2006. It is calculated based on historic interest rates, median home prices and median incomes. Lenders have traditionally limited a mortgage debt payment to 28% and a total debt service to 36% of a borrower's gross income. The figure shows these standard affordability levels. During price rallies, these standards are loosened in response to demand from customers when prices are very high. Debt service ratios above traditional standards are prone to high default rates once prices stop increasing. In 1987, 1988 and 1989 people believed they would be "priced out forever," so they bought in a fear-frenzy creating an obvious bubble. Mostly people stretched with conventional mortgages, but other mortgage programs were used. This helped propel the bubble to a low level of affordability. Basically, prices could not get pushed up any higher because lenders would not loan any more money.

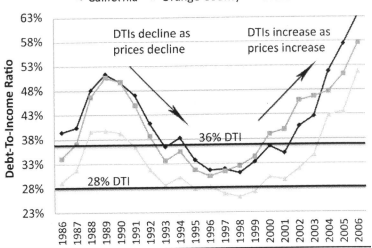

Figure 22: Debt-To-Income Ratio, California 1986-2006

Note: Assumes a Fixed-Rate 30-year conventionally amortized mortgage with 20% down.
Source: US Census Bureau, DataQuick Information Systems, Freddie Mac

Changes in debt-to-income ratios are not a passive phenomenon only responding to changes in price. The psychology of buyers reflected in debt-to-income ratio is the *facilitator* of price action. In market rallies people put larger and larger percentages of their income toward purchasing houses because they are appreciating assets. People are not passively responding to market prices, they are actively choosing to bid prices higher out of greed and the desire to capture the appreciation their buying activity is creating. This will go on as long as there are sufficient buyers to push prices higher. The Great Housing Bubble proved that as long as credit is available there is no rational price level where people choose not to buy due to prices that are perceived to be expensive. No price is too high as long as they are ever increasing.

In market busts, people put smaller and smaller percentages of their income toward house purchases because the value is declining. In fact, it is possible for house prices to decline so quickly that no mortgage program can reduce the cost of ownership to be less than renting. The only thing justifying a DTI greater than 50% is the belief in high rates of appreciation. Why would anyone pay double the cost of rental to "own" unless ownership provided a return on that investment? Once it is obvious that prices are not increasing and even beginning to decrease, the party is over. Why would anyone stretch to buy a house when prices are dropping? Prices decline at least until house payments reach affordable levels approximating their rental equivalent value. At the bottom, it makes sense to buy because it is cheaper than renting. In a bubble market when the market debt-to-income ratio falls below 30%, the bottom is near.

Affordability Limits

Affordability is a measure of people's ability to raise money to obtain real estate. It is often represented as an index that compares the cost to finance a median house price to the percentage of the general population with the income to support this house price. For instance, in Orange County, California, in 2006, only 2.4% of the population earned enough money to afford a median priced home. When affordability drops below 50%, there is a problem in housing; when it drops to 2.4% there is either a severe shortage of housing, or a housing price bubble. Most often, it is the latter.

Figure 23: Affordability / Demand

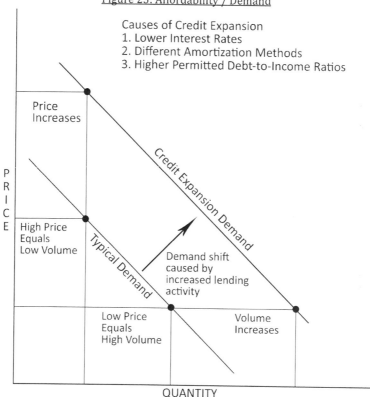

One way to envision affordability is through supply and demand diagrams like those found in introductory economics textbooks. Affordability is the demand curve. There are a small number of buyers who can afford very high prices, and many buyers who can afford very low prices. There is a limit to how high buyers can push prices. This limit is usually determined by lenders who provide the bulk of the money for real estate transactions. During the Great Housing Bubble, these limits were nearly eliminated. In terms of the demand curve, the loose credit standards and low interest rates shifted the demand curve dramatically to the right. Thus many more people were enabled to buy and they were able to do so at much higher prices. In bubble markets, once prices started to rise, they were bid up to levels where affordability was at record lows by historical measures. In a number of other markets, 2005 and 2006 were not the least affordable years in recent history. Markets not historically prone to bubble behavior might have a population which is decreasing (like Detroit,) steady (like Chicago,) or increasing rapidly (like Dallas). In fact, changes in population has very little to do with housing affordability in a particular city.

The expansion of credit took four forms: lower interest rates, lowering or eliminating qualification requirements, different amortization methods, and higher allowable debt-to-income ratios. Lower interest rates expand credit by allowing larger sums to be borrowed with the same payment amount. In 2000, the interest rate on a 30-year mortgage was 8.05%, and in 2003, it was 5.83%. This reduction in interest rates accounts for 20% to 50% of the increase in house prices experienced during the bubble. Subprime lending is an oft-cited example of lowering qualification requirements, but many loan programs included limited documentation that also allowed people with good credit to purchase multiple properties with little or no money down and no real ability to make the payments. Credit was also expanded by borrowers utilizing risky financing options including interest-only and negative amortization. Interest-only loans artificially "add" affordability to the market because it allows for larger sums of money to be borrowed with lower payments. The final component of credit expansion was a willingness of borrowers to take on larger debt-service payments as evidenced by increasing debt-to-income ratios. All of these factors also helped speculators. The acquisition and carrying costs of a speculative flip was greatly reduced. More people were eligible to speculate, and with rapidly rising prices, more people wanted to do so.

Table 7: Interest Rates and House Values

$	244.900	National Median Home Price
$	47.423	National Median Income
$	3.952	National Monthly Median Income
	28.0%	Debt-To-Income Ratio
$	1.106.54	Monthly Payment

Interest Rate	Loan Amount	Value	Value Change
4.5%	$ 218,387	$ 272,984	145%
5.0%	$ 206.127	$ 257.659	137%
5.5%	$ 194.885	$ 243.606	129%
6.0%	$ 184.561	$ 230.701	122%
6.4%	$ 177.046	$ 221.307	117%
7.0%	$ 166.321	$ 207.901	110%
7.5%	$ 158.254	$ 197.818	105%
8.0%	$ 150.803	$ 188.503	100%
8.5%	$ 143.909	$ 179.886	95%
9.0%	$ 137.522	$ 171.903	91%
9.5%	$ 131.597	$ 164.496	87%
10.0%	$ 126.091	$ 157.613	84%

Note: The decline in interest rates from 8.05% to 5.83% explains about half of the national bubble.

86

Nationally, prices during the bubble rally increased by 45%. About half of this increase was due to lower interest rates. However, in the markets most prone to irrational exuberance, prices increased much more than the change in interest rates can explain. These markets also saw a large increase in the use of exotic financing and major increases in debt-to-income ratios utilized by many borrowers. For example, the median household income in Irvine in 2006 was $83,891. Applying a 28% DTI leaves a payment of $1,957. Interest rates at the time were about 6.5%; a payment of $1,957 on a fixed-rate 30-year mortgage at 6.5% would finance $309,691. Short-term adjustable rate mortgages carry lower interest rates than long-term fixed rate mortgages because the lenders have less interest rate risk exposure. The same $1,957 payment on a 5-year ARM at 5.5% would finance $427,081. The interest-only loan terms allows borrowers to increase their loans by 25% thus artificially increasing prices by 25%.

Table 8: Financing Terms and Conditions in Irvine, CA, 2006

$	722,928	Irvine Median Home Price
$	83,891	Irvine Median Income
$	6,991	Monthly Median Income
	6.5%	Interest Rate on 30-Year Fixed-Rate Mortgage
	5.5%	Interest Rate on 5-Year ARM
	3.8%	Payment Rate on Option ARM

Payment	DTI Ratio	30-Year Fixed	Interest Only	Negative Am.*
$ 1,678	24.0%	$ 265,449	$ 366,070	$ 529,838
$ 1,957	28.0%	$ 309,691	$ 427,081	$ 618,144
$ 2,237	32.0%	$ 353,932	$ 488,093	$ 706,451
$ 2,517	36.0%	$ 398,174	$ 549,105	$ 794,757
$ 2,796	40.0%	$ 442,415	$ 610,116	$ 883,063
$ 3,076	44.0%	$ 486,657	$ 671,128	$ 971,369
$ 3,356	48.0%	$ 530,899	$ 732,140	$ 1,059,676
$ 3,635	52.0%	$ 575,140	$ 793,151	$ 1,147,982
$ 3,915	56.0%	$ 619,382	$ 854,163	$ 1,236,288
$ 4,195	60.0%	$ 663,623	$ 915,175	$ 1,324,595
$ 4,474	64.0%	$ 707,865	$ 976,186	$ 1,412,901

Negative Amortization loans (AKA Option ARM)

The most important single factor in the expansion of credit was the negative amortization loan, also known as the Option ARM. The payment rates on Option ARMs differ widely, but for the sake of this calculation, assume a 3.8% teaser rate (they were as low as 1 %). The $1,957 payment finances $309,691 with a Conventional mortgage, $427,081 with an Interest-Only mortgage, and a whopping $618,144 with Negative Amortization. Stop for a moment and ponder the math: the same payment now finances 100% more money. Is it any wonder the real estate in bubble markets like Irvine, California, were 100% overvalued at the top? People purchasing with Option ARMs were buying at the rental equivalent monthly cashflow–at least for a while. From a financing perspective, the market was not overvalued. People were paying exactly what they should have been paying. They were just doing it with loan terms which were going to destroy them–hence the terms "toxic financing" and "suicide loan." This point cannot be overemphasized–Negative Amortization loans inflated the Great Housing Bubble. If this loan product had not been offered and aggressively pushed by lenders, the bubble would not have inflated to the degree that it did.

Figure 24: Market Rally Supply and Demand

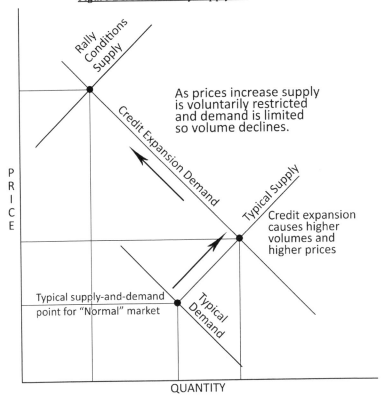

The supply curve is the opposite of the demand curve: sellers will make very few units available at low prices, and sellers will make a great many available at higher prices. Wherever these two curves meet is where supply and demand are in balance and market transactions are taking place. In the initial stages of a market rally both transaction volumes and prices are increasing rapidly. In states with a cumbersome entitlement process like California or in the Northeastern part of the country, delays in bringing supply to the market exacerbates the initial price increase and ignites the speculative frenzy. During the Great Housing Bubble, an increase in demand was caused by a dramatic expansion of lending and credit. As a price rally matures sellers become reluctant to sell because the asset they own is appreciating rapidly, and they do not want to miss the opportunity to profit further. This limits the supply on the market. In terms of the supply and demand diagram, this shifts the supply curve to the left which pushes the balance between supply and demand to a higher price point. The demand curve shifts to the right from the increased liquidity of the lending environment and the supply curve shifts to the left because of seller reluctance; the intersection of these two lines moves prices markedly higher. However, once these two forces come into balance, their intersection is at a point of low transaction volume. There are fewer buyers who can afford the higher prices, so transaction volumes fall. [82]

The first sign of a troubled real estate market is a dramatic reduction in volume known as buyer exhaustion. There are simply not enough buyers able or willing to push prices any higher even at the lower transaction volumes. In a residential real estate market, this phenomenon is particularly pronounced at the entry level. The imbalance between supply and demand first becomes apparent at the bottom of the affordability scale with entry-level buyers because these buyers are not bringing the profits from a previous sale with them to the next property. Affordability is less of a problem for existing homeowners in the move-up market due to this equity transfer.

Figure 25: The Housing Market Pyramid

The real estate market can be visualized as a massive pyramid. There are very few multi-million dollar properties at the top of the pyramid, and a large number of relatively inexpensive entry-level properties forming the base. Like any structure, if the foundation is weakened, the structure may collapse. In the same way, housing markets collapse from the bottom up due to problems with affordability. The foundation of a residential real estate market is the entry-level buyer. Entry-level buyers are generally young people starting to form new households. When homeowners want to sell their house and move up to a nicer one, someone needs to buy their house. If you follow this chain of move-ups backward, eventually you come to an entry level buyer. If there are no entry level buyers pushing the sequence of move ups, the entire real estate market ceases to function. The entry level market was initially boosted the moment 100% financing became available because many more people were enabled to purchase; however, it was imperiled at the same time because of the change in savings incentives. This market was subsequently destroyed the moment 100% financing was eliminated because few entry-level buyers had a downpayment and very few people were in the process of saving to get one. In the past, people would rent and save money until they had the requisite downpayment to acquire a house. The barrier to home ownership was not the ability to make payments; it was having the necessary downpayment money. When downpayment requirements go up, the number of people capable of buying a house declines considerably, particularly for entry-level buyers who must save this money rather than transfer it from a previous sale. Since few potential entry-level buyers were saving money during the rally, sales volumes suffered dramatically in the wake of the bursting real estate bubble.

Figure 26: Affordability Limit

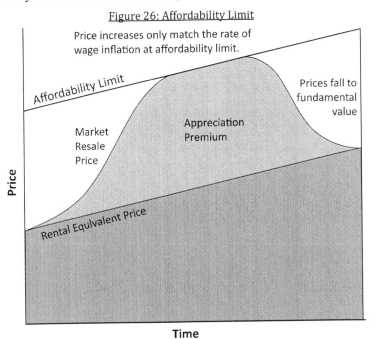

Affordability is the ultimate limit of any asset bubble. If prices are so high that no buyer can afford them, there are no transactions and thereby no market. The fear of many buyers in a financial mania is that prices will remain elevated to the absolute limit of affordability permanently. People who have this fear will put every available resource into getting a house before this happens. This becomes a self-fulfilling prophecy as prices get bid higher and higher by fearful buyers. If prices were to remain at the upper limit of affordability for a long period of time, the rate of price increase would slow dramatically until it only matched the rate of wage growth and inflation because prices could only rise if people had income gains they could use to bid prices up further. If the rate of house appreciation slows down to where it only matches inflation, it fails to have significant investment value. Money would generate much greater returns if invested in other asset classes. During the Great Housing Bubble, certain of the most inflated markets saw prices more than double their rental equivalent value. This significant additional monthly cost provides an economic return while prices are increasing rapidly, but once the rate of price increase slows, the additional "investment" is not providing sufficient returns to justify the use of capital. If price increases do not provide an investment return, many who bought in anticipation of that investment return will decide to sell the asset in order to put their money toward more productive uses. This selling slows the rate of appreciation even further. Also, if prices are not rising in excess of inflation, there is little financial incentive to buy because when affordability is very low, it is much less expensive to rent. If there is no financial incentive to pay more than the cost of rent, people stop buying. The additional selling pressure from those no longer obtaining a return on their investment combined with the diminished buying enthusiasm for the same reason plus the presence of a low-cost substitute (rental,) stops prices from rising and eventually causes a price decline. Once prices start declining, the incentives are even more negative, and prices fall back to levels where they are affordable again.

As prices begin to fall, lenders become more conservative. They do not loan large percentages of the value on a depreciating asset because they do not want to have the loan balance exceed the resale value of the house since the only assurance banks have for getting their money back is the collateral value. Prior to the Great Housing Bubble, lenders demanded 20% down payments to give them a cushion if values declined and they limited debt-to-income ratios to 28% to make sure the borrowers could afford to pay them back. When house values start declining, lenders require more cushion to protect their investments. The demand from lenders for larger downpayments to protect themselves reduces the number of buyers in the market because less people meet the more stringent requirement. Fewer buyers causes even lower prices and a downward spiral of tightening credit. This continues unabated until 20% down payments are the norm, and debt-to-income ratios fall back to their historically "safe" levels for banks (28%).

The Bubble Bursts

When a bubble in a financial market pops, it does not explode in spectacular fashion like a soap bubble; it is more comparable to a breached levee which releases water slowly at first. [83] Once the financial levee is ruptured, the equity reservoir loses money at increasing rates. It washes away the imagined wealth of homeowners who bought late in the rally or used home equity lines of credit to fuel consumer spending until the reservoir is nearly empty and the torrent turns to a trickle. Ultimately, the causes of failure are examined, the financial levee is repaired, and the reservoir again holds value, but not until the dreams and equity of many homeowners are washed away.

Denial runs deep in the financial markets. The vast majority of participants either wants or needs prices to steadily increase. Any facts or opinions that run counter to the idea of ever increasing prices must be quelled in order to prevent a catastrophic collapse of prices due to panic selling. One of the more glaring examples of this phenomenon was the slow leak of information regarding the debacle in the housing market. In February and March of 2007 as the subprime lending implosion became front page news, market bulls were presented with a major public relations problem. It was imperative for the bulls to convince buyers the damage from subprime lending was "contained" and would not "spill over" into other borrower categories and ultimately into the overall economy. [84] The supposition was that the widespread use of exotic loans was not the problem; it was the practice of giving these loans to those with low credit scores. In other words, it was not the loans, it was the borrowers. This was wrong. It was not the borrowers; it was the loans. Exotic loans were given to people of all credit backgrounds. Subprime borrowers where the first to show distress, but the Alt-A and Prime borrowers had the same problems and experienced the same outcome.

Conventional wisdom (or market spin) was that the risk of default from subprime would not spill over into Alt-A and Prime loans. This argument was made because these two categories have historically had low default rates. Of course, this argument ignored the "liar loans" taken out by those with higher credit scores, the unmanageable debt-to-income ratios, and payment resets for interest-only and Option ARM loans which were also given to the Alt-A and Prime crowd. Historically, this group had not defaulted because they have not been widely exposed to these loan types.

An adjustable rate mortgage resets to a different (usually higher) interest rate or payment schedule at a time specified in the loan agreement. The increase in payment may be caused by an increasing interest rate or it may be caused by a recast of the loan to a fully-amortized payment schedule. In either case, the monthly payment will rise. If a borrower is unable to make the new payment because wages did not increase or perhaps the payment increase was simply too large, the borrower will need to refinance to a new loan with an affordable payment structure. If at the time of refinancing the borrower is not eligible for available loan programs because the borrower or the property no longer meets the prevailing loan standards, the borrower may have no choice but to default on the existing loan and go through foreclosure on the property. In short, if borrowers cannot make the new payment or refinance, they will lose their homes. This is how many borrowers lost their homes during the Great Housing Bubble.

Loan standards vary over time as the credit cycle loosens and tightens. Many borrowers in the bubble rally were qualified with low credit scores, very high combined-loan-to-values, high debt-to-income ratios, and little or no income verification. When the ensuing credit crunch occurred, all of these standards were tightened and many of those who previously qualified did not qualify under the new standards. If no other conditions changed, this tightening of standards would have forced many borrowers into foreclosure; however, this credit tightening caused a chain reaction sending market prices for residential real estate which were already falling into an even steeper decline.

Figure 27: Adjustable Rate Mortgage Reset Chart

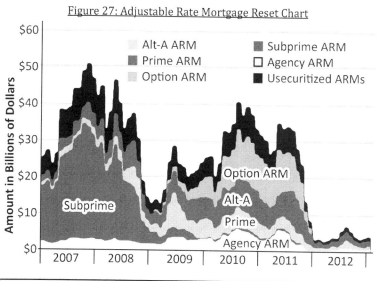

Note: Data as of January 2007
Source: Credit Suisse Fixed Income U.S. Mortgage Strategy.

The Adjustable Rate Mortgage Reset Chart produced by Credit Suisse in 2007 details the dollar amounts of mortgages facing payment resets in the six years from 2007-2012. The bulk of the first two years (24 months on the chart) are loan resets from subprime borrowers who purchased in 2005 and 2006. These subprime borrowers paid peak prices for properties. Most of these borrowers were given 100% financing (if they could have saved up for a downpayment, they probably would not have been subprime,) and they were often only qualified based on their ability to make the initial payment rather than on their ability to make the payment after the reset. There was a special loan program called a 2/28 that most subprime borrowers purchased. [85] This loan fixed a payment for two years; afterward, the payment would increase to a higher interest rate and on a fully-amortized schedule over the remaining 28 years. The payment shock was extreme. This created a condition where most subprime borrowers could not refinance or make their payments, and many of these borrowers defaulted on their loans. Data from early 2008 showed the 2006 and 2007 vintage of subprime loans default rates running close to 50%, and this was before the resets were coming due. Most of these subprime borrowers who went into default lost their properties in foreclosure, and these foreclosures were added to the supply of an already overwhelmed real estate market.

Figure 28: ARM Reset through Foreclosure to Final Sale

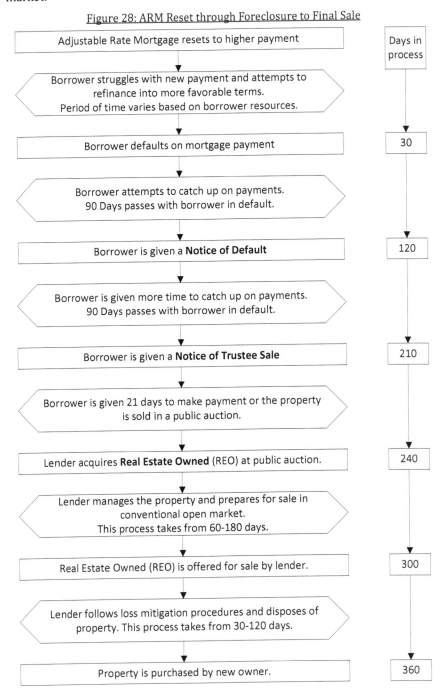

There is a sequence of events which occurs between the mortgage reset and the final sale of a property to a new owner on the open market. After the borrower is faced with a mortgage reset, many try to make the new payment and keep their houses. They may borrow from other sources including credit cards or even their retirement accounts–anything to make the payment and keep their homes. Depending on the resources available and the burden imposed by the new payment, the borrower may stay afloat for an indefinite period of time. Some chose to give up immediately and 30 days later, they are in default. Once a borrower defaults on a loan, in most states the lender is required to wait 90 days to give the borrower a chance to get current on their payments. Once a borrower is 90 days late, he receives a Notice of Default from the lender. Following the Notice of Default, there is another 90 day window where the borrower can make good on their payments. If he is unable (or unwilling) to do so, the lender will file a Notice of Trustee Sale and schedule a public auction for 21 days later. If the borrower cannot pay back the loan or find other ways to delay the process, the property is put up for public auction, generally on the courthouse steps in the jurisdiction where the property is located. At this auction, the lender will generally bid the amount of the outstanding loan and hope another party bids more and pays them off. If the lender is the highest bidder, which is often the case, the lender ends up owning the house.

During the bust, the vast majority of properties at auction went back to the lenders because the loan amounts usually exceeded market value. Properties purchased by the lender at a foreclosure auction are called Real Estate Owned or REO. Lenders are not permitted to keep REOs on their books for long, so these properties are offered at market prices, and they *must* be sold. It will take some time for the property to be prepared for sale. Once the property is finally listed for sale in the conventional resale market, the lender will follow loss mitigation procedures intended to maximize revenue from the property. This often delays the eventual sale 90 days or more. The whole process from mortgage reset to final sale in the market takes at least a year, and it may take much longer.

The subprime borrowers made up the bulk of the mortgage rate resets in 2007 and 2008. Since the default rates were very high, and since prices were already falling before these REOs were added to the market, the subprime foreclosures pushed prices down significantly. This effect was not uniform as subprime borrowers were often concentrated in specific areas or communities. Markets with large concentrations of subprime were decimated first, but all markets are interrelated, as all real estate markets within driving distance are linked together by commuters. When the subprime-dominated markets declined, they created a drag on prices and sales volumes in nearby markets. There was a price differential that enticed people to fringe markets. This created a price drag on the primary markets as some potential buyers were siphoned off by the fringe markets. In California, the collapse of the real estate market was like a land tsunami: it started inland and made it way overland to the coast leveling everything in its path.

The loan reset issue is not confined to those who bought late in the bubble rally. Many borrowers are homeowners who refinanced to take advantage of more favorable loan terms. During the Great Housing Bubble, prices rose dramatically in nearly every market nationally. With such a dramatic increase in prices, one would expect the total home equity for homeowners to increase dramatically as well. If fact, the opposite occurred; home equity declined during the rally of the real estate bubble. By the end of 2007, home equity as a percentage of home values was at record lows. Where did all the equity go? Existing homeowners spent it, and many new homeowners had such low downpayments, that they had very little equity to begin from the start. Refinancing and home equity withdrawal is the primary reason home equity did not rise as prices increased. There was a great deal of conspicuous consumption in the bubble rally, particularly in California. It seemed every house had two luxury cars in the driveway, the malls were always full of shoppers, and every homeowner was busy competing with her neighbor to see who could look richer. Many also spent their "liberated" equity to acquire other properties which was a major driver of the prices in the bubble rally.

Figure 29: Total Home Equity, 1985-2006

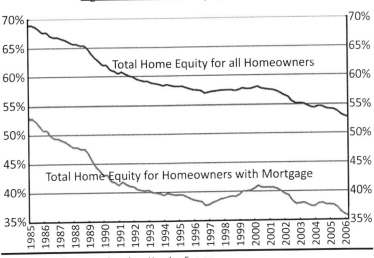

Source: Federal Reserve; American Housing Survey;
Banc of America Securities LLC estimates.

Aggregate home equity statistics can be misleading because approximately 30% of US households have no mortgage at all. Also, during the bubble rally, home ownership increased 5% nationwide, and many of these new homeowners were subprime borrowers who utilized 100% financing. This will have some impact on home equity statistics, but it is not sufficient to cancel out a 45% increase in home prices without massive home equity withdrawal. If the home equity statistics are viewed in the context of those households that have a mortgage, total equity nationwide was around 35% in 2006.

The initial price declines caused by defaulting subprime borrowers set the stage for defaults by Alt-A and Prime borrowers by lowering property values. At the time of this writing, the Alt-A and Prime borrowers have not yet faced the prospect of their loans resetting to higher payments as they start facing resets in 2009 that continue through 2011; however, it is not difficult to speculate on what will happen. Both new homes and foreclosures are must-sell inventory. The presence of must-sell inventory in the market forces prices lower. Builders aggressively cut prices in many markets in 2007 and 2008, and it did not help sales. The builders will be forced to lower prices more in 2009 and beyond until prices bottom in the new home market. Foreclosures increased dramatically in all markets in 2007 as the pressure of large debt loads overwhelmed many borrowers. The number of new units and foreclosures is not a problem in a healthy market, but in a declining market with large numbers of REOs, this must-sell inventory drives prices lower. The lowered property values will make it difficult for these borrowers to refinance because they will no longer meet the more stringent loan-to-value ratios that will be required to refinance. It is likely many of these borrowers will not be able to afford the payment at reset, and they will lose their homes just as the subprime borrowers lost their homes. If Alt-A and prime borrowers had utilized conventional mortgages as they had in the past, they would not be facing the mortgage reset time bomb, and they could simply ride out the subprime debacle just as many homeowners did through the declines of the early 90s. However, it is different this time. This time, the loans they have taken out are going to ruin them. It's not the borrowers, it's the loans.

The Credit Crunch

In 2007, the financial markets were abuzz with talk of a "credit crunch." It was portrayed as some unusual and unpredictable outside force like an asteroid impact or a cold winter storm. However, it was not unexpected, and it was not caused by any outside force. The credit crunch began because borrowers were unable to make payments on the loans they were given. When lenders started losing money, they stopped lending money: a credit crunch.

New Century Financial is the poster child for the Great Housing Bubble. New Century Financial was founded in 1995 and headquartered in Irvine, California. New Century Financial Corporation was a real estate investment trust (REIT), providing first and second mortgage products to borrowers nationwide through its operating subsidiaries, New Century Mortgage Corporation and Home123 Corporation. The company was the second largest subprime loan originator by dollar volume in 2006. On April 2, 2007, the company filed for Chapter 11 bankruptcy protections. 86 The date of their financial implosion is regarded as the day the bubble popped. The death of New Century Financial has come to represent to death of loose lending standards and the beginning of the credit crunch. Subprime lending was widely regarded as the culprit in starting the cycle of credit tightening, and New Century has been linked to this problem, but the scale and scope of the disaster was much larger than sub-prime.

The massive credit crunch that facilitated the decline of the Great Housing Bubble was a crisis of cashflow insolvency. Basically, people did not have the incomes to consistently make their mortgage payments. This was caused by a combination of exotic loan programs with increasing payments, a deterioration of credit standards allowing debt-to-income ratios well above historic norms, and the systematic practice of fabricating loan applications with phantom income (stated-income or "liar" loans). The problem of cashflow insolvency was very difficult to overcome as borrowing more money would not solve the problem. People needed greater incomes, not greater debt loads.

When more money and debt was created than incomes could support, one of two things needed to happen: either the sum of money needed to shrink to supportable levels (a shrinking money supply is a condition known as defla-tion,) or the amount of money supported by the available cashflow needed to increase through lower interest rates. Given these two alternatives, the Federal Reserve chose to lower interest rates. The lower interest rates had two effects; first, it did help support the created debt, and second, it created inflationary pressures which further counteracted the deflationary pressures of disappear-ing debt and declining collateral assets. None of this saved the housing market.

Credit availability moves in cycles of tightening and loosening. Lenders tend to loosen credit guidelines when times are good, and they tend to tighten them when times are bad. This tendency of lenders often exacerbates the growth and contraction of the business cycle. During the decline of the Great Housing Bubble, the contraction of credit certainly played a major role in the decline of house prices. Lenders continued to tighten their standards for extending credit for fear of losing even more money. This meant fewer and fewer people qualified for smaller and smaller loans. This crushed demand for housing and made home prices fall even further.

Figure 30: Personal Savings Rate, 1952-2007

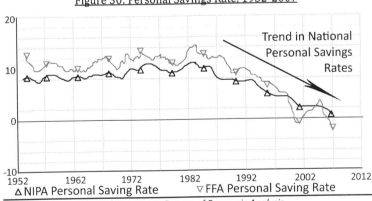

Source: US Department of Commerce, Bureau of Economic Analysis

One of the biggest problems for the housing market was the reinstatement of downpayment requirements. During the bubble rally, 100% financing was made widely available. This made it unnecessary for people to save money to get a house. People respond to incentives (Deming, 2000). This is basic economic theory. The availability of 100% financing removed the incentive to save for a downpayment. People responded; our national savings rate went negative. [87] Potential homebuyers, who ordinarily would have been saving money for a downpayment to get a house, stopped saving, borrowed money and went on a consumer spending spree. This created a situation in the aftermath of the bubble crash where very few potential entry-level buyers had any saved money for the newly required downpayments. This created very serious problems for a market already reeling from low affordability, excess inventory, and a large number of foreclosures.

100% Financing

Once 100% financing became widely available, it was enthusiastically embraced by all parties: the lenders suddenly had a huge source of new customers to generate high fees, the realtors and builders now had plenty of new customers to buy more homes, and many potential buyers who did not have savings were able to enter the market. It seemed like a panacea; for two or three years, it was. There was a problem with 100% financing (which was masked by the rampant appreciation brought about by its introduction): high default rates. The more money people had to put in to the transaction, the less likely they were to default. It was that simple. The borrowers probably intended to repay the loan when they got it, however they did not feel much of a sense of responsibility to the loan when the going got tough. High loan-to-value loans had high default rates causing 100% financing to all but disappear, and it made other high LTV loans much more expensive, so much so as to render them practically useless. It was all part of the credit tightening cycle.

Besides stopping people from saving for downpayments, 100% financing harmed the market by depleting the buyer pool. In a normal real estate market, first-time buyers are saving their money waiting until they can make their first purchase. This usually results in a steady stream of first-time buyers that enter the market each year. When 100% financing eliminated the downpayment requirement, it also eliminated any need to wait. Those who ordinarily would have bought 2-5 years in the future were able to buy immediately. This emptied the queue. This type of financing appears periodically in the auto industry, especially in downturns when it is necessary to liquidate inventory. The term for this is "pulling demand forward," because it reduces demand for new cars in the next few years. This might not have been a problem if 100% financing would have been made available to everyone forever; however, once downpayment requirements came back those who would have been saving were already homeowners, so there were few new buyers available, and any potential new buyers had to start over saving for the downpayment they thought would never be required. The situation was made worse because those late buyers who were "pulled forward" from the future buyer pool overpaid, and many lost their homes. This eliminated them from the buyer pool for several years due to poor credit and newly tightened credit underwriting standards. Thus, most who thought 100% financing was a dream come true found it to be a nightmare instead.

Table 9: Increasing Interest Rates Impact to House Prices

$	244,900	National Median Home Price
$	47,423	National Median Income
$	3,952	National Monthly Median Income
	28.0%	Debt-To-Income Ratio
$	1,106.54	Monthly Payment

Interest Rate	Loan Amount	Value	Value Change
4.5%	$ 218,387	$ 272,984	18%
5.0%	$ 206,127	$ 257,659	12%
5.5%	$ 194,885	$ 243,606	6%
6.0%	$ 184,561	$ 230,701	0%
6.4%	$ 177,046	$ 221,307	-4%
7.0%	$ 166,321	$ 207,901	-10%
7.5%	$ 158,254	$ 197,818	-14%
8.0%	$ 150,803	$ 188,503	-18%
8.5%	$ 143,909	$ 179,886	-22%
9.0%	$ 137,522	$ 171,903	-25%
9.5%	$ 131,597	$ 164,496	-29%
10.0%	$ 126,091	$ 157,613	-32%

Note: An increase in interest rates will have a strongly negative impact on house prices.

Rising Interest Rates

Mortgage interest rates are determined in an open market and are subject to the forces of supply and demand. These rates are the sum of three main components: riskless rate of return, risk premium, and inflation expectation. The Great Housing Bubble was characterized by historic lows in the federal funds rate, risk premiums and inflation expectations which resulted in the very low mortgage interest rates. When credit tightened as prices started to decline, the federal funds rate was lowered in an attempt to provide liquidity to the financial markets. This did temporarily lower one of the three components of interest rates; however, since other central banks around the world did not immediately follow with similar rate cuts, the value of the dollar declined and inflation began to rise. This increased the inflation expectation among investors. The impact of increased inflation expectation was greater than the drop in short-term interest rates, and mortgage interest rates rose steadily. Declining prices also caused losses for lenders as many borrowers defaulted on their loans and the value of the collateral was not sufficient to recover the loan balance. As lenders and investors lost money, they began to demand higher risk premiums. The greater risk premiums and higher inflation expectations caused interest rates to rise and house prices to fall.

Higher interest rates had a dramatic impact on exotic financing as it became more expensive for borrowers. Interest rate spreads grew and the qualification standards tightened to the point they were not usable. This was driven by the defaults and foreclosures. In the heyday of negative amortization loans, lenders qualified borrowers based only on the teaser rate payment without regard to whether or not they could afford the payment at reset. For more sophisticated borrowers, lenders allowed stated income or "liar loans." Basically, borrowers would tell lenders how much they wanted to borrow, and lenders would fill out fraudulent paperwork showing the borrowers were making enough money to afford the payments. This is amazingly irresponsible lending, but it was widespread. Once the price crash began, lenders required borrowers to be able to actually afford the payments; of course, this makes many borrowers unable to obtain financing. When a negative amortization loan costs 13.8% rather than 3.8%, few borrowers wanted it, and if lenders required borrowers to actually afford the 13.8% interest rate, few borrowers qualified. Either way, negative amortization loans died, and the fate of stated income loans was no better.

Mortgage rates for prime customers were very low because they rarely default. During the rally few defaulted because prices were rising; people just sold if they got in trouble. This allowed banks to originate risky loans at very low interest rates because the loans did not appear risky. Once the market stopped rising, the underlying risk started to show with increasing default rates and default losses. When prices crashed, default rates increased for all borrower classes. Prime borrowers did not default at the high rates of subprime borrowers, but they still defaulted at rates higher than in the past; therefore, interest rates increased for prime borrowers as well. The crash in house prices caused all mortgage interest rates to rise. Banks have to make enough money on their good loans to pay for the losses on their bad loans and still make a profit. Higher interest rates make for lower amounts of borrowing, and this in turn leads to lower house prices.

Summary

The ratio of house prices relative to incomes rose considerably during the Great Housing Bubble. Some of this increase was due to lower interest rates, but in bubble markets most was due to supply constraints, regulatory delays, deteriorating credit underwriting standards, and irrational exuberance and the belief that prices were going to rise forever. People stretched to buy real estate as evidenced by the increasing debt service burdens they took on during this time. The rally reached affordability limits where buyers could not push prices any higher. Once these limits were reached, lenders were forced come up with new programs allowing borrowers to take on even more debt to push prices higher, or the rally was going to end. Once prices stopped rising, people lost their incentive to buy and ultimately prices began a decline. This decline is expected to continue unabated until prices fall back to fundamental valuations, or perhaps even lower.

Credit availability moves in cycles. During the Great Housing Bubble, credit was loosened to a degree not seen before, and it facilitated a price bubble of epic proportions. During periods of credit contraction, lenders seek to avoid risk and they make fewer loans. This causes inflated asset prices to drop precipitously. This cycle of credit contraction leading to asset deflation feeds on itself until lending standards become too tight and overly cautious when asset prices are their lowest. Of course, this is when credit should be made available to purchase assets at bargain prices. As safety and sanity returns to a financial market, lenders realize that they became too conservative and loosen their standards allowing more money to flow into capital markets; the whole process repeats, and the credit cycle continues.

Bubble Market Psychology

Financial markets are driven by fear and greed: two basic human emotions. Rationality and careful analysis are not responsible for, or predictive of, current or future price levels in markets exhibiting bubble pricing as the emotions of buyers and sellers takes over.[88] The psychology of speculation drives bubble markets, and because of the nature of fear and greed, most speculators are doomed to lose their money. In contrast, true investors are not subject to the emotional cycles of the speculator, and they are more able to make rational decisions based on fundamental valuations. Of course, many investors also miss the excitement of a runaway price rally in a speculative bubble. The Great Housing Bubble was inflated by people trading houses. Residential real estate took on the character of a commodity, and it became subject to the same chaotic price gyrations as a speculative commodities market. This behavior was caused by lenders who provided the financing terms which enabled speculators to use mortgages as option contracts with the risk of loss being transferred to the lenders.

With any loss, an individual must go through a grieving process. Since markets are the collective actions of these individuals, markets experience the same psychological stages which are apparent in the price action. Efficient markets theory attempts to explain market price action through the collective action of rational market participants. This theory fails to explain the irrational behavior exhibited in bubble markets. Behavioral finance theory seeks to explain irrational exuberance. The price action in a bubble has other impacts on the beliefs and behaviors of individuals and society as a whole. These beliefs and behaviors may become pathological in nature leading to suffering and social problems. As with any form of mass hardship, there are calls for government action which lead to proposals for bailouts and false hopes among the populace.

Speculation or Investment?

Owner-occupied residential real estate is viewed by many people as a good investment. [89] Realtors often use this idea as part of their sales pitch. As mentioned previously, this view is fallacious and it is one of the beliefs responsible for creating an asset price bubble. To understand why houses are not a great investment in most circumstances, one needs to understand the difference between investment and speculation.

An investment is an asset purchased to obtain a predictable and consistent cashflow. This would include things such as bonds and rental properties or even cash in a savings account. The value of the asset is based on the cashflow, and this value can be determined in a number of ways. For a "point in time" analysis simple division will yield the rate of return (return = income / investment). Risk is evaluated by comparing the rate of return of the investment to the safe return one can obtain in a savings account or government bonds. For more complex financial structures the value can be determined by a process known as discounted cashflow analysis. The sales price at the time of disposition is often not a major factor in the investment decision, particularly if the eventual disposition is many years in the future. In fact, true investments need never be sold to be profitable. As Warren Buffet noted, "I buy on the assumption that they could close the market the next day and not reopen it for five years." [90] In contrast to investment, speculation is the purchase of an asset to sell at a later date at a higher price (Actually, you can also speculate by selling first and buying later in a process known as "selling short"). Speculative assets are not valued based on cashflow but instead are valued based on the perceived probability of selling later for a profit. Houses can be purchased as an investment at the right price, but most often when people purchase a property they are engaging in speculation based on the belief they will be able to sell the house for a profit at a later date.

Since 1890 houses have appreciated at 0.7% over the general rate of inflation. Over the long term house values are tied to incomes because most people buy houses with mortgages for which they must qualify based on their income. Inflation keeps pace with wage growth because people will bid up the prices of goods and services with their available income. Therefore, over the long term house prices, wages and inflation all move in concert. There are short-term fluctuations in this relationship due to variations in financing terms, migration patterns, employment, local limits on construction and irrational exuberance, but any such deviations from the mean will be corrected over time by market forces. As an investment, houses serve as a hedge against the corrosive effect of inflation, but over the long term appreciation much in excess of the general rate of inflation is not possible. In this regard, houses are little better than savings accounts as an asset class, and they are inferior to stocks or bonds in the long term.

Leverage and Debt

As a speculative investment, residential real estate has the potential to make or lose vast sums of money due to the impact of financial leverage (debt). Houses are typically leveraged at 80% of their value. During the Great Housing Bubble, this leverage was often provided at 100% by various lenders. Leverage is a powerful ally when prices increase, but leverage works just as strongly against the speculator when prices decrease. For example, if a house is leveraged 80% and it increases in value 5% in one year, the return to the investor is actually 25% due to the 5 times multiplier created by leverage. With the effect of leverage, speculation on housing can far exceed any competing investment strategy. However, the inverse is also true. If a house is leveraged 80% and it decreases in value 5% in one year, the loss to the investor is 25% of her downpayment, not just the 5% the house declined in value. Leverage magnifies both the return and the risk of any speculative venture.

One of the worst mistakes lenders made during the Great Housing Bubble was to allow 100% financing and negative amortization loans. This was a boon for speculators because it allowed them to participate in the market without any of their own capital and it allowed them to hold the speculative assets with a minimal debt service expense. Plus, there was the implicit idea that they would simply default if the deal did not go in their favor (which of course many did). Combine these facts with the near elimination of loan underwriting standards allowing anyone to participate, and the conditions were perfect for rampant speculation, a wild increase in prices and so much speculative demand that many new and existing home purchases would remain vacant.

Why Speculators Fail

Despite the huge price spike in the final two years of the bubble caused by wild speculation, most speculators will lose a great deal of money. The causes are rooted in basic human emotions that work against making the proper decisions to profit in a speculative market. The moment a speculative asset is purchased and the speculator has taken a position in the market, emotions are immediately in play. If the potential resale price in the market is rising, the natural reaction is to want more. Greed takes over and the asset is strongly coveted by the speculator. If possible, the speculator will purchase more of the asset in question. This was common in the bubble when people would take the equity from one property and purchase even more residential real estate. The problem with this natural emotional reaction is that it prevents the speculator from selling the asset and taking profits when they are available. People who successfully make a living participating in speculative markets have learned to override this natural instinct and sell when their emotions are telling them to buy more. The average residential real estate speculator does not have this discipline or awareness. He will hold the asset through the good times.

When prices begin to fall in a speculative market, most speculators immediately lapse into denial. They were so emotionally rewarded by purchasing and holding the asset, they see no reason to believe the first signs of a declining market are anything other than a temporary aberration. As prices continue to fall, the emotions change: fear begins to creep in, and the battle between denial and fear goes on well past the breakeven point where the speculator could have closed the position without losing any money. [91] As prices fall further, the fear begins to take an emotional toll and the speculator starts to feel pain. As prices drop further, more pain is inflicted on the speculator. What is the natural reaction to pain? Push it away. As a speculative investment becomes painful, the natural reaction is to want to get rid of it. This prompts the speculator to sell the asset–only after he has lost money. Speculator's emotions always work against them. When the asset is rising in price they want more of it, and when it is falling in price they want less. This is a natural reaction, and it is a primary cause of losses in speculative markets. This is why most speculators fail.

Figure 31: Speculator Emotional Cycle

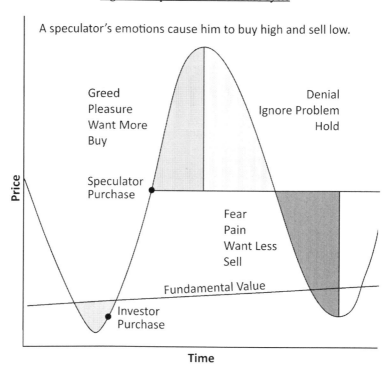

Two Kinds of Real Estate Investors

There are two types of true real estate investors: Rent Savers and Cashflow Investors. These two groups will enter a real estate market without regard to future appreciation because either the cash savings or the positive cashflow warrant the purchase price of the asset. These people are largely immune to the emotional pratfalls of speculators because the value of the investment to them is not dependent upon a profit to be garnered when the asset is sold. They will hold the asset through any price declines because they are not feeling any pain when prices drop. Since these investors will purchase houses even if prices are declining, they are the ones who move in to create a bottom and end the cycle of declining prices.

In a declining market, a market where by definition there is more must-sell inventory than there are buyers to absorb it, it takes an influx of new buyers to restore balance. Since it is foolish to buy with the expectation of appreciation in a declining market, the buyers who were frantically bidding up the values of properties in the rally are notably absent from the market. With the exception of the occasional knife-catcher, these potential buyers simply do not buy. This absence of buyers perpetuates the decline once it starts. Add to that the inevitable foreclosures in a price decline, and the result is an unending downward spiral. It takes Rent Savers and Cashflow Investors entering the market to provide support, break the cycle and create a bottom.

Rent Savers are buyers who enter the market when it is less expensive to own than to rent. It does not matter to these people what houses will trade for in the market in the future. They are not buying with fantasies of appreciation. They just know they are saving money over renting, and that is good enough for them. Cashflow Investors have a different agenda; they want to turn a monthly profit from ownership. For them, the cost of ownership must be less than prevailing rent for them to make a return on their equity investment. Cashflow Investors form a durable bottom. If prices drop low enough for this group to get into the market, the influx of investment capital can be extraordinary.

Buyer Support Levels

When do Rent Savers and Cashflow Investors move in to a market and create a bottom? When comparative rents come into alignment with the total cost of ownership, Rent Savers enter the market and begin purchasing real estate. It makes sense for them to do so because ownership becomes a savings over renting (hence the term Rent Saver). The "return" on the investment is the hedge against inflation the Rent Saver obtains by locking in the cost of housing with a 30-year, fixed-rate, fully-amortized mortgage. As rents in the area continue to increase, these costs are not borne by the Rent Saver. Utilizing the price-to-rent concept, the Rent Savers will enter the market when this ratio falls to 154 (based on financing terms available in 2007). There will be some buyers who enter at higher prices, but there will not be enough of them to stabilize the market. It takes a decline in prices to where it is less expensive to own than to rent before enough new buyers enter the market to create a bottom. However, there are some properties that Rent Savers will not purchase because they really do not want to live in them. This includes transitory housing like apartments or small apartment-like condominiums. Prices on these properties will generally drop below the 154 price-to-rent breakeven for owner occupants until they reach price levels where Cashflow Investors will purchase them as rental properties. Since these investors do not want to merely break even, the price must be low enough for the rental rate to exceed the cost of ownership by enough to provide a return on the investor's capital. Historically, price-to-rent ratios from 100-120 are required to create the conditions necessary to attract Cashflow Investors' capital.

When it comes time to consider purchasing a house, each person should evaluate if their motivation is one of an investor or one of a speculator. Investment in real estate requires an accurate assessment of the revenue (or savings) and the costs associated with the property. If the cashflow from the property warrants the purchase of the investment–without regard to future asset value– then it is a true investment, and the risks of ownership are much reduced. If the property's asset resale value were to decline, the investment value would still be there, and the investor would feel no pain and no pressure to sell. In contrast, speculation is a loser's game, and if the motivation is to capture a windfall from future appreciation, there is a good chance it may not work out as planned because the emotions of a speculator will cause a sale at the worst possible time. A few can put their emotions aside and properly evaluate the market and trade the asset, but most who profit from speculation simply sell at the right time due to life's circumstances. In short, they get lucky. The people who bought late in the rally and are holding on to the asset while they drift further and further underwater–they are not so lucky.

Trading Houses

During the Great Housing Bubble, many speculators tried to make money through trading houses. The vast majority of these traders were not professionals but amateurs who thought they could be professionals. Most amateurs ended up losing money because they did not understand what it takes to be successful in a speculative market. [92] The first and most obvious difference in the investment strategy between professional traders and the amateurs in the general public is their holding time. Traders buy with the intent to sell for a profit at a later date. Traders know why they are entering a trade, and they have a well thought out exit strategy. The general public adopts a "buy and hold" mentality where assets are accumulated with a supposed eye to the long term. Everyone wants to be the next Warren Buffet. In reality this buy-and-hold strategy is often a "buy and hope" strategy–a greed-induced, emotional purchase without proper analysis or any exit plan. Since they have no exit strategy, and since they are ruled by their emotions, they will end up selling only when the pain of loss compels them to. In short, it is an investment method guaranteed to be a disaster.

There is evidence that houses were used as a speculative commodity during the Great Housing Bubble. Since the cost of ownership greatly exceeded the cashflow from the property if used as a rental, the property was not purchased for positive cashflow, and by definition, it was a speculative purchase. Confirming evidence for speculative activity comes from the unusual and significant increase in vacant houses in the residential real estate market.

If markets had not been gripped by speculative fervor, vacancy rates would not have risen so far above historic norms. If houses had been purchased for investment purposes to make money from rental income, the houses would have been occupied after purchase and vacancy rates would not have gone up. A rise in vacancy rates would have resulted in downward pressure on rents, and the investment opportunity–if it had existed initially (which it did not)–would have disappeared with the declining rent. There is only one reasonable explanation for increasing house prices and increasing rents during a period when house vacancy rates increased 64%: people were purchasing houses for speculative gains and leaving them unoccupied while the owners waited for prices to rise. [93]

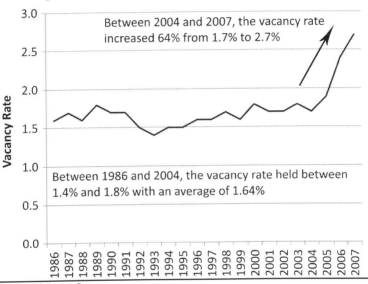

Figure 32: National Homeowner Vacancy Rate, 1986-2007

Source: US Census Bureau

When house prices stopped their dizzying ascent, many speculators found themselves with large monthly debt service costs and no income to offset expenses. Many chose to quit paying their mortgage obligations and allowed the property to be auctioned at foreclosure. Many chose to rent the properties to reduce their monthly cashflow drain, and they became accidental landlords. In the vernacular of the time, they became floplords–flippers turned landlords.

Becoming a floplord was fraught with problems. First, they were not covering their monthly expenses, so the losses on the "investment" continued to mount. For houses purchased near the peak in 2006, rent only covered half the cost of ownership unless the speculator used an Option ARM with a very low teaser rate (which many did). Becoming a floplord was a convenient form of denial for losing speculators because they believed they were buying themselves time until prices rose again, allowing them to sell later either at breakeven or for a profit. Since they bought in a speculative mania, prices were not going to recover quickly and the denial soon evolved into fear, anger and finally acceptance of their fate. Another problem floplords faced was their own inexperience at managing rental properties. Most had never owned or managed a rental property, and none of them purchased the property with this contingency in mind. They often found poor tenants who did not reliably pay the rent or properly care for the property. This created even more financial distress and greater loss of property value as the property deteriorated through misuse.

The problems of renting were not confined to the floplords. Sometimes innocent renters were the ones who suffered. Many floplords collected large security deposits and monthly rent checks from tenants and yet failed to pay their mortgage obligations. This situation is called "rent skimming," and it is illegal in most jurisdictions, but this crime is seldom prosecuted. Most of the time, the first indication a renter had that their rent was being skimmed was finding a foreclosure notice on their front door. By the time of notification, several months of rental payments were gone and the renters were evicted soon after the foreclosure. Renters seldom recovered their security deposits.

Houses as Commodities

Commodities are items of value and uniform quality produced in large quantities and sold in an open market. Although every residential real estate property is unique, these properties became uniformly desired by investors because all real estate prices rose during the Great Housing Bubble. The commoditization of real estate and the active, open-market trading it inspires caused houses to lose their identity as places to live and call home. Houses became tradable stucco boxes similar to baseball playing cards where buying and selling had nothing to do with possession and use and everything to do with making money in the transaction. [94]

In a commodities or securities market, rallies unsupported by valuation measures fall back to fundamental values. It is very clear the rally in house prices was not caused by a rally in the fundamental valuation measures of rent or income. Many people forgot the primary purpose of a house is to provide shelter–something which can be obtained without ownership by renting. Ownership ceased to be about providing shelter and instead became a way to access one of the world's largest and most highly leveraged commodity markets: residential real estate.

Commodities markets are notoriously volatile. In fact, this volatility is the primary draw of commodities trading. If market prices did not move significantly, traders would not be interested in the market, and liquidity would not be present. Without this liquidity, hedgers could not sell futures contracts and transfer their risk to other parties, and the whole market would cease to function. Commodities markets exist to transfer risk from a party that does not want it to a party who is willing to assume this risk for the potential to profit from it. The commodities exchange controls the volatility of the market through the regulation of leverage. It is the exchange that sets the amount of a particular commodity that is controlled by a futures contract. They can raise or lower the amount of leverage to create a degree of volatility attractive to traders. If they create too much leverage, the accounts of traders can be wiped out by small market price movements. If they create too little leverage, traders lose interest.

The same principles of leverage that govern commodities markets also work to influence the behavior of speculators in residential real estate markets. If leverage is very low (large downpayments or low CLTV limits,) then speculators have to use large amounts of their own money to capture what become relatively small price movements. If leverage is very high (small downpayments or high CLTV limits,) then speculators do not have to put up much money to capture what become relatively large price movements. The more leverage (debt) that can be applied to residential real estate, the greater the degree of speculative activity that market will see. Also, the smaller the amount of money required to speculate in a given market, the more people will be able to do so because more people will have the funds necessary to participate. When lenders began to offer 100% financing, it was an open invitation to rampant speculation. This makes the return on investment infinite because no investment is required by the speculator, and it eliminates all barriers to entry to the speculative market. In a regulated commodities market, the trader is responsible for all losses in the account. In a mortgage market dominated by non-recourse purchase money mortgages, lenders end up assuming liability for losses in the speculative residential real estate market.

Mortgages as Options

An option contract provides the contract holder the option to force the contract writer to either buy or sell a particular asset at a given price. A typical option contract has an expiration date, and if the contract holder does not exercise his contract rights by a given date, he loses his contractual right to do so. An option giving the holder the right to buy is a "call" option, and the option giving the holder the right to sell is a "put" option. Writers of option contracts typically obtain a price premium for taking on the risk that prices may move against their position and the contract holder may exercise his right. The holder of an options contract willingly pays this premium to limit his losses to the premium paid if the investment does not go as planned. Most options expire worthless.

Mortgages took on the characteristics of options contracts in the Great Housing Bubble. Speculators utilized 100% financing and Option ARMs with low teaser rates to minimize the acquisition and holding costs of a particular property. The small amount they were paying was the "call premium" they were providing the lender. If prices went up, the speculator got to keep all the gains from appreciation, and if prices went down, the speculator could simply walk away from the mortgage and only lose the cost of the payments made, particularly when this debt was a non-recourse, purchase-money mortgage. Another method speculators and homeowners alike used was the "put" option refinance. [95] Late in the bubble when prices were near their peak, many homeowners refinanced their properties and took out 100% of the equity in their homes. In the process, they were buying a "put" from the lender: if prices went down (which they did,) they already had the sales proceeds as if they had actually sold the property at the peak; if prices went up, they got to keep those profits as well. The only price for this "put" option was the small increase in monthly payments they had to make on the large sum they refinanced. In fact, on a relative cost basis, the premium charged to these speculators and homeowners was a small fraction of the premiums similar options cost on stocks. Of course, mortgages are not option contracts, and lenders did not view themselves as selling option premiums to profit from the premium payments; however, speculators certainly did view mortgages in this manner and treated them accordingly.

The "put" and "call" option features of mortgages during the bubble are the direct result of 100% financing. Speculators and homeowners have too little to lose to behave responsibly when 100% financing is available. Without increasing the cost to speculators through downpayments or a loan-to-value limit on refinances, speculators are going to utilize these mortgage products in ways they were not intended. There are many expensive lessons learned by lenders concerning 100% financing during the Great Housing Bubble.

The Stages of Grief

Markets are the collective actions of individuals, and the psychology of the markets can be broken down to the psychology of the individual participants who make it up. When price levels in a financial market collapse, most people lose money. Any loss has a psychological impact on the individual causing her to experience grief. The grieving process is generally divided into several overlapping stages: denial, anger, bargaining, and acceptance. These stages are also apparent in the mass psychology of the market.

When prices first drop, the individual market participants feel confusion and attempt to avoid the truth. They feel denial. This is motivated by fear (or truth) they may have been wrong to purchase when they did, and they might lose money. They seek ways to quell these fears. Rather than attempt to objectively review facts to ascertain whether or not the unexpected market behavior is the beginning of a new trend, most market participants will seek out data consistent with their original assessment. Denial is a natural reaction, but it is a very costly one when applied to a financial market.

When the initial price drops in the market begin to show the signs of a new trend, market participants become fearful. They work to maintain their denial, but there are moments when the awful truth cannot be contained. The little, fearful voice inside of each buyer gets louder and louder. This boils over into anger, frustration, and anxiety. The individual desperately is seeking ways to maintain denial, but reality becomes stronger than denial. She imagines the possibility that the reality she is trying to deny is the truth. This leads to depression and detachment as reality is too painful to accept. The sadness of the imagined loss is often suppressed or glossed over with a veneer of anger.

Finally, "as the going gets tough, the tough get going," and the individual seeks ways to get out of the problem through emotional bargaining. This behavior often takes the form of a negotiation with Fate or the market. One amusing example of this behavior is the purchase of a St. Joseph statue. [96] Burying this statue in the yard is supposed to secure God's blessing and ensure a quick sale. Some will take more productive action. Perhaps it is lowering an asking price, or taking the property off the market and doing some renovations to "add value." Some will not take action, and they lapse back into denial because the market is "coming back soon." Those owners who chose to lower their price as part of their bargaining may get out with minimal losses (assuming they lower it enough to actually sell). Those that choose other courses of action, lose much more money.

In past market declines each individual reached acceptance of the market reality. Some chose to continue making payments on their "investment" and wait out the bear market. In the aftermath of the coastal bubble of the early 90s, many sellers accepted the market was a buyer's market, and many sellers chose to keep making their payments and keep their properties. Those that chose to keep their property in the Great Housing Bubble did not have the ability to make these payments, and the property became a forced sale at a foreclosure auction. Some individuals reached acceptance and chose to sell their property on their own.

Efficient Markets Theory

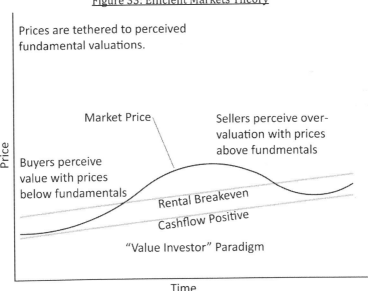

Figure 33: Efficient Markets Theory

The efficient markets theory is the idea that speculative asset prices always incorporate the best information about fundamental values and that prices change only because new information enters the market and investors act in an appropriate, rational manner with regards to this information. [97] This idea dominated academic fields in the early 1970s. Efficient markets theory is an elegant attempt to tether asset prices to fundamentals through the common-sense notion that people would not behave in irrational ways with their money in financial markets. This theory is encapsulated by the "value investment" paradigm prevalent in much of the investment community.

In an efficient market, prices are tethered to perceived fundamental valuations. If prices fall below the market's perception of fundamental value, then buyers will enter the market and purchase the asset until prices reach their perceived value. If prices rise above the market's perception of fundamental value, then sellers will enter the market to sell the asset at inflated prices. Efficient markets theory explains the majority of market behavior, but it has one major flaw which renders it inoperable as a forecasting tool: it does not explain those instances when prices become very volatile and detach from their fundamental valuations. This becomes painfully obvious when adherents to the theory postulate new metrics to justify fundamental valuations that later prove to be completely erroneous. [98] The failed attempts to explain anomalies with the efficient markets theory lead to a new paradigm: behavioral finance theory.

Behavioral Finance Theory

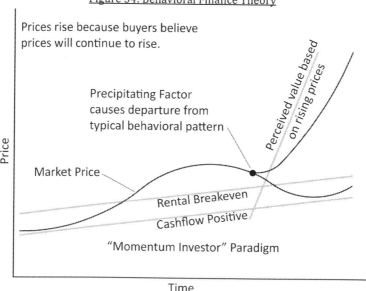

Figure 34: Behavioral Finance Theory

Prices rise because buyers believe prices will continue to rise.

Precipitating Factor causes departure from typical behavioral pattern

Perceived value based on rising prices

Price

Market Price

Rental Breakeven

Cashflow Positive

"Momentum Investor" Paradigm

Time

Behavioral Finance abandoned the quest of the efficient markets theory to find a rational, mathematical model to explain fluctuations in asset prices. Instead, behavioral finance looked to psychology to explain asset valuation and why prices rise and fall. The primary representation of market behavior postulated by behavioral finance is the price-to-price feedback model: prices go up because prices have been going up, and prices go down because prices have been going down. If investors are making money because asset prices increase, other investors take note of the profits being made, and they want to capture those profits as well. They buy the asset, and prices continue to rise. The higher prices rise and the longer it goes on, the more attention is brought to the positive price changes and the more investors want to get involved. These investors are not buying because they think the asset is fairly valued, they are buying because the value is going up. They assume other rational investors must be bidding prices higher, and in their minds they "borrow" the collective expertise of the market. [99] In reality, they are just following the herd. This herd-following has long been a valid investment technique employed by traders known as "momentum" investing. [100] It is not investing by any conventional definition because it relies completely on capturing speculative price changes. Success or failure often hinges on knowing when to sell. It is not a "buy and hold" strategy.

The efficient markets theory does explain the behavior of asset prices in a typical market, but when price change begins to feedback on itself, behavioral finance is the only theory that explains this phenomenon. There is often a precipitating factor causing the break with the normal pattern and releasing the tether from fundamental valuations. During the Great Housing Bubble, the primary precipitating factor was the lowering of interest rates. The precipitating factor simply acts as a catalyst to get prices moving. Once a directional bias is in place, then price-to-price feedback can take over. The perception of fundamental valuation is based solely on the expectation of future price increases, and the asset is always perceived to be undervalued. There are often brave and foolhardy attempts to justify these valuations and provide a rationalization for irrational behavior. Many witnessing the event assume the "smart money" must know something, and there is a widespread belief prices could not rise so much without a good reason. Herd mentality takes over.

Psychological Stages of a Bubble

Once a bubble starts to form, it will go through several identifiable stages: enthusiasm, greed, denial, fear, capitulation, and despair. Each of these stages is characterized by different speculator emotional states and different resulting behaviors. There are outside forces that also act on the market in predictable ways in each one of these stages. Most often, these outside factors serve to reinforce the market's herd behavior and exacerbate changes in price.

Precipitating Factor

There is often a precipitating factor causing the initial price rally that pushes prices above their supported fundamental values. A bubble rally is usually kicked off by some exogenous event, but it may occur simply because prices have been rising and investors take notice, or it can be merely the result of a lack of investor fear and the widespread belief prices cannot go down. [101] In a typical market, there is a significant selloff when prices exceed fundamental valuations. This selloff is a natural reaction to inflated prices as a decline to fundamental valuations is normal and expected. Many seasoned market observers will "sell short" here to profit from the initially inflated values caused during the take-off stage. However, in a financial mania, this sell off is short-lived, and it traps many who are bearish on asset pricing on the wrong side of the trade. This "short squeeze" may prompt a feverish activity of buying as short sellers cover their positions before their losses get too great. A short squeeze may act as a precipitating factor. In a securities market, a precipitating factor may be a very large order hitting the trading floor, and in a real estate market it may be a dramatic lowering of interest rates as it was in the Great Housing Bubble. Regardless of its cause, the initial price rise has the potential to spark sufficient interest to prompt further buying and set a series of events in motion which repeat with a remarkable consistency. Market bubbles can be found in all financial markets and on multiple timeframes.

Figure 35: Psychological Stages of a Bubble Market

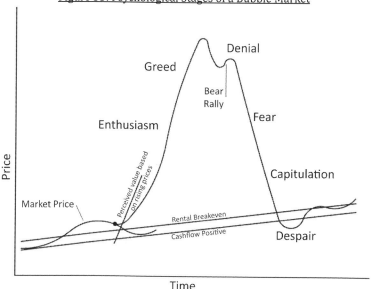

Enthusiasm Stage

At the beginning of the enthusiasm stage, prices are already inflated, so there is cautious buying from traders looking for trends and momentum. If prices fail to drop to fundamental valuations and instead push higher, media attention is often drawn to the speculative market. The general public starts to take notice of the money being made by people who have bought the featured asset and they begin to participate in larger numbers. Of course, this stimulates more buying and prices continue to climb. The market sentiment turns very bullish. Buyers are everywhere and sellers are scarce. At this point, prices are completely detached from fundamental valuations, but people are not buying because of the underlying value, they are buying because prices are going up.

In residential real estate markets, the enthusiasm stage is often greeted by lenders with open arms. With prices rising, there is little risk of loss from default. If a borrower gets in trouble, they can simply sell into rising prices, and neither party takes a loss. With neither party fearing loss, and since lenders make most of their money on the transaction itself through origination fees, there is an inevitable lowering of standards to meet market demand. This in turn creates more market demand leading to further lowering of standards. The credit cycle reinforces the bullish psychology in the market and helps push prices even higher.

Greed Stage

In the greed stage, the bullish sentiment reaches a feverish pitch and prices rise very rapidly. Every owner in the market is making money and most believe it will go on forever. As prices continue to climb, buyers become very enthusiastic about owning the asset, and they tell all their friends about their great investment. The word-of-mouth awareness and increased media coverage bring even more buyers to the market. Egomania sets in as everyone thinks she is a financial genius. Any intellectual analysis at this stage is merely a cover for emotional buying and greed. During the Great Housing Bubble, there were many instances of properties receiving a dozen or more offers the day they were listed, with many in excess of the asking price. Encouraged by realtors, some buyers wrote emotional letters to sellers to convince them why they should be bestowed with the honor of home ownership. [102]

Most people who are bullish already own the asset, but for prices to continue to rise there must be more buying. For buying to occur, someone who was either bearish or ignorant of the rally must be convinced to buy. In other words, a greater fool must be found. Once everyone is made aware of the market rally and is convinced to buy, you simply run out of new buyers. Once there is a shortage of potential buyers, prices can only go down.

Denial Stage

When the limit of affordability is reached and the pool of available buyers is exhausted, prices start to decline. At first market participants are still overwhelmed by greed, and they choose to ignore the signs that the party might be over. In 2007 most real estate markets were in the denial stage as prices had not dropped enough to cause real fear. Denial is apparent in polls in mid-2007 where 85 percent believed their home would rise in value during the next five years, and 63 percent believe a house is a good investment. That is denial. It is also apparent in the number of homes purchased during the greed stage that are held for sale at breakeven prices–even if this is above market. When the inventory is large, and houses stay on the market for a long time, prices are too high. Sellers who refuse to lower their prices to take a small loss are in denial about the state of the market. They believe bids will increase and some buyer will come along and pay their price–after all, that is the way it was just a couple of years prior. Buyers who bought in the enthusiasm stage are still ahead, so they feel no urgency to sell. They have made good money already and they will hold on with hopes of making a little more. Since they believe the asset will appreciate again (and they have no exit strategy), this group of buyers does not sell. [103] In contrast, the few traders who still hold positions liquidate and go back into cash. Successful traders recognize the emotion of denial as a signal to exit their positions to lock in profits or prevent further damage.

In the denial stage of a residential real estate market, many speculators are unable to obtain the sale price they desire. [104] The accumulation of unrealistically priced houses starts to build a large inventory of homes "hanging" over the market. Overhead supply is a condition in a financial market when many units are held for sale at prices above current market prices. Generally there will be a minor rally after the first price decline as those who missed the big rally but still believe prices will only go up enter the market and cause a short-term increase in prices. This is a bear rally. It is aptly named as those bullish on the market buy right before the bear market reverses and quickly declines. For prices to resume a sustained rally, the overhead supply must be absorbed by the market. Once prices stopped going up and actually began to fall, demand is lessened by diminished buyer enthusiasm and the contraction of credit caused by mounting lender losses. With increasing supply and diminished demand prices cannot rally to absorb the overhead supply. The overall bullish bias to market psychology has not changed much at this point, because owners are in denial about the new reality of the bear market; however, the insufficient quantity of buyers and the beginnings of a credit crunch signal the rally is over and the bubble has popped.

Fear Stage

In the grieving process there is a shift from denial to fear when the reality being denied becomes too obvious to be ignored or pushed out of awareness. There is no acceptance of reality, just the idea that reality might be fact. The fact that an investment might turn out to be a very poor financial decision with long-term repercussions to the speculator's financial life is generally very difficult to accept. The imaginings of a horrifying future creates fear, and this fear causes people to make decisions regarding their investments.

The most important change in the market in the fear stage is caused by the belief that the rally is over. Price rallies are a self-sustaining price-to-price feedback loop: prices go up because rising prices induces people to buy which in turn drives prices even higher. Once it is widely believed that the rally is over, it is over. Market participants who once only cared about rising prices suddenly become concerned about valuations. Since prices are far above fundamental values and prices are not rising, there is little incentive to buy. The rally is dead.

Another major psychological change occurs in this stage after people accept the rally is dead: people reassess and change their relationship to debt.

During the rally, debt becomes a means to take a position in the housing commodity market. Nobody cares how much they are borrowing because they never intend to pay off the loan through payments from their wage income. Most believe they will pay off whatever they borrow in the future when they sell the house for more than they paid. Once prices stop going up, people realize they are simply renting from the bank, and the only way to get ahead and build equity is to pay off a mortgage. The desire to borrow 8 to 10 times income diminishes rapidly as people realize they could never pay off such a large sum. What started in the denial stage as an involuntary contraction of credit, in the fear stage becomes a voluntary contraction of credit as people simply do not want to borrow such large amounts of money.

In August of 2007, a more serious credit crunch gripped financial markets, and during the times that followed there was increased liquidation of bank held inventory. Banks tried to get their wishing prices through the prime selling season, but by the end of the year, there was pressure to get these non-performing assets off their books. The sales of bank foreclosures and the ongoing tightening of credit drove prices down an additional 5% to 10%. This caused some major problems for owners of residential real estate. Fear began to grip the market.

By the time a financial market enters the fear stage, greed stage buyers are seriously underwater. Comparable properties may be selling for 10% less than their breakeven price, and there is little hope that prices will rally. Some sell at this point and take a loss, but most do not. People who bought in the enthusiasm stage come up to their breakeven price and face the same decision the greed stage buyers faced earlier: sell now or hold out for a rally. Even though there is good reason to fear, most do not sell here. They regret it later, but they hold on. Speculators generally only sell an asset when the pain of loss becomes acute. The pain threshold is different for each individual, but there is no real pain until the investment is worth less than the purchase price, so few sell for a profit or at breakeven. Inventories grow in the fear stage because many would like to sell, but sales volumes are light because few are willing to sell at prices buyers are willing to pay.

Prices do not rally here because there are even fewer buyers in the market and a reduced appetite for debt due to the change in market psychology. There are more and more sellers either choosing to sell or being forced to sell, and since there are more sellers than buyers, prices continue to drop. During the fear stage, a majority of buyers during the rally go underwater on their mortgages and endure the associated pain and stress. In the past, since the bubbles of the 80s and 90s were largely built on conventional mortgages, people just held on. During the Great Housing Bubble, people used exotic loan financing terms, and they simply could not afford to make their payments. They borrowed from other sources until their credit lines were exhausted and they imploded in foreclosure and bankruptcy. During this stage many renters who would otherwise have purchased a home put off their purchase and save more money because they correctly see the decline in prices has momentum and prices should continue to drop further.

Capitulation Stage

The transition from the fear stage to the capitulation stage is caused by the infectious belief that the rally is over. There is a tipping point where a critical mass of market participants either decide to sell or are forced to sell. In residential real estate, people are compelled to sell by anxiety, and the mechanism for force is foreclosure. Once a critical mass of selling is reached, the selling causes prices to decline further which in turn causes more selling. This convinces even more people the rally is over yielding even more selling: a downward spiral. The same price-to-price feedback mechanism that served to drive prices up during the rally works to drive prices down during the crash. Collectively, everyone in the market accepts prices are going to drop further, and they need to get out: Now! Of course when everyone knows prices are going to drop, and everyone is trying to sell, there are very few buyers. Each market participant has a different threshold for pain. Some give up early; some give up later; some stubbornly try to hold on, but in the end, by choice or by force, everyone who cannot afford their home sells out and capitulates to the forces of the market. Each seller accepts the market rally was a bubble, and the frenzy of selling activity clears out the overhead supply. The capitulation stage is the counterpart of the greed stage. Sellers are everywhere and buyers are scarce. This puts prices into free-fall until a critical mass of buyers is ready to buy again.

Since buyers in the aftermath of a bubble tend to be the risk averse who did not participate in it, they will make cautiously low offers on properties. Buyer caution is reinforced by lender caution. In stark contrast to the days of bubble lending, large downpayments are suddenly required, appraisals are carefully reviewed, eligibility is tighter, and most exotic loan programs are gone. This cautious buying together with desperate sellers causes the market to drop below normal valuation standards. The market enters the despair stage. Here the market participants think nobody wants the asset, and nobody ever will again. Of course, nothing could be farther from the truth as those who recognize the fundamental value of the asset are buying it in preparation for the next cycle.

Despair Stage

From a perspective of market psychology, it is difficult to tell when the capitulation stage ends and the despair stage begins. Both stages have an extremely negative bearish sentiment. It is called the despair stage because most who own the asset are in despair and wish they did not own it, and the general public is still selling. Most who still own their homes are able to afford the monthly payments, but realize they will face a large loss if they sell their house anytime soon. They feel like prisoners in their own homes because they are unable to relocate for a better job or any other reason. One distinguishing feature of the despair stage is the increased buying activity of investors–true investors, not the speculators who were wiped out during the price decline.

Investors are not in despair during this stage. This is the time they were anticipating to make their purchases.

There is an extreme emotional toll paid by those who participated in the mania. Losing a home to foreclosure is devastating. The emotional ties to a home go beyond seeing it as an investment. A home is supposed to be a safe haven where people raise a family. It is a unique reflection of the family, adorned with mementos and family photographs. Being forced to leave the family home is difficult for reasons that have nothing to do with money. Unfortunately, this is often followed by personal bankruptcy, and the difficulties in bankruptcy have everything to do with money.

In some ways, those who endure foreclosure may be the lucky ones as they get to leave their debtor's prison and go find an affordable rental. The income that used to go toward housing is now freed up to go toward living a life. Those homeowners who hang on, who are desperately underwater, and who are putting 50% or more of their income toward a house worth less than they owe on it, their circumstances are arguably even more dire. There is no light at the end of their tunnel; they must live with their pain every day.

The despair stage is not desperate for everyone. What makes the despair stage different from the capitulation stage is that buyers who focus on fundamentals like rental savings or positive cashflow return to the market and begin buying. Affordability has returned to the housing market, and those who did not participate in the mania finally get their chance to become homeowners–at reasonable prices. These buyers are not concerned with appreciation; they simply want an asset which provides a savings or a cash return on their investment. They are not frightened by falling prices because their financial returns are independent of the asset's market valuation. It is the return of these people to the market that creates a bottom.

Bubbles as Cultural Pathology

What is a Cultural Pathology? There are certain beliefs if widely held and acted upon by a group of people leads inevitably to collective suffering and personal destruction. One example of a cultural pathology is demonstrated by the American auto industry. Before the age of imported cars, the American auto industry believed the quality of their product did not matter; people bought their product irrespective of quality. For many years, the industry was successful despite this pathology. This belief allowed offshore competitors to enter the market, build market share, and finally take over the industry. The American auto industry's belief system had had a pathologic effect on their business which caused much suffering in Detroit. This commitment to quality in the industry is still suspect, and it may lead to the bankruptcy and destruction of our major automakers.

The best treatise on the pathology of cultural beliefs was George Orwell's novel, 1984. [105] In Orwell's vision, a totalitarian State had convinced the populace of the following:

- WAR IS PEACE
- FREEDOM IS SLAVERY
- IGNORANCE IS STRENGTH

Although these statements are clearly contradictory, in the story the slogans do make sense to the State. For example, through constant "war", the State can keep domestic peace; when the people obtain freedom, they become enslaved to it, and the ignorance of the populace is the strength of the State. Just as Orwell's Big Brother convinced the populace the above contradictions were true, Californians and other bubble participants have convinced themselves of the following:

- APPRECIATION IS INCOME
- CREDIT IS SAVINGS
- DEBT IS WEALTH

Just as these statements are contradictory and ridiculous, the proof that these statements are believed is that they are reflected in the actions of many homeowners during the Great Housing Bubble. For example, through borrowing against increasing home values, appreciation is turned to income; when people obtain more credit, they spend it like available savings, and a large amount of debt used to finance a large, opulent home makes one wealthy. To many buyers and homeowners during the Great Housing Bubble this made perfect sense.

The problem is rooted in a basic misunderstanding of what separates the rich from the poor: the habit of saving. There is an old expression, "the rich get richer and the poor get poorer." It is more accurate to say the rich save money and the poor spend it: in the end, the rich will have money, and the poor will have none. [106] This is not one of life's inequities, but rather one of life's simple truths. When the average Joe says he wants to be rich, what he is really saying is he wants unlimited spending power. He wants the ability to *spend* like the rich people he sees wearing Rolexes and driving BMWs to their mansions. This is why, when given the chance, poor people will emulate the rich by spending beyond their means in order to *be* rich. Of course, in the process, they spend themselves poor.

Appreciation is Income

There is a noticeable difference between the behavior of rich and poor when it comes to home price appreciation. The rich view home price appreciation as adding to their net worth. If lower interest rates allow them to refinance, they will restructure their debt to pay off the loan more quickly in order to increase their wealth. Poor people view home price appreciation as income; free money for them to spend. If lower interest rates allow them to refinance, they will restructure their loan to pull as much home equity as possible and reduce their payment as much as possible so they can spend more. If any net worth happens to accumulate, they obtain a home equity line of credit and spend the appreciation as quickly as possible–it makes them feel rich even though it really makes them poor.

Credit is Savings

So how do the rich and poor deal with credit? The rich do not carry consumer debt. Why would they pay interest on a credit balance when it almost always costs more than the income they earn on their savings? The rich will use credit sparingly and most often pay off any credit balances each month as the bill comes due. In contrast, the poor carry as much consumer debt as they can afford to service. Whenever they receive an increase in a credit line, they believe they have more money to spend, just like it was savings. In a strange way, a credit account is like a savings account, only it has a negative balance. In a savings account, the saver earns money; in a credit account, the spender pays money. Again, the rich have savings, and the poor have credit.

Debt is Wealth

There are a great many homeowners who live in big houses, and they believe that makes them rich. To them, the possession and use of an expensive house makes them wealthy even if they have no equity in the property. The rich buy less home than they can afford and work to pay off the debt in order to maximize their net worth. The poor stretch their finances to possess more home than they can afford with loan terms which never retire the debt, or in the case of negative amortization loans, actually increases their debt held against the property. This ensures they never gain any equity or only gain it by appreciation, and as mentioned previously, if prices appreciate they quickly withdraw the gain to fuel more consumer spending.

It's a California Thing

So what happens when you give poor people money? They spend it. The stories of people who won the lottery and managed to spend themselves into bankruptcy a few years later are classic examples of the pathology of the beliefs of spenders. [107] A great many Californians are spenders. This is why California has a strong cultural pathology. The main psychological reason house prices in California were bid up to such dizzying heights during the Great Housing Bubble was because there was a high percentage of the population in California that subscribed to the spending habits just described. They went out and borrowed as much money as they could with exotic loans, bought up all the real estate they could get their hands on, and in the process drove real estate prices into the stratosphere. In other areas of the country, reckless spending was not so trendy, and home prices were not bid up so high.

Pretentious displays of conspicuous consumption are less common in the Midwest, and consumerism is often viewed with contempt rather than envy. In short, there is a smaller percentage of the general population in the Midwest with the aforementioned pathologic beliefs. [108] To substantiate this claim, observe the profile of Minnetonka, Minnesota, a suburb of Minneapolis with very similar income and demographics to Irvine, California. The median income in Minnetonka, Minnesota in 2006 was $84,024, and the median income in

Irvine, California, in 2006 was $84,253. [109] This is close enough to be a good comparison. The median home price in Minnetonka in 2006 was $305,600, and the median home price in Irvine in 2006 was $722,928. [110,111] If the thesis is correct, one would expect to find a much higher percentage of home loans utilizing exotic loan terms in Irvine as compared to Minnetonka. In 2006 the Minneapolis area had 8.7% of its loan originations were negative amortization, while Orange County had 32%.[112] In all of California more than 80% of loan originations in 2006 were either Option ARM or interest-only. Here are two groups of people with the same median income, and with the same access to credit making very different choices. Potential homebuyers in Minnetonka and Irvine faced the same decision on taking out an exotic loan and buying more house than they can afford or choosing to live within their means. Very few in Minnetonka chose to overextend themselves, so they did not bid up the values of their houses. Residents of Irvine (and the rest of California) chose to utilize exotic financing and thereby real estate prices were bid much, much higher. The high utilization of exotic financing was the *cause* of the price increase, not the result of it. Nobody was forced to buy.

Perhaps Californians were just more financially sophisticated than the rubes back on the farm in the Midwest? If many in California were spending freely, feeling rich, and enjoying life, where is the pathology? The beliefs and resulting behavior is pathological because it is not sustainable. There is an inevitable Day of Reckoning when all debts must be paid. Charles Ponzi was the most excessive example of this pathology. So extreme were his activities, that the term Ponzi Scheme has become synonymous with the use of ever increasing amounts of investment or debt. [113] This scheme is also encapsulated in the expression "robbing Peter to pay Paul." The twentieth century economist Hyman Minsky wrote about the "Minsky Moment" when borrowers must liquidate assets to pay off debts which in turn lowers asset prices and creates more margin calls and even more asset liquidation. [114] At some point, the debt becomes so large that no lender is willing to loan more money, no greater fool can be found to bail them out, and the whole system comes crashing down. However, while the debt was building, the debtor becomes accustomed to a certain lifestyle and level of spending. When the credit is cut off, the debtor can no longer spend, and a great deal of suffering ensues. This is Armageddon for debtors: the spending stops, they lose their homes and with it their illusion of wealth, and they definitely are not enjoying life. The cause of all the weeping and gnashing of teeth is not an exogenous event, but rather a direct result of the circumstances they themselves created.

The California Social Contract

Satire is often more revealing than detailed explanations. The pathology of a collection of beliefs becomes apparent when the natural end result of a group of people acting on those beliefs is an absurd contradiction and an obviously unsustainable state. The following is a satirical essay written from the point of view of a desperate homeowner trying to sustain the Ponzi Scheme of the Great Housing Bubble:

You fence-sitters are failing to fulfill your part of the California Social Contract. Your failure to continue buying homes is disrupting the social order, and it is causing those of us who bought before you psychological, emotional and financial damage. It is time for you to get off the fence and buy–NOW!!!

In any social contract, you give up something personally for the greater good. When those of us who bought before you purchased our homes, we had to commit unrealistic percentages of our income to housing, lie on mortgage applications, and take out financing on unstable mortgage terms in order to do our part for the continuing social good. We made these sacrifices willingly because the benefits of maintaining the social contract are worth the price we paid. Look what those who bought before us received in return:

1. Dramatic increases in wealth through home equity. I think we can all agree this is desirable. You want to be rich, right?

2. The ability to spend more than what is earned through productive activities like work. Think of all the BMWs, Mercedes, vacations to Maui, Coach Bags, designer jeans, Rolex watches and other items purchased with home equity lines of credit. You want to double your spending power, right?

3. The ability to buy furniture and home improvements without saving or spending income. Your house should be a self-sustaining asset which provides the ability to maintain itself with perpetual appreciation. Who would not want that?

We provided all of this to the buyers who came before us, and all we ask is that you do the same for us. Is not this a fair bargain? You want the same for yourself, right? If you do this, the next generation of buyers will learn from your example, and they will be willing to do the same.

Some have argued it is our fault that the social contract is falling apart. If we recent homebuyers had simply made our payments, the contract would not have been broken. This is rubbish. The lenders failed us. They knew we could not make those payments when we took out the loans. They knew we were not truthful on our loan applications. They knew they were going to have to provide opportunities for serial refinancing of ever increasing amounts of debt. They failed us. They are the ones who broke the social contract, not us.

The tightening of credit just means you will have to make more significant sacrifices to keep the social contract. You may need to borrow money from family members or solicit larger gifts. You may need to become more creative in your attempts to inflate your income or assets. All we had to do was sign some fraudulent paperwork, but you may have to forge some documents or buy a seasoned credit line or find a hard-money lender who does not record the debt (loan sharks).

It is going to be tough, but look at the benefits listed above. Is it not worth the sacrifice?

It is time for you to buy now. Trees really can grow to the sky; prices really can go up forever–if you hold up your end of the California Social Contract. To paraphrase Winston Churchill,

> Let us therefore brace ourselves to our duties, and so bear ourselves that if the {California Social Contract} last for a thousand years, men will still say, 'This was their finest hour.'

This is your chance to stand up for what is right and perpetuate a system that is beneficial to our society. History will remember what you do. Will you be the generation that lived up to its duties, or will this be the end of the world as we know it? You decide.

Bailouts and False Hopes

One of the more interesting phenomena observed during the bubble was the perpetuation of denial with rumors of homeowner bailouts. Many homeowners held out hope that if they could just keep current on their mortgage long enough, the government would come to their rescue in the form of a mandated bailout program. Part of this fantasy was not just that people could keep their homes, but that they could keep living their lifestyle as they did during the bubble. What few seemed to realize was any government bailout program would be designed to benefit the lenders by keeping borrowers in a perpetual state of indentured servitude. With all their money going toward debt service payments, little was going to be left over for living a life.

All of these plans had benefits and drawbacks. One of the first problems was to clearly define who should be "bailed out." The thought of bailing out speculators was not palatable to anyone except perhaps the speculators themselves, but with regular families behaving like speculators, separating the wheat from the chaff was not an easy task. If a family exaggerated their income to obtain more house than they could afford in hopes of capturing appreciation, did they deserve a bailout? The credit crisis that popped the Great Housing Bubble was one of solvency, and there was no way to effectively restructure payments when a borrower could not afford to pay the interest on the debt, and this was a very common circumstance. None of the bailout programs did much for those with stated-income (liar) loans, negative amortization loans, and others who are unable to make the payments, and since this was a significant portion of the housing inventory, none of these plans had any real hope of stopping the fall of prices in the housing market.

The main problem with all of the plans is the moral hazard they created because those who did not participate in the bubble and instead behaved in a prudent manner would be penalized at the expense of those who were cavalier about risk. In one form or another either through free market impacts or direct subsidies from the government paid by tax dollars, these bailout plans all asked the cautious to support the reckless. [115]

Many of the early bailout plans called for changing the terms of the mortgage note. This might have been easy in the days when banks held mortgages in their own portfolios, but it was much more difficult once these mortgages were bundled together in collateralized debt obligations and sold to parties all over the world. Even if it would have been possible to easily change the terms, the resulting turmoil in the secondary mortgage market would have caused higher mortgage interest rates. When an investor faces the risk of the government changing the terms of their contract, and these changes would not be in their favor, the investor would demand higher returns. Higher investor returns means higher mortgage interest rates which would raise the cost of borrowing. This was the opposite of what the government bailout plans were trying to accomplish.

Hope Now?

The first of the numerous bailout programs was "Hope Now" introduced in October of 2007. As the name suggests, Hope Now was sold to the general public as a reason for them to hang on and continue making crushing payments for as long as possible. It was a false hope, but even false hope gave homeowners a little emotional relief, and it provided a few more payments to the lenders. According to their website, "HOPE NOW is a cooperative effort between counselors, investors, and lenders to maximize outreach efforts to homeowners in distress." [116] The plan was to streamline the process of negotiating workouts between lenders and borrowers to keep borrowers making payments and ostensibly to stop them from losing their homes. The emphasis was on making payments and maximizing investor value in collateralized debt obligations. Very few people benefited from the program, despite government claims to the contrary, and no rights or benefits were conferred to borrowers that they did not already contractually have. There was much fanfare when it was first announced, but the program did far too little to have any impact on the housing market.

The next bailout was aimed directly at the lenders with the Super SIV program introduced in October of 2007 (Paulson, 2007). An SIV is a special investment vehicle. It is an off-balance-sheet investment designed to hold investments a company (usually a lender) does not want to show on its own balance sheets. It is a smoke-and-mirrors device used primarily to get around regulations intended to stop lenders from taking excessive risk. The Super SIV program was intended to purchase assets from the troubled SIVs and provide liquidity for lenders who desperately needed it. The problem with the Super SIV was simple: nobody wanted these assets. Moving bad mortgage paper around was akin to rearranging the deck chairs on the Titanic. Few in the general public knew what this program was for, and even fewer cared. Most wanted to know their government was doing something to solve the problem, and the Super SIV announcement provided them with much wanted denial.

In December of 2007, the government offered a more direct homeowner bailout plan. The proposal was to freeze the interest rates on certain loans for certain borrowers for five years. This was greeted as a panacea by all parties, and the beast of homeowner denial was fed once again. As with the Hope Now program, few people qualified, and it did nothing to hold back the tide of increasing defaults and foreclosures. The denial was short lived, and this unnamed bailout plan quickly fell from the headlines.

In February of 2008 Congress and the President signed the Economic Stimulus Act of 2008 temporarily increasing the conforming loan limit for Fannie Mae and Freddie Mac, the government sponsored entities (GSEs) that maintain the secondary mortgage market. The GSEs provide insurance to mortgage backed securities, and by raising the conforming limit, the GSEs were able to insure large, so called "jumbo" loans. This enabled the holders of jumbo loans who were unable to sell these mortgages access to capital in the secondary market. All of this was seen as another reason for homeowners in severely inflated bubble markets to hope the government was going to rescue the housing market.

Forgiveness of Debt

Perhaps the most outrageous suggestion put forth was the suggestion by the FED Chairman Ben Bernanke when he proposed lenders forgive mortgage debt in early 2008 (Bernanke B. S., Reducing Preventable Mortgage Foreclosures, 2008). The moral hazards were obvious. Would people stop making their payments to make sure they qualified? Would more people buy homes they could not afford then appeal for debt relief? Rational people became frightened when they heard the head banker in the United States propose massive debt forgiveness as they realized this meant the entire banking system was in peril. The implications of this proposal were lost on the typical homeowner who only saw how they might benefit from it. Debt forgiveness was the ultimate fantasy of every homeowner. They could be relieved of their financial burdens and get to keep their houses and their lifestyles. It did not matter to the financially troubled that the proposal made no sense and had no possibility of happening, the thought of it would motivate them to hang on a little longer to see if maybe they could hit the jackpot.

Housing and Economic Recovery Act of 2008

In late July 2008, Congress passed and the President signed the Housing and Economic Recovery Act of 2008 that included the following provisions: Federal Housing Finance Regulatory Reform Act of 2008, HOPE for Homeowners Act of 2008, and the Foreclosure Prevention Act of 2008. At the time of this writing, these programs have not been fully implemented, and it is too soon to determine if they are successful. Of course, success can mean different things to different parties. For homeowners, success means keeping their house, getting a lower payment, and profiting from its eventual sale. For lenders and holders of mortgages, success means keeping a steady flow of money coming in from previously insolvent debtors. For the government, success means doing something to make angry homeowners less likely to vote them out of office and keep our financial system from complete collapse. As with many pieces of legislation, it is an ugly series of compromises, and ultimately, none of the concerned parties may deem it successful.

In the Savings and Loan disaster of the late 1980s, the government was liable to investors for their losses through the Federal Savings and Loan Insurance Corporation (FSLIC). The government had no choice but to compel taxpayers to cover the costs of the industry bailout. The Great Housing Bubble had no such direct government liability until this burden was assumed by the government retroactively. The Federal Housing Finance Regulatory Reform Act of 2008 established a regulator to watch over the GSEs. This was too late to do anything about the serious problems facing the GSEs, and it acted as an interim step toward a direct GSE bailout of lenders and investors at the expense of the taxpayers. If one of the GSEs would have failed prior to this legislation, many in Congress would have resisted a taxpayer bailout because the activities of the GSEs were not strictly regulated. Once the regulatory framework was in place, Congress had greater political cover to justify a taxpayer bailout.

In early September 2008, not long after the legislation was passed, the Department of Treasury took over "conservatorship" of the GSEs. It is unclear what will happen once under government control–other than the taxpayers of the United States will be directly responsible for all losses. In time, the government's interests in the GSEs will likely be sold, and the GSEs will become private companies again, but this time with greater governmental oversight. With any regulatory framework, enforcement is pivotal to its success. If another bubble starts inflating, enforcement may not take priority over profits, particularly when the GSE lobbyists start donating heavily to key Congressional leaders.

The HOPE for Homeowners Act of 2008 and the Foreclosure Prevention Act of 2008 are of primary interest to homeowners. [117] It falls well short of what most homeowners wanted: direct debt relief from the government. However, it does provide incentives for lenders and investors to forgive the debts of homeowners, but it makes homeowners agree to take out an FHA loan with a higher interest rate and give half the profits on the eventual sale to the FHA. Neither of those provisions will be palatable to borrowers. Both the lender and the homeowner must voluntarily participate. If the lender is determined to foreclose or if the borrower is determined to give up paying back the loan, neither party is compelled to work with the other. For lenders facing taking a property back in foreclosure, writing off a significant portion of the original loan may be preferable to taking a larger loss in a foreclosure. Desperate owners facing foreclosure may like the idea of debt forgiveness, but their payments will not go down much, and giving up half their appreciation will not go over well when they go to sell the property.

Emergency Economic Stabilization Act of 2008

In early October 2008, the Congress passed and the President signed the Emergency Economic Stabilization Act of 2008. The purpose of the bill was "to restore liquidity and stability to the U.S. financial system and to ensure the economic well-being of Americans." The law authorized the Secretary of the Treasury to establish a Troubled Asset Relief Program (TARP) to purchase the toxic waste poisoning the balance sheets of lenders and other financial institutions. This measure was passed in response to an unprecedented seizure of the short-term credit markets. Banks quit lending money to other banks once it became apparent that few of them were solvent. This fear spread to all short-term commercial paper and threatened to bring down the entire financial system. It is unclear whether or not this new program will save the institutions holding the toxic waste.

When this legislation was first introduced, there was widespread public disapproval of what amounted to be a transfer of wealth from taxpayers to rich bankers on Wall Street. There was no mention of bailing out troubled home-owners who were the cause of all the financial distress in the lending industry. Since desperate homeowners were not being given any new false hope, they saw no reason to support the bailout. A series of dramatic drops in the equities markets while the legislation was being debated helped turn the tide of public opinion.

The impact of this legislation is unknown at the time of this writing; however, it appears to be designed as part of a controlled implosion of the banking system. With $700,000,000,000 at his disposal and complete discretion on how to spend it, the Treasury Secretary, with cooperation from the Chairman of the Federal Reserve, will be able to sort out the healthy banks from the unhealthy ones, broker mergers and acquisitions and recapitalize the survivors. By October of 2008, the need for bailouts and false hopes had gone beyond foolish borrowers; the banks were the ones who needed some denial.

Zero Coupon Notes

Of all the intervention programs put forward, only one had any chance of providing any real relief to homeowners if it had been implemented, but the terms would not have been to the liking of homeowners, and the long-term implications would not have been pleasant: convert part of the mortgage to a zero coupon bond. A zero coupon bond is a bond which does not make periodic interest payments. Think of it a zero amortization loan. The borrower pays neither the interest nor the principal, and both accumulate for the life of the loan. The loan would be due upon the sale of the house.

There were many borrowers who were capable of making the payments on a conventional 30-year mortgage when their loans reset, but they were unable to refinance because they owed more on their mortgage than was allowed to qualify for refinancing. For this group of borrowers, the government could have instituted a "loan guarantee" program similar to what they did for Chrysler in the 80s. It would have been in both the lender's interest and the borrower's interest to make the loan and have the borrower continue to make payments, and some banks would have done this on their own (or would have been forced to in a "cram down"); however, many other banks would not, so a government program would have been necessary to prevent further disruption in the market.

Here is how it would have worked for our typical homeowner: Assume a borrower utilized 100% financing and took out a $500,000 interest-only mortgage with a 2% teaser rate that is due to adjust to 6%. Further assume the borrower's real income (not what was reported on the liar loan) could support a $1,500 payment on a $250,000 conventional 30-year mortgage at 6%. The bank could convert $250,000 to a conventional mortgage, and convert the other $250,000 to a zero coupon bond at 6% due on sale. The homeowner could have made their payment and kept their house; however, when they later sold their house, they would have owed the bank a great deal of money. If they sold the house in 20 years, they would owe $800,000 on the zero coupon bond note. In other words, all the equity gain on the value of the home would have gone to the bank.

This would have solved a multitude of problems: First, it would have provided a mechanism whereby people who were victims of predatory lending could have kept their homes. This would have made the homeowner happy, and it would have kept government regulators out of the lender's business. Second, it would have made the lenders more money in the long run because they still would have been making their interest profit even if they did not see it until after the home was sold. (Many may not be aware of it, but lenders book income on the increase in principal on a negative amortization loan). Third, since foreclosures were the primary mechanism facilitating the crash, it would have kept home prices from crashing by reducing the number of foreclosures.

Sounds like a panacea, but there would have been some problems. The first problem would become apparent when people start selling their houses. People are greedy. They would not have wanted to give the bank all their equity when they sold. They would have conveniently forgotten the debt relief and avoiding foreclosure and all the problems they had earlier. All they would have seen is that they sold the house for much more than they paid for it, and they did not make any money. And what happens when the appreciation does not match the term of the note? Would they have completed a short-sale 20 years down the line? This would have caused a huge uproar and more calls for congressional intervention. In other words, for everyone involved the day of reckoning would be delayed, not avoided.

This solution would have done nothing for the affordability problem. If prices did not crash, a great many people really would have been priced out forever. To solve that problem, banks would have had to make zero coupon bonds available to everyone, and eventually everyone would have had them. Think about where we would have been then: we would have become a society of homeowners who had collectively agreed to give all our equity to the bank for the pride of ownership: starts to sound a bit like Pottersville from It's a Wonderful Life. [118] Is that the way we all would have wanted to live?

The zero coupon bond solution would have effectively eliminated the move-up market because people would not have had any equity to take with them from house to house. Unless a prospective move-up buyer has saved a substantial sum or obtained a large pay increase to afford a larger payment, they could not get a more expensive home. This would have resulted in a dramatic flattening of prices. In other words, the low end would have been supported at inflated levels while the high end would have stagnated or declined.

Also, based on the problems above, it would have been difficult to find a new equilibrium in prices. How would people have calculated how much anything was worth? How would all price ranges have been supported equally? Small changes in the interest rate on the zero coupon bond would have made the difference between hundreds of thousands of dollars at the time of sale, particularly on a long-term hold. Does anyone think this would have turned out in favor of the borrower? We would have undoubtedly seen many short-sales as the banks graciously agreed to take all the gains and forgive the rest of the debt. This would take us back to our first problem with angry, greedy sellers.

Finally, this would have been only a short to medium term solution to the foreclosure problem. For as much as we are addicted to credit in this country, there is a point where people would have said "enough is enough." When a house fails to have any investment value, people would not have been so excited about home ownership. People can blather on about pride of ownership all they want, but people want to make money when selling their houses. Inflated valuations are only supported by greed. If home ownership becomes less desirable, prices would have ended up falling back to their rental equivalent values because the demand would not have been there. In the long run, we would have ended up with prices where they should have been anyway, it would have been a much more prolonged and painful journey very similar to the Japanese experience of the 1990s.

Zero coupon bond structures and other exotic financing terms are quite common in complex real estate deals. Exotic loan terms are the exclusive purview of sophisticated investors who understand what they are doing. They are not intended for consumption by the general public. Given the profusion of interest-only, and negative amortization loans in the market, is not a surprise the financial innovations of the Great Housing Bubble turned out badly.

Let Markets Work

It is difficult not to become cynical about all the various bailout programs, and the proposals outlined were not the only ones discussed in the public forum. There was a steady drumbeat of public plans and announcements that were never substantial, and their only purpose seemed to be to foster denial among those who needed it.

There is no possible bailout program without the commensurate moral hazards and unfair benefits they would contain. The best course of action would be to ease the transition of people from overextended homeowner to renter and not to attempt to manipulate the financial markets for the benefit of a few. There is nothing that can be done to prevent of the collapse of financial bubbles. The solution lies in easing the pain of their deflation and in preventing them from inflating in the future.

Summary

The motivations for purchasing real estate or any asset differ considerably between investors and speculators. Since speculators rely on capturing the change in asset price, they are much more emotionally involved with the gyrations of market resale value, and since their emotions work against them, they most often sell at a loss. Trading houses became epidemic in the Great Housing Bubble. Houses became commodities to buy and sell and lost their intrinsic value as a shelter or a place to call "home." People utilized 100% financing and treated mortgage obligations as little more than options contracts.

The emotional cycle of an asset price bubble emanates from the emotional cycle of individual speculators. Efficient markets theory would say these emotions are irrelevant as each investor acts rationally based on fundamental market data. Behavioral finance theory argues our herd instincts coupled with irrational beliefs and expectations are primary forces at work in financial markets. Efficient markets theory fails to explain asset price bubbles, whereas behavioral finance theory does. When the bubble bursts, each speculator must go through the stages of grief as she comes to accept her loss. These stages have analogous counterparts in the price cycle of an asset bubble, and it is through the actions of these grieving speculators that the timing of the cycle takes place.

Asset price bubbles can distort the values and behaviors of entire segments of society. Pathological beliefs can take root and grow into an unsustainable system doomed to crash down around all those who subscribe to the cultural pathology. The activity of governments can serve to reinforce pathological behaviors, and when called upon by a desperate public, the government can pander to the emotional needs of the citizenry through generating false hopes and supporting denial.

Many people like it when houses go up in price. During a rally the bulls become intoxicated with greed and obsessed with owning real estate as an investment. However, once houses become an investment, the prices of houses begin to behave like an investment, and volatility is introduced into the system. When houses trade with the volatility of a commodities market, it causes more harm than good. Price volatility is a very disruptive feature in a housing market: the upswings are euphoric, and the downswings are devastating–and there are downswings. Declining house prices are emotionally and financially draining both to individuals and to the economy as a whole. The upswings create massive amounts of unsustainable borrowing and spending, and the downswings create economic contraction, foreclosures and personal bankruptcy. Is the ecstasy of a rally worth the despair of a crash?

Houses should not be viewed as a commodity to trade. Most people lack the financial sophistication to successfully trade in commodity markets. Buying and hoping prices go up is not a successful strategy. Volatility in housing prices is harmful to the community as the financial and emotional costs of the inevitable price crash are just too great. Everyone pays a price. Renters who chose not to participate are forced to wait to obtain the security of home ownership at an affordable price, and buyers who endure the crash... well, their pain is obvious.

Future House Prices

For all our wisdom and collective experience, none of us knows what the markets will do next. Like an ocean current or a raging river, a financial market charts its own course. It is fickle and feckless and flows without regard to our hopes and dreams. The ebbs and flows of financial markets are meaningful to us, but in reality they are just movements in price; nothing more. Price rallies make homeowners blissful and renters bitter, while price declines make homeowners gloomy and renters gleeful. These feelings and emotions are independent of movements in price. The market just moves, that is all it does. It is benign, yet dangerous; it is indifferent, yet demonstrative; the market is a paradox which we must simply accept.

During the rally of the Great Housing Bubble, buyers did not concern themselves with the day they were going to become sellers. Why would they? There was an endless demand for properties, and buyers were paying whatever was asked. If they wanted a price above current market values to pay off a loan, all they had to do was wait. Once the bubble burst and home prices started to decline, the conditions people were accustomed to during the rally dramatically changed. Anyone considering buying a home in the aftermath of a crash should think about the buyer who is going to buy their home from them at some point in the future, and more specifically, what debt-to-income ratio and loan terms this future buyer will utilize. This is important, because the amount of money this take-out buyer will pay for the home is completely dependent upon these variables. At most, a house is only worth what a buyer can pay for it. In a declining market with few qualified buyers, many of those qualified buyers will only make offers if the deal is exceptional or simply wait for further price declines.

In a market environment where prices are detached from fundamental valuations, bubble buyers face a daunting challenge just to break even on their purchase when the time comes to sell it. A future buyer must have favorable borrowing terms allowing for a high degree of leverage or they may not be able to borrow the prodigious sums borrowers during the bubble rally were able to obtain. If a future buyer is not able to borrow as much with their income as bubble buyers, then wages must increase over time to permit future borrowers to borrow the same sum and allow a bubble buyer to avoid a loss. Unfortunately, it will take many years for wages to catch up to bubble prices. Even when this occurs, and a seller can recover their purchase price, inflation will have diminished the value of those dollars. If the prices are adjusted for inflation, many bubble buyers will never see an inflation adjusted breakeven price.

How Far to Fall

This book was written as the market crash was just beginning, and although there was already significant history to discuss, the price levels where the markets ultimately found stability had not yet been reached. The remainder of this chapter is a projection of what should happen if the residential real estate market responds as history would suggest. There will undoubtedly be unexpected twists and turns that impact the various variables influencing housing prices, and changes to these variables will change the timing and the depth of the crash. The projections and discussion which follows is based on first a return to historic norms and finally a look at what could happen if the crashing market causes an "overshoot" of fundamental valuations as often occurs in the collapse of a financial bubble.

All methods of predicting future price action rely on the same basic premise: prices are tethered to some fundamental value, and although prices may deviate from this value for extended periods of time, prices eventually return to fundamental valuations. This premise has been reinforced by market observation; in fact, many estimates of fundamental value are based on market action. Since many market participants believe in buying and selling based on fundamental values, there is also an element of self-fulfilling prophecy contained therein. The efficient markets theory is based on this idea, and although the behavioral finance theory is needed to explain the wide deviations from fundamentals real-world prices exhibit, both theories share the same notion of an underlying fundamental valuation on which prices are ultimately based. The challenge to market prognosticators is to select a fundamental valuation to which prices will return, and then extrapolate a period of time in which the return of prices to fundamental valuation will take place.

There are a number of ways to project how far and how fast prices will fall. One is to look at the price charts themselves and try to project reasonable trend lines to approximate bottoming valuations. This is not an accurate methodology as it is based on the assumption of a repetition of past performance without examining the reasons for this past performance; however, it does serve as a useful rough estimate. A more accurate and detailed method is to examine the variables that determine market pricing and see how changes in these variables impact resale values. This process involves assessing current fundamental values to make a statement as to where prices should be–and would have been if there had not been a residential real estate bubble–then estimating how long it will take for these variables to return to their historic norms. Also, there are a number of exogenous forces that act on market pricing in an indirect manner. These include debt-to-income ratios, availability of credit and changes in loan terms, mortgage interest rates, unemployment rates, foreclosure rates, home ownership rates, possible government intervention in the markets, and other factors. These forces do not directly impact house prices as changes in these variables do not have strong correlation with house prices; however, these variables can and do impact the variables that do correspond with house prices, therefore an evaluation is provided of the role these factors play in market pricing.

The timing of the decline is the most difficult parameter to evaluate and estimate. [119] House prices are notoriously "sticky" during price declines because sellers are loath to sell at a loss. The timing of a decline is impacted both by psychological and technical factors. The motivations of sellers based on their personal circumstances and emotional states will determine if there is a heightened sense of urgency to sell which would push prices down quickly. During the price correction of the coastal bubble of the early 90s, prices declined very slowly as unmotivated sellers held on and waited for prices to come back. The market experienced denial and fear, but there was not a stage of capitulatory selling that drove prices down quickly as is typical in the deflation of a speculative bubble. The primary technical factor impacting the rate of price decline is the presence of foreclosures and real estate owned (REO). REOs are a form of must-sell inventory (as are new homes). If there is more inventory of the must-sell variety than the market can absorb, prices are pushed lower. The more of this must-sell inventory there is on the market, the faster prices decline. If the pattern of the early 90s is repeated, the price decline of the Great Housing Bubble may drag out slowly while fundamentals catch up to market pricing. In fact, this is probably what will occur on the national market unless the foreclosure numbers and resultant REOs overwhelm market buyers. In the extreme bubble markets like Irvine, California, the combination of high foreclosure rates and general market panic will likely push prices lower much more quickly. [120] Even though the percentage decline in house prices is projected to be double the decline witnessed in the coastal bubble of the early 90s, the duration of the decline may be similar as capitulatory selling pushes prices lower at a faster rate.

Price Action

Most market participants focus on price action. The price-to-price feedback mechanism largely responsible for bubble market behavior gathers its strength from an awareness of market pricing, and the widespread belief that short-term, past price performance is predictive of long-term, future price performance. It is a fallacy that is often reinforced in the short-term as irrational exuberance takes over in a market, but over the long term, short-term price movements rarely correspond to long-term price trends, and when they do, it is only by chance.

Predicting future prices based on price action is based on the premise that long-term price trends are reflective of fundamental valuations because they represent the collective wisdom of the market. As with all methods of predict-ing pricing, deviations from the long-term fundamental valuation almost always result in a return to this value. The weakness in this theory is in its failure to provide a causal mechanism. To note that prices return to long-term valuations without postulating why prices do this provides no mechanism for estimating when prices will return to fundamental value, and it provides no way to determine if there is a significant change to the market's valuation to establish whether or not prices will return at all. In short, past price action itself is very limited in its ability to predict future price action. Despite the shortcomings of the methodology, predictions based on past price performance are widely used and often woefully inaccurate.

Figure 36: National Projections from Historic Appreciation Rates, 1984-2012

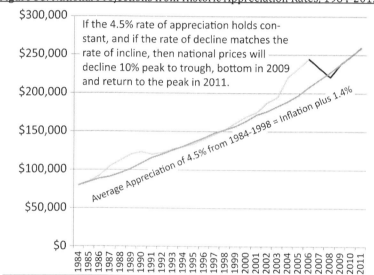

Source: US Census Bureau, US Department of Labor

From 1984 through 1998, national house prices appreciated at a rate of 4.5%. There is a strong correlation between this rate of price increase and observed market prices. There is only one deviation from this rate of apprecia-tion during the period. The effect of the coastal bubble of the late 1980s on national prices creates a small rise from the historic appreciation rate and a sideways drift of prices until values resume their 4.5% annual rise. Since prices consistently match this rate of appreciation, and since prices deviate once from this rate in a prior price bubble and return to it, there is a compelling argument that prices will drop to this level of long-term appreciation and begin rising again. If this proves to be true, national home prices will decline 10% from the peak, bottom in 2009, and return to the peak by 2011. This is the market's best-case scenario.

Figure 37: Irvine, CA, Projections from Historic Appreciation Rates, 1984-2026

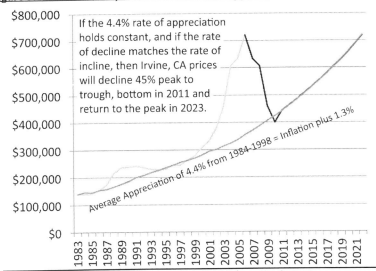

If the 4.4% rate of appreciation holds constant, and if the rate of decline matches the rate of incline, then Irvine, CA prices will decline 45% peak to trough, bottom in 2011 and return to the peak in 2023.

Average Appreciation of 4.4% from 1984-1998 = Inflation plus 1.3%

Source: California Association of Realtors, DataQuick Information Systems

The story for the most inflated markets such as Irvine, California, is much the same as the national forecast. If the 4.4% rate of appreciation seen from 1984-1998 is repeated, then prices will decline 45% from the peak, bottom in 2011 and return to the peak in 2023. Since prices peaked in 2006, this method of price projection shows an 18 year peak-to-peak waiting time: not a comforting forecast for Irvine homeowners.

Figure 38: Growth in Income and House Prices, 1981-2006

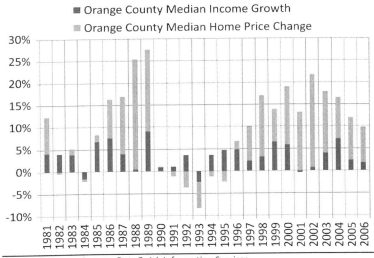

■ Orange County Median Income Growth

■ Orange County Median Home Price Change

Source: US Census Bureau, DataQuick Information Services

The key assumption in this analysis is that market prices will resume the rate of appreciation seen from 1984 to 1998. This rate of house price appreciation is 1.4% above the rate of inflation, 1.2% above the rate of wage growth, and 0.7% above the very long-term rate of house price appreciation. House appreciation cannot exceed wage growth forever: trees cannot grow to the sky. People have to earn money to buy a home (unless of course we become a nation of the landed gentry in which real estate is only transferred through inheritance). Over the last 25 years, house appreciation in Orange County has outpaced wage growth. Wage growth has averaged 3.4% while house price appreciation has averaged 6.9%. The coastal bubble years (1986-1989) where house prices outpaced income growth were followed by bust years (1990-1995) where wage growth made modest recoveries.

House prices outpaced wage growth for two reasons: first, debt-to-income ratios rose as people put higher percentages of their income toward making payments; second, interest rates declined allowing people to finance larger sums with less money. Much of the reason house prices appreciated at a rate in excess of its normal relationship to inflation is due to the gradual decline of interest rates during the period. As interest rates decline, the amount people can borrow increases. If people can borrow more, they can bid prices higher. House prices appreciated at a rate greater than its long-term average due to declining interest rates. If interest rates stop declining (which is likely), or if interest rates begin a cycle of long-term incline, the rate of house price appreciation will be impacted negatively; the drop of prices from the deflating bubble will be deeper, and the date of ultimate price recovery will be much later.

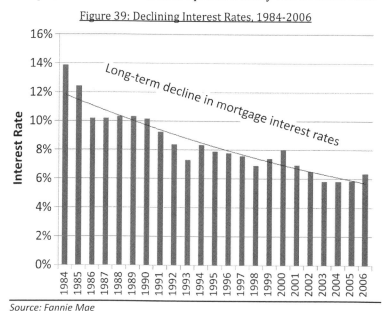

Figure 39: Declining Interest Rates, 1984-2006

Source: Fannie Mae

The median sales price measures the general price levels at which buyers are active in the market, but it does not reflect the quality of what is purchased and it does not reflect the price changes of individual properties. The S&P/Case-Shiller indices measure price changes in individual properties through its use of repeat sales in calculation of the index. Market participants are primarily concerned with how their property is changing in price rather than some aggregate measure of the market. The S&P/Case-Shiller index is the best market measure for approximating the price change on individual properties.

Figure 40: National Projections based on S&P/Case-Shiller Indices

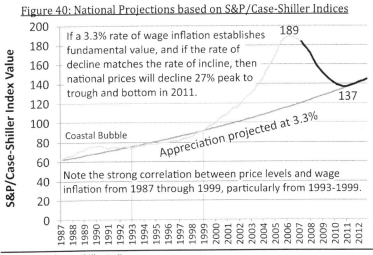

Source: S&P/Case-Shiller Indices

It is more difficult to use an aggregate appreciation rate on the S&P/Case-Shiller indices because there is no single period where a particular average correlates well with market pricing, plus small changes in the rate of appreciation can make large differences in where the bottom is found. There are two issues to be addressed with any projection of appreciation when there is low correlation to the data: the starting point, and the rate of increase. The S&P/Case-Shiller indices did not start collecting data until 1987, but this date is arbitrary. The most recent market low was in 1984, and by 1987, there was some detachment from fundamental valuations. The point of origin for the projection of appreciation may more appropriately be below the first data point in 1987; however, to simplify the analysis, the 1987 data point was used as the origin. The 3.3% rate used in the projections was the historic rate of wage growth from 1987 to 2006. Since people finance house purchases with payments made from wages, this is a reasonable rate to use. Another method that can be used is to assume the very long-term rate of appreciation of 0.7% over inflation. The question then is what rate of inflation should be used. The average rate of inflation from 1987 to 2007 has been just over 3%, but inflation rates have been much higher and more volatile prior to this time. So an argument can be made that 3.7% is a more appropriate number. If this rate is

141

used with the lower origin point to allow for the small degree of house price inflation already evident in 1987, the two support curves differ slightly, but the difference between the two is not significant to the outcome.

Figure 41: Los Angeles Projections based on S&P/Case-Shiller Indices

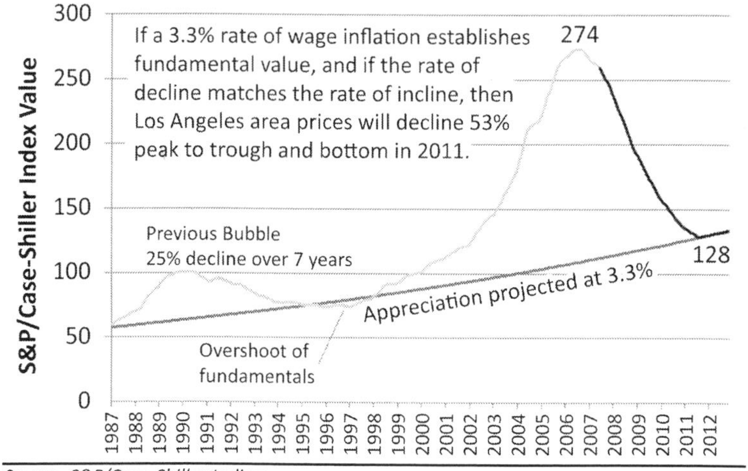

Source: S&P/Case-Shiller Indices

Based on projections from S&P/Case-Shiller indices using a 3.3% rate of wage growth as a support level, prices of individual properties will decline 27% from their peak valuations in 2006, finding a bottom in 2011 and reaching the previous peak in 2025. This is arguably the market prediction of most concern to homeowners that purchased during the bubble because it reflects the price change of individual properties like theirs. There is very little comfort in the thought of a 27% decline and a 19 year waiting period until prices regain their previous peak.

The degree of detachment from fundamental valuations in the extreme bubble markets like those in California is truly remarkable, and the decline in house prices will be as unprecedented as the rally that preceded it. Based on projections from S&P/Case-Shiller indices using a 3.3% rate of wage growth as a support level, prices of individual properties will decline 53% from their peak valuations in 2006, finding a bottom in 2011 and reaching the previous peak in 2033. Twenty-Eight years is a long time to wait for peak buyers to get their money back.

Price-to-Rent Ratio

Comparative rent is the primary method of evaluating the fundamental value of any property. The price-to-rent ratio links the cost of ownership with the cost of rental. This link is direct because possession of property can be obtained by either method. The cost of ownership encapsulates all of the financing terms and other variables associated with possession of real estate as does the cost of rental. Price-to-rent ratio fluctuates over time as changes in the cost of ownership and terms of financing makes financing amounts vary and house prices vary as well.

Figure 42: Projected National Price-to-Rent Ratio, 1988-2021

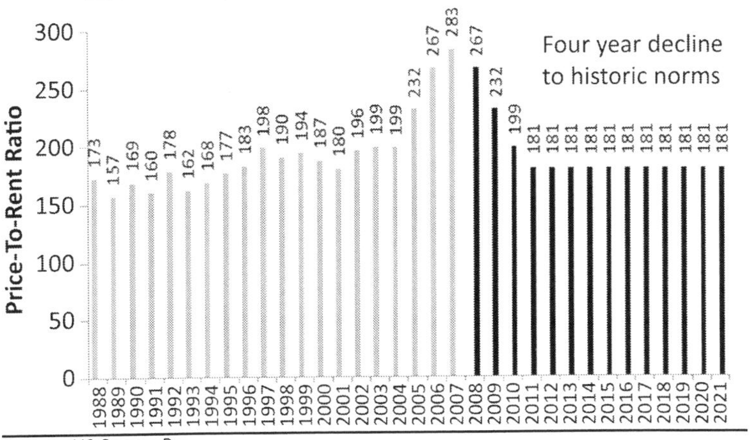

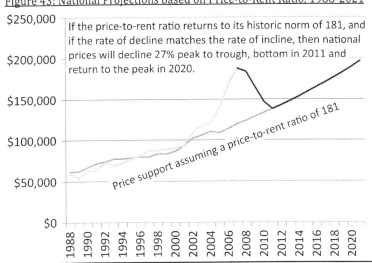

Source: US Census Bureau

Figure 43: National Projections based on Price-to-Rent Ratio, 1988-2021

If the price-to-rent ratio returns to its historic norm of 181, and if the rate of decline matches the rate of incline, then national prices will decline 27% peak to trough, bottom in 2011 and return to the peak in 2020.

Price support assuming a price-to-rent ratio of 181

Source: US Census Bureau

One of the major components of any projection using price-to-rent ratios is the projection of future rents. On a national level rents have been rising at a 3.6% rate from 1988 to 2007. [121] This is 0.6% greater than the rate of inflation and 0.3% greater than the rate of wage growth. In Orange County, California, rents have been rising at the rate of 4.7% from 1983 to 2007. This is 1.7%

greater than the rate of inflation and 1.3% greater than the rate of wage growth. Any difference between the rate of rental growth and the rate of wage growth cannot be sustained forever; however, the differential on the national level is small, and it can be attributed to changing customer behavior as people demonstrate an increased willingness to spend more on housing related costs. The rate of rent growth over wage growth in Orange County is a bit more troubling. Orange County is second only to Honolulu, Hawaii as the most expensive place to rent in the United States and the continued growth of rents in excess of wages is not sustainable.

The unprecedented spike in the national price-to-rent ratio is clear evidence of a massive, national real estate bubble. As the ratio demonstrates, there was no increase in rents justifying market pricing. The only other explanation which would deny a market bubble would be a dramatic lowering of ownership costs through other means. Although lower interest rates did lower ownership costs somewhat, the resulting savings due to lower interest rates only explains about one-third to one-half of the increase in prices. The remainder is caused by the use of exotic financing and irrational exuberance. Predictions based on the price-to-rent ratio are arguably the most robust because the ratio has been stable over long periods of time, and for good reason; the comparative cost of ownership to rental is a logical basis for valuation. If house prices return to their historic average of the 1988 to 2004 period of 181, then national prices will fall 27% peak-to-trough, bottom in 2011 and return to the peak in 2020.

Figure 44: Projected Orange County, CA Price-to-Rent Ratio, 1983-2020

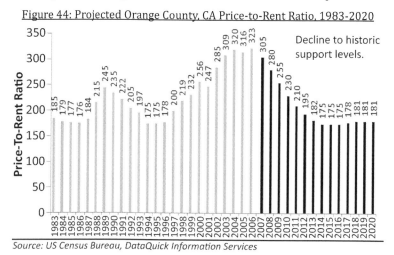

Source: US Census Bureau, DataQuick Information Services

The ratio of price-to-rent in Orange County, California, where the city of Irvine is located, has shown more variability than national figures. There was a coastal bubble taking off in the late 80s and collapsing in the early 1990s. The premise of prices reverting to fundamental valuations can be clearly seen in the changes in the price-to-rent ratio in Orange County. In the mid 1980s, the market was bottoming out from the first coastal residential real estate bubble associated with the inflationary times of the late 1970s. From 1983 to 1987, the price-to-rent ratio stabilized between 176 and 185, a range of about 6%. After the coastal bubble, prices stabilized in 1994 to 1996 in a range from 175 to 178. Projections using the price-to-rent ratio assume prices will fall again to the range from 175 to 185 before stabilizing. The reason prices stabilize in this range is because it is here that the cost of ownership approximates the cost of rental, and Rent Savers buy real estate and form a support bottom. If house prices in Orange County return to their historic price-to-rent stability range, prices will fall 22% peak-to-trough, bottom in 2013, and return to the previous peak by 2019; however, if rental increases do not sustain their 4.7% historic rate, the bottom may be somewhat lower, and the return to the previous peak would be delayed.

Figure 45: Orange County Projections based on Price-to-Rent Ratio, 1988-2020

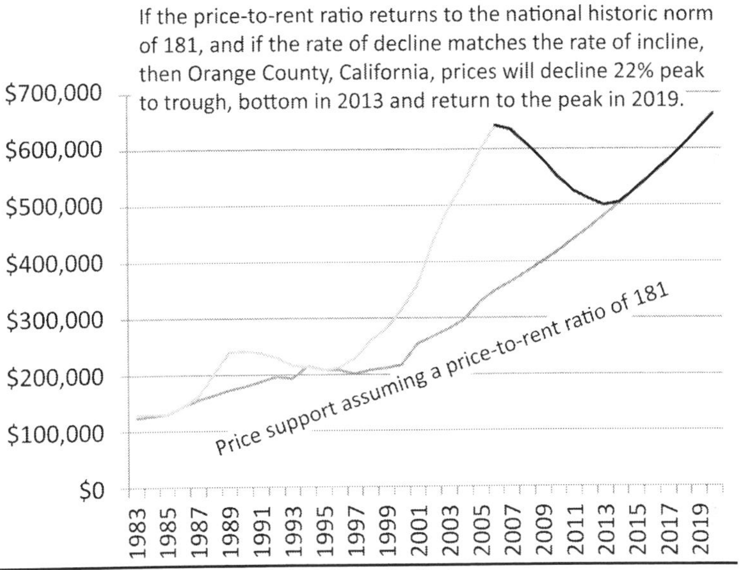

If the price-to-rent ratio returns to the national historic norm of 181, and if the rate of decline matches the rate of incline, then Orange County, California, prices will decline 22% peak to trough, bottom in 2013 and return to the peak in 2019.

Price support assuming a price-to-rent ratio of 181

Source: US Census Bureau, DataQuick Information Systems

Price-to-Income Ratio

Since incomes and rents are closely related, evidence for the Great Housing Bubble that appears in the price-to-rent ratio also appears in the price-to-income ratio. National price-to-income ratios are quite stable. There has been a slight upward drift with the decline of interest rates since the early 1980s peak, but from the period from 1987 to 2001, this ratio remained in a tight range from 3.9 to 4.2. The increase from 4.1 to 4.5 witnessed from 2001 to 2003 can be explained by the lowering of interest rates; however, the increase from 4.5 to 5.2 from 2003 to 2006 can only be explained by exotic financing and irrational exuberance.

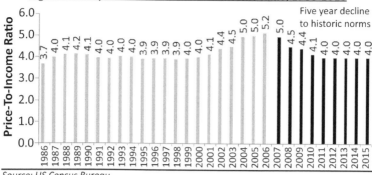

Figure 46: Projected National Price-to-Income Ratio, 1988-2015

Source: US Census Bureau

If national price-to-income ratios decline to their historic norm of 4.0, prices nationally will fall 9% peak-to-trough, bottom in 2011 and return to peak pricing in 2014. A 10% decline and a nine year waiting period would be difficult on homeowners nationally, but the magnitude and the duration will not be nearly as severe for most as it will be for homeowners in the extreme bubble markets like Irvine, California.

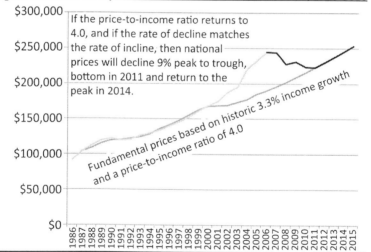

Figure 47: National Projections based on Price-to-Income Ratio, 1986-2015

Source: US Census Bureau

The volatility in price-to-income ratios caused by bubble behavior is clearly visible in the historic price-to-income ratios from Irvine, California. During the coastal bubble of the late 80s, in which Irvine participated, the price-to-income ratio increased from 3.7 to 4.6, a 25% increase. In the decline of the early 90s, price-to-income ratios dropped to a range from 4.0 to 4.1 and stabilized there from 1994 to 1999 before rocketing up to an unprecedented 8.6–a 115% increase. This new ratio was achieved by the extensive use of exotic financing, in particular negative amortization loans that rendered the new ratio inherently unstable.

Figure 48: Projected Irvine, California Price-to-Income Ratio, 1986-2030

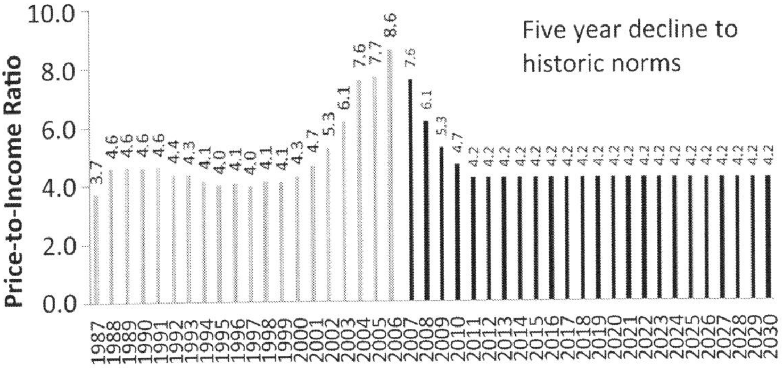

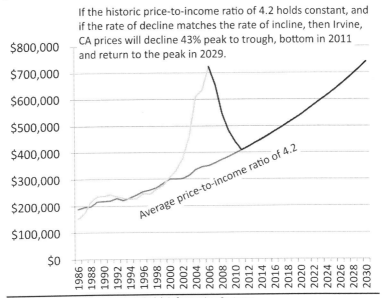

Source: US Census Bureau, Data Quick Information Systems

If house prices in Irvine decline to the point where the price-to-income ratio reaches its average of 4.2–a ratio higher above this historic range of stability between 4.0 and 4.1–prices will decline 43% peak-to-trough, bottom in 2011 and return to the peak in 2029. The magnitude of this decline would be catastrophic to homeowners who purchased during the bubble. Twenty-four years is a long time to wait for peak buyers hoping to get out at breakeven.

Figure 49: Irvine, California Projections from Price-to-Income Ratio, 1986-2030

If the historic price-to-income ratio of 4.2 holds constant, and if the rate of decline matches the rate of incline, then Irvine, CA prices will decline 43% peak to trough, bottom in 2011 and return to the peak in 2029.

Average price-to-income ratio of 4.2

Source: US Census Bureau, DataQuick Information Systems

147

Hyperinflation

The Federal Reserve under Ben Bernanke began aggressively lowering interest rates at the end of 2007 in response to the severe economic downturn caused by the collapse of house prices and the related difficulties falling house prices had on the banks and other institutions that made loans using houses as collateral. [122] Bernanke, prior to taking the position as the chairman of the Federal Reserve, was an academic who studied the Great Depression and wrote extensively on the failures of monetary policy by the Federal Reserve at the time. He also wrote about the crisis of deflation Japan faced when their combined stock market and real estate bubbles deflated throughout the 1990s. [123] Bernanke believed that quick and decisive action on the part of the Federal Reserve was necessary to prevent a destructive deflationary spiral as was witnessed in the United States during the Great Depression and in Japan during the 1990s. [124] By lowering interest rates and creating price inflation, Bernanke hoped to devalue the currency and provide market liquidity through both domestic and foreign investment. Once the real rate of interest was below the level of inflation, borrowing would be strongly encouraged as the value of the currency was falling faster than the interest rate being charged. The increased borrowing would stimulate business growth and the general economy minimizing the deflationary impact of falling home prices. In theory, the lower interest rates would also serve to blunt the decline in housing prices as borrowers would again be able to finance large sums to support inflated prices.

Figure 50: CPI Adjusted Median Home Prices, 1986-2006

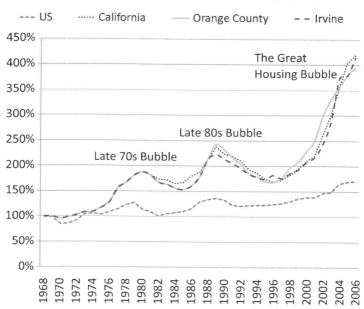

Source: DataQuick Information Systems; National Association of Realtors;
US Department of Labor

At the time of this writing, the results of the policies of the Federal Reserve have not become history so the consequences cannot be fully evaluated. The primary foreseeable consequence of Federal Reserve policy is rampant price inflation. An economy that relies for 70% of its value on the spending of consumers will be strongly impacted by price inflation. When a country knowingly devalues its currency, it causes a severe recession as the prices of imported goods and raw materials increase significantly. Perhaps a severe recession and price inflation is preferable to an economic depression like the one of the 1930s in America, but it is certainly not desirable. Since stagflation of the 70's, the FED has shown a willingness to push the economy into recession before it allows inflation to get out of control. When the FED started lowering interest rates at the end of 2007, it appeared as if they may be moving down the path of hyperinflation; however, it seems unlikely they would take it to extreme. One of the primary functions of the FED is to provide a stable financial system. Once the Federal Reserve begins to see economic growth and liquidity in the debt markets, interest rates may rise as quickly as they fell in order to stop hyperinflation from occurring.

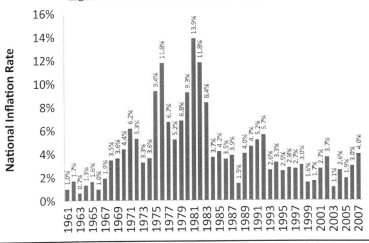

Figure 51: National Inflation Rate, 1961-2007

Source: US Department of Labor, Bureau of Labor Statistics

There will be some benefits to a devalued currency. A less valuable currency is a boon to exporters. The United States has run a chronic trade deficit for many years, and much of the recent deficit has come from inexpensive goods imported from China. The trade imbalance may correct itself with currency devaluation. Of course, this rebalancing of trade will come at the cost of more expensive imported foreign goods and a commensurate decline in spending power from US consumers. Also, prior to currency devaluation, wages in the United States were so high that jobs were being outsourced to foreign countries where people can be paid much less. Wages could not rise significantly from where they were without devaluing the dollar to prevent wage arbitrage from moving jobs overseas. [125] The devalued currency provided some room for wage increases, and these wage increases could theoretically provide additional support for housing prices.

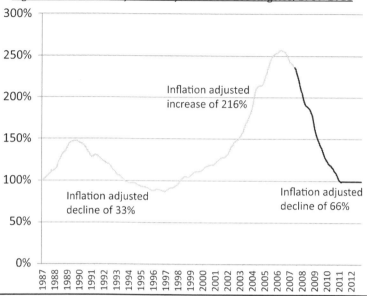

Figure 52: Inflation-Adjusted Projections for Los Angeles, 1987-2012

Inflation adjusted increase of 216%

Inflation adjusted decline of 33%

Inflation adjusted decline of 66%

Source: S&P/Case-Shiller Indices, US Department of Labor

Currency devaluation and inflation eats away at the buying power of money. Although this may support house prices at marginally higher nominal price levels, real price levels, the price level adjusted for inflation, will remain unchanged. Imagine if the Federal Reserve allowed inflation to cut the spending power of the dollar in half by 2011, and imagine if this level of inflation allowed house prices to remain stable at 2006 price levels for those 5 years. Many homeowners would feel relieved their homes did not decline in value, but this relief would be an illusion as the buying power of their money tied up in the value of their houses was cut in half. Irrespective of the nominal decline in prices, the inflation adjusted prices will decline significantly going forward. In the Los Angeles market as measured by the S&P/Case-Shiller index, a decline in prices to levels of historic rates of appreciation as previously described will result in a 66% decline in inflation adjusted terms. [126] On an inflation adjusted basis, buyers during the bubble will never get back to breakeven unless there is another real estate bubble similar to the Great Housing Bubble.

An Educated Guess

Each of the four methods of house price valuation described previously makes an independent prediction of how far prices will fall, and when they will recover. Some of these will prove more reliable and accurate than others, but an average of the results of these four methods makes it possible to make an educated guess as to the percentage decline in house prices and when prices will get back to peak levels. Unfortunately, there is no reliable method for projecting the rate of this decline, but if the experience of the coastal bubble of the early 90s is a good guide, then prices should fall for 6 to 7 years before reaching a bottom. This puts the bottom of prices sometime in or around 2011 based on the peak in various markets occurring in 2005 or 2006. Prices will flatten at the bottom because it will take time to absorb the inventory of foreclosures resulting from the drop. Market psychology and the rate of foreclosures will largely determine the rate of price decline, and these forces are difficult if not impossible to model. It is possible to construct a graph that illustrates the path of house prices over time based on the methods of price valuation and assumptions about the timing of the decline.

Table 10: Summary of Predictions for National Home Prices

Method	Total Decline	Appreciation Rate	Recovery Year
S&P/Case-Shiller Inflation Support	33%	3.3%	2025
Median House Price and Historic Appreciation	10%	4.5%	2011
Price-To-Rent Ratio	27%	3.6%	2020
Price-To-Income Ratio	9%	3.3%	2014
	20%	3.7%	2018

The range of predictions for the decline of national home prices is from 9% to 27% with an average of 20%. The predicted time of peak-to-peak recovery ranges from 2011 to 2021 with an average of 2018. Some will argue price drops of this magnitude are not likely, and these would be unprecedented declines; however, the increases were unprecedented as well. The Great Housing Bubble was a unique and unprecedented event.

Figure 53: National Median House Price Prediction, 2004-2019

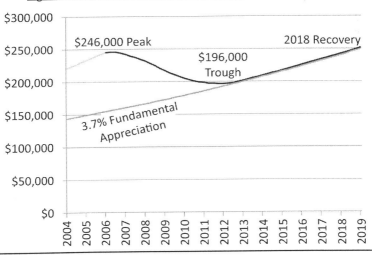

The predictions for national prices are based on a 3.7% rate of fundamental appreciation for some combination of wage growth, rental increases and other factors. The origin point for the graph is based on the last period in which fundamentals were aligned in the 1986-1999 period (not shown on the figure). The amount of the decline, 20%, is based on the average prediction of the four methods. The rate of decline was interpolated from the date of the peak to the date of the predicted bottom based on the experience of the coastal bubble of the 1990s. National prices peaked at an approximate value of $246,000 in 2006; they should bottom out at around $196,000 in 2011, and if fundamental appreciation rates hold, they will reach the previous peak in 2018.

Table 11: Summary of Predictions for Irvine, California Home Prices

Method	Total Decline	Appreciation Rate	Recovery Year
S&P/Case-Shiller Inflation Support	55%	3.3%	2039
Median House Price and Historic Appreciation	45%	4.4%	2023
Price-To-Rent Ratio	22%	4.7%	2019
Price-To-Income Ratio	43%	3.2%	2029
	41%	3.9%	2028

* The appreciation rate of 3.9% moved up the recovery year to 2025

The range of predictions for the decline of home prices in Irvine, California, is from 22% to 53% with an average of 41%. The predicted time of peak-to-peak recovery ranges from 2019 to 2033 with an average of 2028. Of course, since Irvine is in the heart of a bubble-prone market, recovery may happen more quickly, but then again, that would mean prices have entered another unsustainable price bubble.

Figure 54: Irvine, California, Median House Price Prediction, 2004-2025

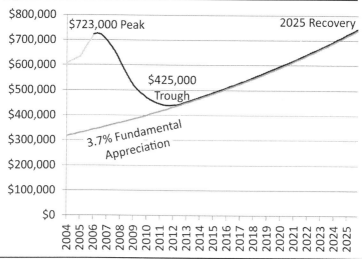

Source: US Census Bureau

Predictions for Irvine, California, are based on a 3.9% rate of fundamental appreciation as wage growth and rental rate growth have consistently outpaced national averages. The origin point is the intersection of the last two stable bottoming periods in 1984-1987 and 1995-1999. The 41% decline is the average of the four analysis methods, and the rate of decline is projected in the same manner as the national statistics. In Irvine, California, prices peaked around $723,000 in 2006, and they should bottom out in 2011 along with the rest of the country. If the fundamental appreciation rate of 3.9% is accurate, the previous peak will be reached in 2025–a 19 year span from peak to peak.

Price Decline Influences

There are a number of factors that will influence the timing and the depth of the price decline. There are a number of psychological factors and technical factors in play. [127] These include:

- Smaller Debt-to-Income Ratios
- Increasing Interest Rates and Tightening Credit
- Higher Unemployment
- Foreclosures
- Decrease in Ownership Rates
- Government Intervention

Smaller debt-to-income ratios impact the market because buyers tend to put a smaller percentage of income toward housing payments during price declines. Increasing interest rates decrease the amount borrowers can finance and use to bid on real estate, and tightening credit decreases the size of the borrower pool and thereby lowers demand. A deteriorating economy and higher rates of unemployment means there are fewer buyers with the income to purchase homes, and more homeowners are put in financial distress. High rates of financial distress caused by unemployment or the resetting of adjustable rate mortgages in a higher interest rate environment leads to more foreclosures. Large numbers of foreclosures adds to market inventories and works to push prices lower. The ultimate unknown factor is the meddling of the US Government in the financial markets. A bailout program for homeowners or lenders could radically alter the course of price movement.

Debt-to-Income Ratios

The debt-to-income ratio is a measure of how far buyers are "stretching" to buy real estate. Buyers have historically committed larger sums to purchase real estate when prices are rising in order to capture the appreciation of rising prices. Conversely, buyers have historically committed smaller and smaller percentages of their income toward buying real estate when prices are declining because there is little incentive to overpay. Some may look at this phenomenon as a passive effect of the rise and fall of prices, but since buying is a choice, the fluctuation in debt-to-income ratios is an active force on prices in the market.

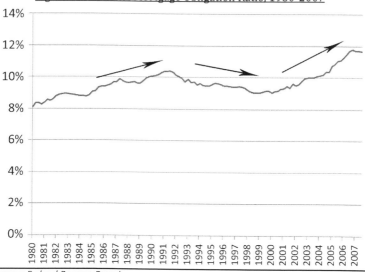

Figure 55: National Mortgage Obligation Ratio, 1980-2007

Source: Federal Reserve Board

This change in buyer behavior based on the trend in house prices is apparent in the national mortgage origination ratio. This statistic kept by the Federal Reserve Board is a measure of the total national mortgage debt service as a percentage of gross income. Since over 30% of houses in the United States are owned outright, this national percentage is far lower than the debt-to-income ratio of most individuals who have a mortgage. In the coastal bubble rally of the late 80s, people took on larger debts to buy homes, and when prices began their decline, people did not stretch to buy. If people had continued to put a high percentage of their income toward housing, prices would not have fallen as far as they did. The Great Housing Bubble witnessed a 30% increase in the average mortgage debt ratio on a national basis as people bought out of fear and greed in order not to be priced out forever and capture the capital gains of home price appreciation. If history repeats itself, this ratio will decline as house prices decline.

Table 12: National Payments and Prices at Various Debt-to-Income Levels

$	244,900	National Median Home Price
$	47,423	National Median Income
$	3,952	Monthly Median Income
	6.0%	Interest Rate

Payment	DTI Ratio	Value	+ 20%
$ 1,107	28.0%	$ 184,561	$ 230,701
$ 1,186	30.0%	$ 197,744	$ 247,180
$ 1,462	37.0%	$ 243,884	$ 304,855

Table 13: Irvine Payments and Prices at Various Debt-to-Income Levels

$	722,928	Irvine Median Home Price
$	83,891	Irvine Median Income
$	6,991	Monthly Median Income
	6.0%	Interest Rate

Payment		DTI Ratio	Value		+ 20%	
$	1,957	28.0%	$	326,487	$	408,109
$	3,495	50.0%	$	583,013	$	728,766
$	4,334	62.0%	$	722,936	$	903,670

House prices are sensitive to small changes in debt-to-income ratios when interest rates are very low as they were during the Great Housing Bubble. For instance, a 2% increase in the debt-to-income ratio can finance a loan that is 10% larger. Each borrower deciding to put a little more of their income toward housing can bid up prices very quickly. Prior to the bubble rally, lenders would limit DTIs to 28%, but during the bubble rally the only limit to DTIs were the degree to which borrowers were willing to exaggerate their income on their stated-income loan application. The debt-to-income ratio in Irvine, California, in 2007, was 64.4%. Even if it is assumed every buyer was putting 20% down (which they were not), the DTI ratio is 50.1%. This is gross income; as a percentage of take-home pay, the number is much higher. Most financed these sums through some combination of "liar loans" and negative amortization loan terms. Since these two "innovations" have likely been eliminated forever, bubble buyers who used these techniques are not going to be bought out by a future buyer using the same financing methods and thereby using the same debt-to-income ratio.

Higher Interest Rates

Another key factor impacting the fundamental value and thereby the bottom is interest rates. Interest rates went down during the price decline in the early 90s. That softened the impact and made the decline take somewhat longer. When interest rates are declining, bubbles take longer to deflate, and the bottom is at a somewhat higher price point. When interest rates are increasing, bubbles deflate faster, and the bottom is at a lower price point. Mortgage Interest rates during the Great Housing Bubble were at historic lows so a repeat of the steady decline in rates witnessed during the 90s is not very likely. Higher interest rates translate into diminished borrowing, lower prices and a lower bottom.

The lowering of the fed funds rate to 1% during the bubble prompted the lowering of mortgage interest rates to 5.8% by driving down the yield on the 10-year Treasury bill. [128] The difference between the 10-year Treasury bill and mortgage interest rates is due primarily to the risk premium which was near historic lows during the Great Housing Bubble. As lenders and investors in Mortgage Backed Securities (MBS) lost money during the decline, they demanded higher risk premiums. This increased the spread between the 10-year Treasury bill yield and mortgage interest rates. The spreads for jumbo and subprime both became larger, and the funding for many exotic loan programs dried up.

Figure 56: Mortgage Interest Rates, 1972-2006

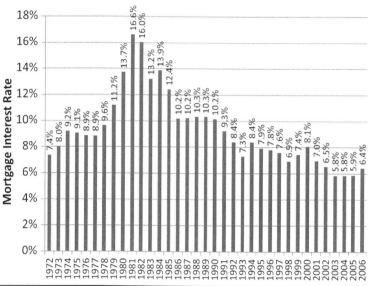

Source: Fannie Mae

As the FED lowered interest rates, the increased risk premiums demanded by lenders and MBS buyers drove up mortgage interest rates along with the heightened inflation expectation the lower FED funds rate caused during the cycle. Unless the FED wants to start paying people to borrow by lowering rates below 0%, base rates cannot go much lower. If all three parameters that make up mortgage interest rates were at historic lows during the bubble rally, there was little or no hope of mortgage interest rates falling below 5.8% in the bubble's aftermath. The combination of a higher FED rate, higher inflation expectations and larger risk premiums could easily push interest rates back up to near the 8% historic norm or even much higher. An increase in interest rates from 6% to 8% would reduce buying power 18%, and an increase to 10% would reduce buying power 32%. This would be disastrous for housing prices.

Mortgage interest rates have been on a slow but steady decline since the early 1980s. Interest rates were at historical highs in the early 80s to curb inflation, and the decline from these peaks to the 7% to 9% range was to be expected. This initial decline in interest rates coupled with low inflation caused house prices to begin rising again in the late 80s culminating in the bubble that burst in 1990 leading to six consecutive years of declining prices.

FUTURE HOUSE PRICES

Table 14: Impact of Rising Interest Rates on Prices

$	244,900	National Median Home Price
$	47,423	National Median Income
$	3,952	National Monthly Median Income
	28.0%	Debt-To-Income Ratio
$	1,106.54	Monthly Payment

Interest Rate	Loan Amount	Value	Value Change
4.5%	$ 218,387	$ 272,984	18%
5.0%	$ 206,127	$ 257,659	12%
5.5%	$ 194,885	$ 243,606	6%
6.0%	$ 184,561	$ 230,701	0%
6.4%	$ 177,046	$ 221,307	-4%
7.0%	$ 166,321	$ 207,901	-10%
7.5%	$ 158,254	$ 197,818	-14%
8.0%	$ 150,803	$ 188,503	-18%
8.5%	$ 143,909	$ 179,886	-22%
9.0%	$ 137,522	$ 171,903	-25%
9.5%	$ 131,597	$ 164,496	-29%
10.0%	$ 126,091	$ 157,613	-32%

Note: An increase in interest rates will have a strongly negative impact on house prices.

During the early 90s while prices were declining, interest rates were also declining from 10.6% in 1989 to 7.2% in 1996. These 30% declines in interest rates made housing more affordable and helped limit the price declines in the early 90s. If interest rates had not declined, house prices certainly would have dropped further than they did. It is not very likely that interest rates will decline 30% from the 5.8% they were during the bubble down to an unprecedented 4.1% to match the debt relief of the early 90s. The actions of the FED could not and did not keep house prices from falling.

Figure 57: Mortgage Interest Rates, 1986-2006

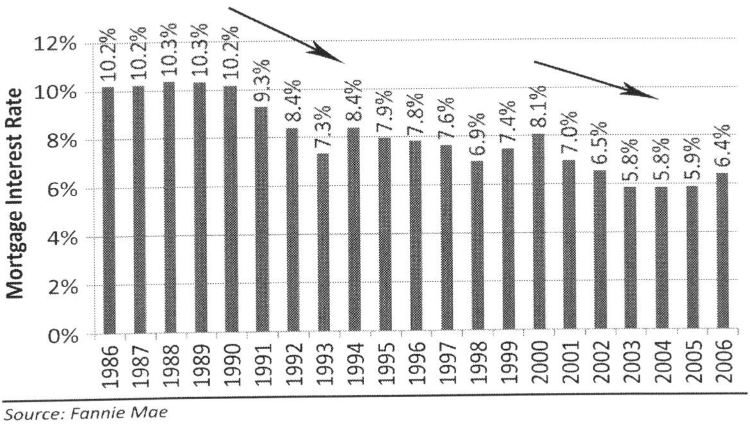

Source: Fannie Mae

Future Loan Terms

One of the primary mechanisms for inflating the Great Housing Bubble was the widespread use of exotic loan terms including interest-only and negative-amortization adjustable rate mortgages. The appeal of interest-only and negative-amortization loans is the lower payments they offer, or their ability to finance larger sums of money with the same payment. Adjustable rate mortgages are very risky; it is a risk that has been forgotten, ignored, or not understood by a great many buyers. In an era of steadily declining interest rates, the risks of adjustable rate mortgages do not become problems and many forget (or never realized) the risks were there. Once prices decline to a point where the loan balance is greater than the value of the property, mortgage holders are unable to refinance when their mortgage reset comes due. Most often this will result in a foreclosure. In fact, this is the primary mechanism of the decline, and it will also prevent any meaningful appreciation for years to come.

Of all the factors that contributed to the inflation of the Great Housing Bubble, the negative amortization loan with its offers of extremely low initial payment rates was the primary factor that pushed prices higher than anyone could previously imagine. Toxic loan products, or as the lending industry likes to call them, affordability products, distort the traditional measure of the debt-to-income ratio. The debt-to-income ratio is calculated with an assumption of a 30-year fixed rate mortgage, when in reality, borrowers were using interest-only and negative amortization loans to keep their debt-to-income ratio to manageable levels.

Table 15: Loan Amounts based on Amortization Method and Debt-to-Income Ratio

$	722,928	Irvine Median Home Price
$	83,891	Irvine Median Income
$	6,991	Monthly Median Income

6.0%	Interest Rate on 30-Year Fixed-Rate Mortgage
5.0%	Interest Rate on 5-Year ARM
3.8%	Payment Rate on Option ARM

Payment	DTI Ratio	30-Year Fixed	Interest Only	Option ARM*
$ 1,957	28.0%	$ 326,487	$ 469,790	$ 618,144
$ 2,289	32.7%	$ 381,831	$ 549,425	$ 722,928
$ 3,012	43.1%	$ 502,410	$ 722,928	$ 951,221
$ 4,334	62.0%	$ 722,928	$ 1,040,236	$ 1,368,732

* Negative Amortization loans (AKA Option ARM)

The table above illustrates the impact of various amortization methods on the debt-to income ratio and the resulting loan amount. The first line shows the typical debt-to-income ratio of 28% prior to the bubble and the amounts this payment would finance using a 30-year fixed, an interest-only and a negative-amortization loan. The fact that this payment amount, even using exotic financing does not reach the median sales price is testament to the high debt-to-income ratios utilized by bubble buyers. Using an Option ARM (negative amortization) it takes 32.7% of a median household's gross salary to purchase a median home; using interest-only takes 43.1%, and using conventional financing takes an astounding 62% of gross income. The widespread use of Option ARMs in Irvine is not surprising. Irvine, California, is the center of the subprime lending universe, and many mortgage brokers who strongly believed in the viability of this product live and work in Irvine and used them to purchase their primary residences.

Since adjustable-rate mortgages of all types performed poorly during the collapse of house prices, and in particular the negative amortization loans, it is likely these loan terms will be curtailed or eliminated in the future. These loans are inherently unstable and prone to high default rates due to the escalating payments that can, and often do, result from their use. The widespread use of these loans destabilizes home prices by detaching them from fundamental valuations. The use of these loans creates the very conditions in which they poorly perform. People who purchased during the bubble rally at inflated prices using these loan terms were risking that these terms would always be available to buyers in the market because without these terms, future buyers would not be able to finance the inflated sums necessary to allow a bubble rally buyer to get out with a profit. Without these exotic loan terms the bubble could not stay inflated.

Unemployment

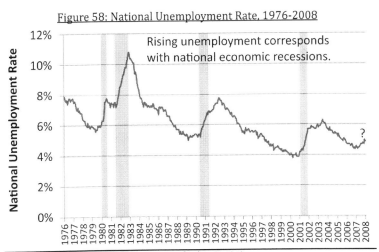

Figure 58: National Unemployment Rate, 1976-2008

Source: US Department of Labor, Bureau of Labor Statistics

Prior to the Great Housing Bubble, house price declines had only been associated with economic downturns and increases in unemployment. [129] When the economy softens, wage growth slows down as employers are less able to pay higher wages and the competition for available work makes people less able to demand higher wages from their employers. The economic slowdown is thereby responsible for slower rates of house price appreciation. If the down-turn is more severe, rising unemployment serves to push prices lower because the unemployed cannot afford to make their house payments, and their houses often fall into foreclosure. As unemployment increases so does the number of foreclosures, and since there are fewer buyers in a recession, the number of foreclosures cannot be absorbed by the market without a lowering of prices to meet diminished buyer demand.

There is evidence that housing market downturns may actually be the cause of many recessions. [130] There is a strong correspondence between the times when the country enters and exits a recession and when the times when residential construction spending drops off and picks up. The recession of 2008 was clearly caused by the problems in the credit markets and the resultant slowdown in consumer spending related to the collapse of house prices during the Great Housing Bubble. The result of this recession is unknown as of the time of this writing. If the unemployment rate rises significantly, people are out of work and unable to make their housing payments. This will lead to many more foreclosures even among people who did not take out exotic financing or extract all of their home equity for consumer spending.

Figure 59: California Unemployment Rate. 1976-2008

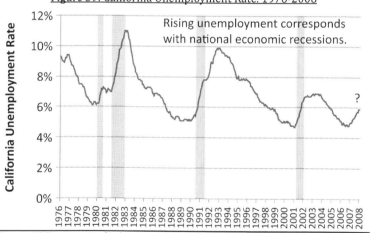

Source: US Department of Labor, Bureau of Labor Statistics

Many layoffs came to Irvine and Orange County, California, in 2007. New Century Financial went bankrupt along with numerous other subprime lenders based in Orange County. Real Estate related employment went from 15% of the workforce to 18% during the bubble. Most of these workers were laid off when the housing market slowed significantly. Many of the realtors and mortgage brokers in Orange County, California, and Irvine in particular, made hundreds of thousands of dollars a year off real estate transactions during the bubble. Most of these workers were not W-2 employees counted in regular government statistics. Transaction volumes declined 80% from the peak in 2005 to the end of 2007 in Orange County. Prices declined 15% as well. This resulted in a decline in income for realtors and mortgage brokers which put many of them in financial difficulty. Also, many if not most of these members of the real estate industry invested heavily in real estate and acquired multiple properties. Faced with the near elimination of their income, an inability to borrow more money and payments far in excess of any potential rental income, many of these individuals financially imploded and let all of their properties go into foreclosure.

One of the largest contributors to the Irvine, California, economy also does not show up in the unemployment statistics: people's houses. Median house prices went up in value an amount equal to or greater than the median household income for 5 consecutive years from 2002-2006. It was as if every homeowner had another breadwinner in the family. With home equity withdrawal, this money could be taken out at any time without IRS withholding. On a cash basis, a family's house was actually contributing more cash to spend than the household wage income. Not everyone took out this money and spent it, but a great many did. When prices fell and credit tightened, the mortgage equity withdrawal spigot was shut off. Imagine the impact on the local economy when half of its "workers" lose their incomes.

With the diminishment of wage income, commission income, and mortgage equity withdrawal, many businesses in Orange County began to suffer. This had ripple effects through the local economy. The lower income began to show up in weakening rents and higher vacancy rates at the major apartment complexes, but the major problem for the housing market was the unemployment. As the unemployment numbers went up, so did the number of foreclosures.

Foreclosures

The wildcard in this analysis is the impact of foreclosures. The number of foreclosures will affect both the timing and the severity of the drop because it is foreclosures that drive prices lower quickly. Foreclosures control the timing of the crash because they directly impact the must-sell inventory numbers: the greater the number of foreclosures, the greater the rate of decline in house prices. By early 2008, the markets in Southern California had already surpassed the peak set in the price decline of the early 90s of Notices of Default and Trustee Sales (foreclosures).

Lenders faced high foreclosure rates in the early 90s because they were too aggressive with their lending practices in the rally of the late 80s: it was their own doing. Lenders overheated the market then, and they got burned. Apparently, they did not learn the lesson of history. One of the problems with the collapse of a financial bubble is the causes get incorrectly identified. When the housing market in California collapsed in the early 90s, the recession and job layoffs were blamed for the problems with the housing market. The recession and layoffs came *after* the housing market was already in trouble. Unemployment slowed the recovery and added to the foreclosure problem, but it was not the primary cause of the entire pricing downturn. The ultra-aggressive lending

161

practices of the Great Housing Bubble caused a huge spike in foreclosures by early 2008. [131] Just as in the early 90s, the increase in defaults and foreclosures is being caused by the past sins of the lenders: karma on grand scale.

Figure 60: NODs and Trustee Sales as a % of Total Sales, San Diego, CA, 1990-2007

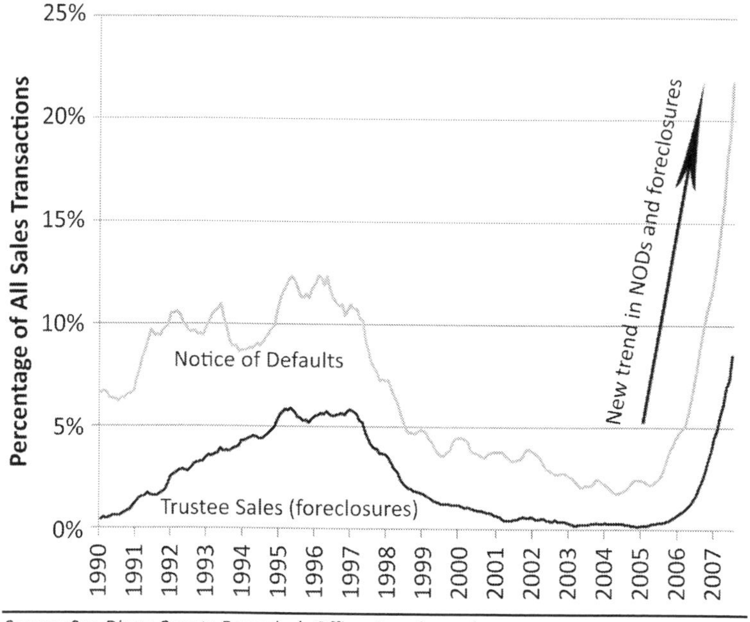

Source: San Diego County Recorder's Office, Foreclosureforum.com

The importance of the foreclosures cannot be overstated: sellers do not lower their prices voluntarily. Prices do not drop without massive numbers of foreclosures to push them down. The entire "soft landing" argument boils down to one supposition: the number of buyers in the market is able to absorb the must-sell inventory on the market. If this is true, prices do not drop. If this is not true, prices do drop until enough buyers are found to purchase the foreclosures. There are always a number of buyers when prices are declining; some are long-term homeowners who are present in any market, but many are speculators betting on the return of appreciation. These people are few in number, but they buoy the market if there are not many foreclosures. If foreclosure numbers really spike, prices fall until Rent Savers and Cashflow Investors enter the market and absorb the excess. If current trends continue, the number of foreclosures will be too great for long-term owners and speculators to absorb. Foreclosures also control the depth of the decline to some degree. Once prices fall down to their fundamental values, new buyers enter the market and begin to absorb the inventory. If there are not enough buyers at this price level to absorb all the foreclosures, prices could overshoot fundamentals to the downside; in fact, this does tend to happen at the bottom of the real estate cycle.

Figure 61: Projected NODs and Trustee Sales as a % of Total Sales, San Diego, CA, 1990-2012

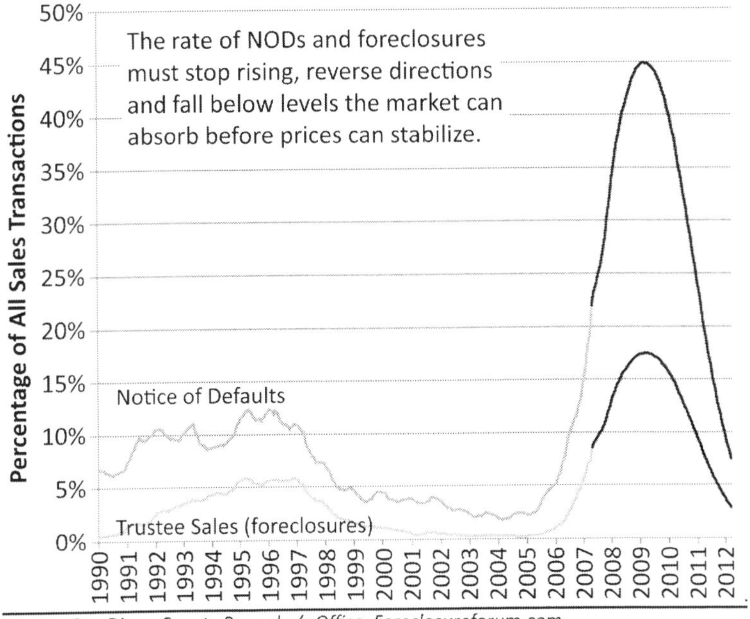

Source: San Diego County Recorder's Office, Foreclosureforum.com

Decrease in Home Ownership Rates

There is a strong correspondence to the growth of the subprime lending industry and an increase in home ownership rates. [132] This is a direct result of lending money to those borrowers previously excluded from the housing market either because the borrower did not have the downpayment, or they lacked good credit. The collapse of the subprime lending industry in 2007 and the subsequent foreclosures on the millions of subprime loans caused a decrease in home ownership rates. Foreclosures are associated with bad credit; those with bad credit are eliminated from the buyer pool until their credit improves. Therefore, people who lose their homes to foreclosure move into a rental, and the previously owner-occupied home often enters the rental pool. (A popular misconception is that rents will go up. The number of rentals will increase along with the number of renters).

Prices fall below rental parity in conditions of decreasing home ownership rates because Rent Savers, who are typically owner occupants, are not numerous enough to absorb the foreclosure inventory, hence the decline in home ownership rates. This means a significant number of the houses due to hit the market due to foreclosure will be purchased as rentals. This is the Cashflow Investor support level. Prices often fall below fundamental valuations at the

163

end of a speculative bubble due to short-term supply and demand imbalances. If this occurs at the bottom of the price cycle of the Great Housing Bubble, the measures of house values may all be lower than the projections and estimates provided herein.

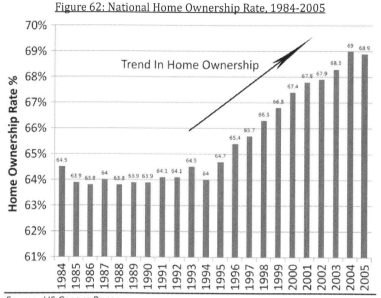

Figure 62: National Home Ownership Rate, 1984-2005

Source: US Census Bureau

Doomsday Scenario

The analysis presented in this section is intended as a conservative estimate of the magnitude and duration of the decline and recovery following the Great Housing Bubble. Due to the relatively extreme declines contained in the projections, it does not appear as conservative as it really is. When bubbles collapse, they often drop lower and last longer than most can imagine. Few thought the NASDAQ would drop from 5200 to 1200 from 2000-2003, few thought house prices in California would drop from $200K to $177K from 1991-1996 in the deflation of the last coastal real estate bubble, and few thought real estate prices in Japan would drop 64% between 1991 and 2005. [133] The Doomsday Scenario is an examination of what could happen if all the potential problems for the real estate market negatively impact price levels. It is not likely this scenario will come to pass, but it is certainly a possibility.

Appreciation rates are not fundamental laws of physics. They are dependent upon a solid economy to provide income growth and the willingness of people to put money toward housing payments from their income. If the economy slows and if people choose not to spend large percentages of their incomes toward housing payments (or if people are not permitted to by tighter lending standards,) house prices are not supported. The projection of a worst-case scenario shows the impact of an economic recession and a slow recovery due to tightening credit and a reduced willingness on the part of borrowers to take on new debt.

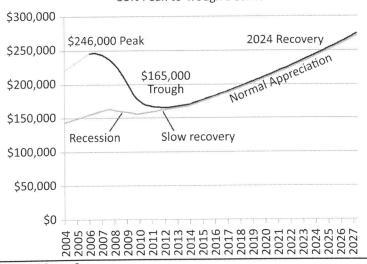

Figure 63: National Doomsday Scenario

Source: US Census Bureau

The primary mechanism of the decline is the high rate of foreclosures. This is caused by rising unemployment and the resetting of adjustable rate mortgage payments to much higher amounts due to higher interest rates and the inability of people to refinance into affordable payments, and the inability to make further home equity line of credit withdrawals to make mortgage payments. There are trillions of dollars worth of mortgage obligations in adjustable rate mortgages due to reset by 2011. When many of these borrowers are unable to refinance or make their payments, they will lose their homes to foreclosure. The impact of all these foreclosures will drive prices down quickly, and the depth of the decline may overshoot fundamental valuations due to the temporary imbalance between demand and supply. As each of these borrowers succumbs to the weight of his housing payments, the rate of recovery will be slowed until the bad loans are purged from the financial system. If this scenario becomes reality, on a national basis prices will decline 33% or more from their peak bottoming out at a median price of $165,000 in 2012 or later. The slow recovery at historic appreciation rates will not bring national prices back up to their peak again until 2024.

In Irvine, California, and other extreme bubble markets the forecast is even grimmer. The doomsday scenario would see a 51% decline from peak to trough with prices bottoming at a median price of $351,000 in 2012. Prices will not recover to the previous peak until 2030. Price declines of this magnitude are not likely, but the scenario is not unrealistic. The only requirement is the confluence of all the negative forces working on the market.

Figure 64: Irvine, California, Doomsday Scenario

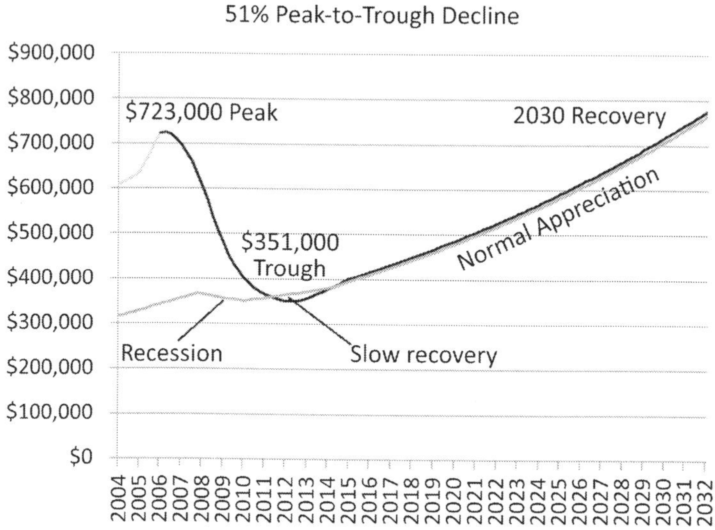

51% Peak-to-Trough Decline

Source: US Census Bureau

Lingering Problems

As with any illness, the recovery is often plagued by symptoms of the disease and unwanted side effects. The recovery from the Great Housing Bubble will be no exception. The main problems will be experienced by those who bought at peak prices and did not go through the cleansing foreclosure process. As painful as foreclosure is to those who must endure it, foreclosure is the cure to the disease of the market. After foreclosure, a borrower is no longer burdened by high housing payments, and is free to move to find new work and spend income on consumer goods.

Houses will become America's new debtor's prisons. By the end of 2008, anyone who purchased between 2004 and 2007 will be underwater. Everyone who is underwater and making crushing home payments will be stuck in their homes until values climb back above their purchase price. Since there are a great many people in these circumstances and since each of these people are in at a different price point, each one will have a different term in debtor's prison, but when their sentence is up, many will opt to sell to get out from under the crushing payments. Each of these people selling their homes keep prices from rising. This is the impact of overhead supply. It is also why the market will not see meaningful appreciation without capitulatory selling. People trapped in their homes cannot move to accept promotions or advancements in their careers, and people who are making large debt service payments have less discretionary income to spend. In an economy heavily dependent upon consumer spending, the impact of this loss of spending power will serve as a drag on economic growth. [134] Aside from the broader economic ramifications, the heavily indebted will need to adjust to a lifestyle within their available after-tax and after-debt income. This will be a disheartening adjustment to many, particularly those who had become dependent upon mortgage equity withdrawal to sustain their lifestyles.

Summary

During the decline of house prices in the deflation of the Great Housing Bubble, price levels will fall to fundamental valuations of historic levels of appreciation, price-to-rent ratios, and price-to-income ratios. The nominal price declines may be impacted by inflation and monetary policy of the Federal Reserve, but inflation adjusted prices will fall precipitously. As people put less money toward housing payments either by choice or by tightening lender standards, prices will not be supported at inflated levels. The combination of unemployment, higher interest rates and the elimination or severe curtailment of exotic financing terms will make refinancing more difficult and the resulting unaffordable mortgage payments will put many borrowers into foreclosures adding large amounts of must-sell supply to the market, driving prices lower. If prices follow their historical pattern, they will fall down to their fundamental valuations by 2011. There are a number of variables which will influence the depth and timing of the decline, and most of the risks are to the downside. There will likely be an overshoot of fundamental valuations at the bottom. Despite all the nuance and analysis, everything comes down to one simple indicator: to paraphrase James Carville and Bill Clinton, "It's the Foreclosures, Stupid!"

So what implication does all of this have on a future buying decision? Buyers should not count on appreciation. If a buyer needs to factor in appreciation to make the math work on a home purchase, she will buy too early, and she will pay too much. When the cost of ownership is equal to the cost of rental it is safe to buy. Even if prices drop further–which they might–buyers will not be hurt because they will be saving money versus renting. If buyers are counting on increasing rents or house price appreciation to get to breakeven sometime later, they will probably get burned.

Buyers should think about what terms and conditions a future buyer will face. During the bubble prices were bid up to unsustainable heights. Prospective buyers should not purchase when conditions are not favorable. If interest rates are low, debt-to-income ratios are high, and exotic financing is the norm, it is a bad time to buy. It seems counter-intuitive, but a wise buyer wants to purchase when credit is tight and values are depressed. Buyers should be patient and wait for the conditions to be right because a future buyer can pay more when credit is loose and prices are inflated. A house is only worth what a buyer will pay for it.

Buying and Selling During a Decline

During the bubble price rally, sellers and realtors, the agents of sellers, had everything going their way. It was easy to price and sell a house. A realtor would look at recent comparable sales, and set an asking price 5% to 10% higher and wait for multiple bids on the property–some of which would come in over asking. The quality of the property did not matter, and the techniques used to market and sell the property did not matter either. As far as buyers and sellers were concerned house prices always went up, so the sellers were thought to be giving away free money; obviously, the product was in high demand. As the financial mania ran its course, buyers became scarcer; all the ones who could buy did buy. The buyer pool was seriously depleted leaving prices at artificially high levels. When the abundance of sellers became greater than the number of available buyers qualifying for financing, prices began to fall.

Residential real estate markets generally move very slowly and trend in a single direction for long periods of time. Once these markets reach an inflection point, the direction of price movement changes, and the balance of negotiating power shifts from an advantage to one side to an advantage for the other. However, most market participants do not recognize this change for some time. Sellers continue to price and attempt to sell using tactics that worked during the rally, and they find they are unable to sell their properties. It often takes two years or more before sellers accept the reality of the new market and adjust their attitudes and behaviors to the new dynamics of a buyer's market.

In a buyer's market, buyers have the upper hand, and sellers need to adjust their pricing tactics to reflect this fact. During a rally, many buyers must compete with each other for the property of a few sellers. In a price decline, many sellers must compete with each other for the money of a few available buyers. It is common for sellers to ask their realtor to find a buyer who will appreciate the "unique qualities" of their property. Every seller thinks their property is the finest in the neighborhood and certainly commands a premium 5% to 10% more than their neighbors. These fantasies are reinforced by the behavior of buyers during the rally. At the risk of losing the listing, the realtor must find a diplomatic way to convince a would-be seller their property is average at best and needs to be priced accordingly. It is a difficult challenge for an experienced realtor to persuade an owner her castle is a cottage. Failure to educate the sellers to the reality of the market wastes the seller's time and the realtor's resources. Experienced realtors who thrive in bear markets earn their commissions.

Selling for Less

Sellers in declining markets must compete on price. Only the best properties can command prices equal to recent comps. In a buyer's market, there are no premiums: getting the price of recent comps reflects a premium because prices are declining. Properties with negatives must price 10% or more below recent comps to attract the attention of buyers. There are many books and articles written about staging a property and various techniques a seller should employ to sell their home. Most of these writings pander to the ego and false hopes of sellers who refuse to compete on price. No amount of sales and marketing is going to convince a buyer to overpay in a buyer's market. Price is the ultimate amenity.

Paying off a Mortgage

Once a price decline gets underway many buyers who were late to the price rally find they are in a property worth less than they paid for it. As prices continue to fall, many find themselves "underwater" owing more on their mortgage than their property is worth. When these late buyers want to become sellers, they cannot sell and pay off the mortgage balance with the proceeds from the sale. Then they have a real problem. It is a problem with only 4 plausible solutions:

1. The borrower can keep making the mortgage payments until prices go back up. This is the "hold and hope" strategy. If the borrower uses exotic financing–which most buyers did in the later stages of the Great Housing Bubble–it may be difficult to continue making mortgage payments because these payments are likely to increase substantially. If the property is not owner-occupied, the borrower may try to rent it out to cover expenses; however, this is generally not feasible. Buyers who purchased during the mania paid too much money relative to prevailing rents and available income. If this were not the case, it would not have been a financial mania. Since the payments are too high, renting the property does not cover the expenses. Renting out the property lessens the pain, but it does not make it go away. Also, since housing market corrections often last 5 years or more, it may be a very long time before prices recover to peak bubble levels. Keeping the property is a "death by a thousand cuts," or perhaps a death by a thousand payments.

2. The borrower can write a check at the closing to pay off the portion of the mortgage not covered by the proceeds from the sale. Many people do not have the amount necessary in savings, as few thought such a loss was even possible, and even fewer are willing to go through with the sale knowing they will have to pay for the loss. The undesirability of this option usually forces the borrower to keep the property and try to endure the pain, or let it go up for auction at a foreclosure.

3. The borrower can try to convince the lender to agree to a short sale. A short sale is a closing where the lender accepts less than the full mortgage amount at the closing.

4. The borrower can simply stop making payments and allow the property to go to public auction in foreclosure. Both short sales and foreclosures have strongly negative impacts on credit scores and the availability of credit in the future.

In the price declines of the early 90s, most people opted for option number one. Downpayment requirements were high, and the use of exotic loan programs was less common in the preceding rally, so many homeowners had equity in their properties and were able to make their payments. They accepted debt servitude as part of the price of home ownership. When faced with the four options presented to them, most chose to stay in their homes and keep making payments. As the slowdown in the housing market helped facilitate a recession in the early 90s, a recession compounded in California with defense industry layoffs, many people lost their jobs and as a result, lost their ability to make high mortgage payments. This created a problem with foreclosures that pushed prices lower. The decline in prices in the early 90s, though extreme in certain fringe markets, was not so deep to cause many people to voluntarily walk away from their mortgages. Most buyers during this period were required to put 20% down. This represented years of savings and sacrifice for many, so they were not willing to lose it. Since the total peak to trough correction was a bit less than 20% statewide in California and even less in other states, many homeowners still had some equity in their homes. The combination of high equity requirements and a relatively shallow correction made staying in the home the best choice for many. This kept foreclosures to high but manageable levels. In contrast, the Great Housing Bubble was characterized by low or non-existent equity requirements, and very steep initial drop in house prices. These conditions made foreclosures, both voluntary and involuntary, a tremendous problem.

Much of the purchase money in the bubble rally was debt. As 100% financing became common, the average combined loan-to-value on purchase money mortgages climbed to more than 90% (Credit Suisse, 2007). With so many people with so little in the transaction, it did not take much of a price decline to cause people to give up. By late 2007 prices had already fallen 10% or more in many markets, and there was no sign this would change in the immediate future. It was becoming obvious that those with little at risk were well underwater and they were going to be that way for the foreseeable future. This inevitably lead to one of the unique phenomena of the Great Housing Bubble–Predatory Borrowing. Many simply stopped making payments they could afford because the value of their property had declined significantly. Nowhere in the terms of the mortgage did it state the payments would be made if, and only if, resale values increased, but many borrowers acted as if it did. When borrowers quit making payments they were capable of making simply because they were not going to make money on the deal, their behavior was predatory to the lender who ultimately had to absorb the loss. These borrowers often had so little of their own money invested in the form of a downpayment they felt little actual damage from just walking away from the property and mailing the lender the keys. Many borrowers simply stopped making payments, did not respond to letters or phone calls from the lender, and moved out. Short sales and foreclosures were not the end of the nightmare for sellers. It is the last contact they had with the property, but in many circumstances the debt–and debt collectors–followed them until the debt was repaid or discharged in bankruptcy.

Short Sale

A short sale is a property closing where the proceeds from the closing do not satisfy the outstanding debt on the property. The lender must agree to accept less money at the closing table for the closing to occur. From a credit perspective, there is little or no difference between a short sale and a foreclosure. Both a short sale and a foreclosure will show a series of missed payments and a secured credit line (or multiple credit lines) with a permanent delinquency and discharge for what is generally a very large sum of money. Both will have a strong, negative impact on the borrower's FICO credit score that will persist for many years.

Because of the potential for fraud and the bureaucratic tangle of various parties involved, it is very difficult to get a short sale approved. If a lender is going to lose money, they are going to want to be sure the borrower is not selling the property to a friend or relative or engaging in some other kind of fraudulent conveyance. Also, the lender will want to be sure the borrower cannot pay back the money. They often require additional financial information like updated W-2s, 1040 tax returns, and a statement of assets certified by an accountant. In most cases, the borrower will have to stop making payments as evidence of their inability to do so in the future. Further, the property will also need to be listed for some period of time at a sales price which would result in sufficient funds to pay off the loan. Once it is demonstrated to the lender that the borrower has stopped making payments, cannot reasonably make future payments, and the property cannot be sold for a breakeven amount, then the lender may grant a short sale request. None of this happens quickly. If a buyer is found who is willing to purchase the property, the process of approving a short sale is so long and cumbersome, most buyers will move on to one of several other available properties on the market.

In the end, a short sale is only in the best interest of the borrower if they believe the bank will try to collect on the shortfall from the property sale. If a borrower is in a position where he will have to pay back any losses, a short sale may result in a smaller loss than a foreclosure and subsequent auction. If the borrower is not in a position where the lender either can or will go after the deficiency, there is little incentive for the borrower to even attempt a short sale. In these instances, the borrower generally lets the property go into foreclosure.

Foreclosure

Foreclosure is the forced sale of a property owned by the borrower in order to satisfy the debt(s) secured by the property. Foreclosure laws are complex, and they vary from state to state. There are no federal laws governing foreclosures. The borrower is the legal owner of the property who has entered into a mortgage agreement with a lender to pay back all borrowed money, fees and interest due. The Mortgage is a security instrument that pledges the property as the security for the loan. This document provides the lender the ability to force the sale of property to satisfy the debt if the borrower fails to pay in accordance with the terms of the agreement. The lender does not own the property; they merely own a lien on the property which can be exercised to force a sale to satisfy the debt. At the time of a sale, all proceeds first go to settling this indebtedness before any residual "equity" goes to the seller. Foreclosures are always public auctions where the lender must notify the general public in advance, and the general public must be allowed to bid on the property. This public auction is necessary to prevent the lender from forcing the borrower to sell the property at a below market price to the lender who could then resell it for a profit on the open market.

Lenders do not want to own real estate. Lenders are in the business of loaning money and collecting fees and interest. At a foreclosure auction the lender will generally bid on the property up to the value of the loan. [135] This ensures auction bids will be high enough to satisfy the outstanding loan amount. The lenders do not want to be the highest bidder. They would rather someone else bid over the loan amount and make them whole. If they end up being the highest bidder, then they must manage the property and ultimately arrange for its sale in the non-auction real estate market. There are costs and fees associated with this endeavor which eats in to the final disposition amount garnered from the final sale of the property. These fees generally increase the loss for the lender.

Recourse vs. Non-Recourse Loans

Loans used to purchase real estate assets can be either recourse loans or non-recourse loans. A recourse loan is one where the lender can sue the borrower for any amount owed in the terms of the loan contract. As with foreclosure laws, whether a loan is recourse or non-recourse varies from state to state. In California, all purchase money mortgages are non-recourse loans. In most states, including California, all refinances, home equity lines of credit or

173

other loans not used to purchase the property will be recourse loans. This distinction becomes very important in a foreclosure or short sale. If a loan is non-recourse, the lender cannot collect from the borrower for deficiency under any circumstances. The sale and closing of the property is the end of the matter: the debt does not survive. If the loan is a recourse loan the lender may have the right under certain circumstances to go after the borrowers assets after a foreclosure. This depends on whether the foreclosure was judicial or non-judicial.

Judicial vs. Non-Judicial Foreclosure

Foreclosure proceedings in most states can be either judicial or non-judicial at the lenders discretion. The lender has the right to sue the borrower in a court of law for repayment of the debt on the property. This legal action is a judicial foreclosure. A judicial foreclosure is slower and costlier than a non-judicial foreclosure. The mortgage agreement has a provision where the borrower authorizes the lender to sell the property at a public auction if the borrower fails to pay the debt. A lender can exercise this right without a court order, and therefore it is considered a non-judicial foreclosure. It is faster and less expensive to perform a non-judicial foreclosure because no attorneys are involved and there is no waiting for a case to come up on a court's schedule; however, there is a problem with non-judicial foreclosure, in most states the lender waives their rights to obtain money in a deficiency situation because no deficiency judgment is entered in the court record. When faced with deciding between a judicial or non-judicial foreclosure, the lender must weigh the cost and time of a judicial foreclosure against the probability of actually collecting any money with a deficiency judgment. If a borrower is insolvent, which they often are if they are going through a foreclosure, they may not have enough money or other assets for the lender to collect on the deficiency judgment. In these circumstances, the lender will foreclose with a non-judicial procedure to minimize their losses. In these circumstances the borrower is not liable for repayment on the deficiency.

Tax Implications

Prior to the Great Housing Bubble, if a mortgage debt was forgiven, the amount of forgiven debt was subject to taxation as ordinary income. Since people who lost their house under these circumstances were already financially ruined, this tax provision was seen as unduly burdensome to those it was levied against. The President signed into law the Mortgage Forgiveness Debt Relief Act of 2007 to relieve the federal income tax burden on debt forgiven in a short sale, foreclosure, dead in lieu of foreclosure, or a loan restructuring where the principal amount was reduced. This tax relief is only given to an owner's principal residence and only for debt used to acquire the property. Speculative properties purchased as second or third homes are not covered, and debt incurred after the purchase through refinancing or opening new credit lines is not covered. This tax change made it easier for some borrowers to make the decision to go through a foreclosure because it removed one of the negative consequences of the decision.

A Buyer's Market

When the market turned up in the late 1990s the market shifted. During the last decline, the buyers had an advantage. During the bubble the advantage went to the sellers. The seller's market went on for so long and became so feverish that people have forgotten (or may never have known) what it was like to see buyers in control of the action. Buyers need to be re-educated on how to behave in a buyer's market. Buyers must remember they are the ones in control. Buyers are the scarce resource in the marketplace. The seller is one of many for the buyer to choose from, and all sellers are desperate. Sellers need buyers. Buyers do not need sellers. No matter which seller the buyer purchases from, the buyer is going to leave all the other sellers disappointed because they are going to continue to be trapped in their homeowner's prison. [136] Buyers cannot please everyone, so they should focus on pleasing themselves.

Buyers should not become concerned with the sellers needs, wants and problems. Does it matter if this house is the seller's entire savings for retirement? Should a buyer care if a sale below a certain price puts the seller into bankruptcy? Buyers need to ask themselves, "Would I give the seller money if I were not buying their home?" Unless the buyer is running a charity, the answer should be no, and she should not care about the consequences of the seller's financial decisions. The seller created her own problems; it is not the buyer's responsibility to solve these problems by overpaying for a house.

Pay the Lowest Possible Price

This may sound like common sense, but the behavior of many buyers during the early part of the decline demonstrated a lack of understanding of this principal. Buyers should not ask for or take any incentives, and they should pay their own closing costs. They are paying for all these incentives; it is just buried in the loan. They will be paying interest on this purchase for the next 30 years, and the buyer will be paying property tax on these costs for as long as they own the house. Buyers are far, far better off lowering the price and foregoing the incentives and paying their own closing costs. A buyer's brokerage typically kicks back 2% at closing. Work out a deal with them in advance where they will agree to take a 1% commission at the closing so the price can lowered by 2%. Again, the buyer is paying taxes on the purchase price, so they should make this as low as possible.

The First Offer is the Best Offer

This is the most counter-intuitive part of buying in a buyer's market. Ordinarily sellers, or more accurately the seller's realtor, try to create a sense of urgency to buy the house. They want the buyer to think other people are looking, there is going to be a bidding war, and the buyer needs to get an offer in today. Realtors thrive by creating fear in buyers. They will use lines like:

- It is a good time to buy!
- Hurry. This one won't last.
- Don't throw away your money on rent.
- If you are serious, you had better buy now or you might be priced out of the market.
- They are not making land anymore.
- If you see a property you love, you really need to make an offer.
- The more earnest money you put down, the more seriously your offer is taken.
- Things have been a bit slower than last year, but the last two weeks we have seen a lot more traffic.
- Rates are at all time lows and buyers have more choice than ever!
- Rates are creeping up, so you better get in now.
- If you wait until the bottom, you will miss out on getting a property that you really like.
- This property is priced at below market value.
- Incentives this good won't be available after...
- Don't worry about the asking price: just offer what you're willing to pay.
- Don't worry. You can afford this house.
- I will show my client the offer, but I just want to let you know that we have another offer for more coming in this afternoon.
- Trust me.
- It's not just the commission. I really care about you.

In a buyer's market these ploys are all lies (the truthfulness of these statements is questionable in all market conditions). Generally, the buyer is the only prospective buyer, and they can take as long as they want to buy the house. The buyer's task in negotiating is to create a sense of urgency and panic in the seller. This is why buyers should make their first offer their best offer.

There are many properties priced over market in a buyer's market. Sellers resist the realities of the market environment. Asking prices that are much too high do not warrant buyer consideration. Most sellers will not reduce their asking prices more than 15% to consummate a transaction, so "lowballing" a seller with an offer 25% from their asking price is a waste of everyone's time. If the asking price is not within 15% of the price a buyer is willing to pay, the buyer should not even instigate a negotiation. If the asking price is within range, buyers should start with a bid at least 10% below asking price. This is the best offer. The buyer should lower the opening bid as follows:

- If actively bidding on the property, the buyer should make all offers expire in 3 days, and these offers should be delivered on a Tuesday. The buyer should not allow the seller to think about things over the weekend. If the buyer is still interested in the property after the offer expires, resubmit a fractionally-lower offer (1% is a good rule) on the following Tuesday (make them sweat over the weekend). The new offer should not be so much lower as to lose consideration, but it should be enough lower so that the seller gets the message they need to accept the offer before it drops further.

- If the seller makes a counter offer, the buyer should retract the offer and resubmit a lower one. This works the same as the time decay offer above. After the buyer has lowered an offer a few times, the seller may panic and take the offer before it goes any lower. This is what buyers are after.

- Buyers should lower their offers 1% each time they speak with the seller's realtor. Every time the seller's realtor communicates with the buyer, the realtor will pressure the buyer to increase their offer. If the buyer lowers their bid each time the realtor speaks, the buyer sends a message that the realtor pressure is not working, and it is, in fact, hurting the deal. Buyers should lower their offer 2% if the realtor uses one of the standard lies mentioned above.

- If the realtor tells the buyer there is another bidder on the property, the buyer should immediately withdraw their offer and tell the realtor to call if the deal falls out of escrow with the other buyer. Since this statement from the realtor is almost certainly a lie, it will cause them to have to explain to their client why the only buyer around has pulled their offer.

Closing the Deal

When the seller starts to counter-offer, it is very tempting for buyers to agree to their price to close the deal, particularly if the counter offer is below the original offer. Buyers should not do it. In a buyer's market, the seller will come to meet the buyer's terms. Buyers have the power. However, if the seller is now asking below the original offer, and if the buyer really, really wants the house, the buyer may raise the offer one time. Even after a price agreement has been reached, the deal can still be made better. The buyer should go through the inspection sheet and establish holdbacks for all repairs. The buyer should do this as an incentive for the owner to get this work done before move-in.

Not everyone has what it takes to implement all of these price-shaving techniques. However, the more of these that buyers put into practice, the lower the price they will pay for the home they want. A buyer will never see the seller or the seller's realtor ever again. It does not matter if they are offended. In the end, they will be relieved the buyer took the house even if that buyer made their lives hell in the process.

Summary

Many would-be sellers failed to sell their homes at inflated bubble prices. This might not have been a financial burden depending on how they managed their mortgage debt. They may have regretted missing the windfall they could have received by selling at the peak, but they stayed comfortably in their homes and forgot about the excitement of the real estate bubble. The sellers who missed the peak sales prices and fell underwater on their mortgage faced more difficult choices. Many borrowers concluded a foreclosure was the best course of action because they owed more on their loan than their property was worth. Also, due to the exotic loan terms utilized by many borrowers, they were experiencing increasing loan payments and decreasing property values. With the prospect for recovery bleak, many decided to give up paying their mortgages and allowed the lender to foreclose. One can argue the morality of this decision, but financially, it was the best course of action given the conditions.

In a buyer's market, the buyer has the power in a negotiation. Buyers should take advantage of this power and negotiate the lowest possible price. Since the price determines the loan amount and often the taxes on the property, the buyer benefits through lower interest costs and lower taxes by minimizing the purchase price. Buyers are not responsible for fixing the prior financial decisions of sellers. Overpaying for real estate to cure the financial mistakes of sellers is not in a buyer's best interest. Financial transactions with real estate are not relationship building exercises. Buyers almost never maintain a relationship with sellers after the transaction is complete, and paying extra money for a house to be a "good neighbor" or nice person is not to a buyer's financial benefit.

Preventing the Next Housing Bubble

The pain of the deflation of a housing bubble cannot be avoided by trying to keep the bubble inflated, or by trying to deflate it slowly. [137] The only way to avoid these problems is to prevent the bubble from inflating in the first place through some form of intervention in the mortgage market. Intervention can take the form of a market-based intervention demanded by investors and ratings agencies, and it can also come about through direct government regulation. [138]

Necessary Intervention

The regulated free-market system in place at the turn of the millennium allowed the creation of the Great Housing Bubble. Some combination of market-based and regulatory reforms is necessary to prevent the same circumstances that created the bubble from creating another one; it is imperative to prevent the next bubble in order to avoid the problems from the bubble's deflation. [139] The kind of intervention proposed here is not a bailout plan. A substantive bailout plan to rescue homeowners would be fraught with problems and unintended consequences. In September of 2008, the banking system neared collapse due to the problems of the fallout, and a banking system bailout became necessary. This outcome argues more forcefully for an intervention to prevent future bubbles from occurring in the housing market.

Economic Problems

The foremost problem resulting from the deflation of the Great Housing Bubble was the imperilment of our banking and financial system. The Great Depression was precipitated by the collapse of margin trading and the subsequent decline of the stock market beginning in 1929; however, this decline is not what made the Great Depression so severe. The policies responding to the upheaval caused many banks to fail, and it was the failure of banks that led to the dramatic decline in business activity and asset deflation of the Great Depression. To prevent a repeat of those problems, Congress passed a number

179

of banking reforms granting the Federal Reserve broad powers over our currency and effectively abandoned the gold standard. One of the most successful of these policies was the establishment of the Federal Deposit Insurance Corporation (FDIC) to guarantee the safety of deposits in banking institutions and prevent panic-induced, mass depositor withdrawals (aka "bank runs") from decimating our banking system. Since the FDIC has been in effect, mass depositor withdrawals at American banks have been relatively uncommon. Just as the deflation of the stock market asset bubble of the Great Depression imperiled the banking system, the deflation of the Great Housing Bubble endangered the banking system because the bank losses were so severe that most became insolvent and many went bankrupt or were taken over by other lenders. Whenever the banking system is put in jeopardy, economic growth is curtailed, and other major economic problems develop.

Another source of economic problems caused by housing market bubbles is the immobility of workers. These problems were witnessed in the deflation of the coastal bubble during the early 1990s, and they occurred again in the deflation of the Great Housing Bubble. When people owe more on their mortgage than their house is worth, they could not move freely to accept promotions or work in other areas. In such circumstances the borrower had limited options. The borrower could have tried to rent the property, but those who bought at bubble prices paid in excess of its rental value so renting the property did not cover the costs of ownership. They were losing money each month trying to keep the house. If they tried to sell the house to avoid the monthly loss, they could not get enough money in the sale to pay off the debt. The borrower would either pay the lender the difference or accept the negative consequences of a short sale or foreclosure. Most often they chose the latter option. Since none of the options available to borrowers were very palatable, many passed on promotions or other opportunities because they were trapped in their homes. Employers also faced difficulties when house prices were much higher than local incomes. When an employer wanted to expand and hire new people, the potential new employee was repelled by the high house prices and either demanded a higher wage or refused to accept employment. Both circumstances were detrimental to the economy when an employee was trapped in their home and could not move and when an employer could not attract new employees because local house prices were very high.

Like all financial bubbles, the bubble in residential real estate caused the inefficient use of capital resources. When prices rose, it signified an increase in demand, and the supply chain went to work to deliver more supply to meet this demand and capture the profits from increased prices. When the demand was artificial, as was the case in a bubble, the market became oversupplied, and this supply was not of the type or quantity the market really needed. For instance, in the NASDAQ stock market bubble, billions of dollars of investment capital flowed into internet companies. This money went into all forms of unproductive uses which ultimately provided little or no return on the investment capital. In the Great Housing Bubble, the inflated prices prompted builders to construct many large houses known as McMansions. The economics favored this because the largest homes had the lowest cost per-square-foot to construct, and these houses obtained some of the highest revenues per-square-foot on the market. The result was entire neighborhoods of homes that were very resource wasteful. If the construction resources had been allocated based on true market need, which would have happened in the absence of price bubble distortions, fewer construction resources would have gone into each home, the ongoing cost of maintenance would have been reduced, and fewer total homes would have been built. The temporary demand of construction resources in a financial bubble also impacted human resources. There was a nationwide increase in construction employment to meet the bubble demand. When the bubble burst, many of these people were laid off causing both economic and personal turmoil.

Financial bubbles also witnessed the birth, growth and death of unsustainable financial models. The NASDAQ bubble had internet companies, and the Great Housing Bubble had subprime lending. The subprime lending model was profitable despite a 10% to 15% default rate among its customers. The industry was able to sustain this rate of default because the default losses they sustained were small as long as prices were rising. As soon as prices stopped rising, their loan default rates increased, and their default losses drove the entire industry into oblivion. [140]

In the aftermath of the coastal housing bubble of the early 90s, the economy experienced a period of diminished consumer spending because many homeowners who bought during the bubble and did not go into foreclosure were making payments that represent a high percentage of their income. The extra money going toward their mortgage payment, the money in excess of normal debt-to-income guidelines was money the borrower did not have available to spend on other things. The diminished discretionary spending income from this population of borrowers slowed economic growth in an economy heavily dependent upon consumer spending such as the United States. [141] Many borrowers during the Great Housing Bubble became accustomed to supplementing their income through mortgage equity withdrawal. When house prices fell, mortgage equity withdrawal was curtailed. This forced many to adjust their lifestyles to live within the money provided by their wage incomes after paying the large debt-service payments. This loss of spending power was not just a difficult economic problem, it was a deeply personal problem for those who wished to spend freely.

Personal Problems

The economic problems caused by asset price bubbles often lead to personal problems in the wake of the deflating bubble. Statistics about unemployment, foreclosure and bankruptcy are impersonal. The events that result in any one of these outcomes was anything but impersonal: these things happened to real people who had very real emotional responses. Many people during the fallout of the Great Housing Bubble experienced all three. Any one of these outcomes can lead to depression, suicide, divorce and a whole host of traumatic personal problems. All of it was preventable if the bubble was not allowed to inflate in the first place.

The volatility of price action during a bubble had a profound and capricious impact on people's financial lives. Many people became enriched by fortuitous timing. Some of these people were market savvy individuals who knew when to buy and sell in a volatile market; however, since the mindset of a successful trader was rare, and since most housing market participants were amateurs with emotional responses almost guaranteed to produce a loss, the majority of bubble participants lost a great deal of money. Some were lucky. Some people bought and sold at the right time due to life circumstances beyond their control. Those who transferred out of bubble markets for their careers and sold their houses at the peak reaped huge windfalls. Of course, for every seller who reaped a windfall, there was a buyer who faced major financial difficulties. The unequal distribution of gains and losses from bubble market volatility is not a positive feature.

Another group of people deeply impacted by bubble market volatility are those who chose not to participate. Some of these people recognized the bubble for what it was, and some could not set aside common sense to accept the fallacious beliefs of bubble mentality. This group was forced to rent during the bubble and subsequent decline. Many of these people would have preferred ownership, preferred to have the freedom to customize a property to their liking, and preferred to obtain the intangible benefits of ownership such as a feeling of community and belonging. These people had to endure the patient "waiting game" and feelings of groundlessness renting can entail.

Addressing the Cause

Before a doctor prescribes a treatment, the patient must first be evaluated and a disease must be diagnosed. Similarly, implementing a new policy in either the public sector or private sector to prevent future housing bubbles can only take place after the causes of the housing bubble are accurately identified. If the root causes are not identified correctly, policy initiatives may not have the desired effect. The Great Housing Bubble was a credit bubble, and some form of restriction of credit must be part of any policy initiative. A common criticism of past initiatives restricting credit availability to homeowners is that these initiatives tended to limit opportunities for home ownership without properly addressing problems with lending practices. [142] The goal of any policy initiative with regards to preventing future housing bubbles is to limit or constrain irrational exuberance without impacting the smooth operation of the financial market. It is no easy task.

Before a policy can be formulated, there needs to be an open discussion of the goal of maximizing home ownership. Owning a home has become synonymous with the American Dream. Every Presidential administration has had the expansion of home ownership as one of its goals. The tax code is structured to give tax breaks to home owners to encourage home ownership. The idea of home ownership is deeply embedded in our culture.

PREVENTING THE NEXT HOUSING BUBBLE

Managing the rate of home ownership is analogous to managing the rate of economic growth. It is not the policy of our government or the Federal Reserve to maximize economic growth. Instead, the Federal Reserve balances economic growth with inflation and tries to manage economic growth to keep it on a sustainable path. This policy grew out of our painful history of economic cycles of boom and bust. It was realized that economic growth must be tempered to a sustainable level to minimize the damage of economic downturns. Similarly, the rate of home ownership should not be maximized. Home ownership will never reach 100%, and this should not be the goal of housing policy. Just as economic growth is tempered by the rate of inflation, home ownership rates are tempered by the rate of default of mortgage loan programs.

The harsh reality is that a certain percentage of the population lacks the desire, discipline or responsibility requisite to be a homeowner. There is a percentage of the population who do not want to be homeowners. Many people require mobility to pursue career opportunities or other goals. Some people like the freedom of renting and do not want the responsibilities of home ownership that go beyond monthly payments. There are some people who simply do not make housing payments consistently. This group is not capable of sustaining home ownership. There may be opportunities for policy initiatives to increase education to make this group smaller, but there will always be some people who cannot or will not do what is necessary to keep a house: make their payments. There is a percentage of the general population who should be renters.

There is a natural, sustainable level of home ownership. Home ownership rates in the United States increased markedly at the end of World War Two as the 30-year fixed-rate mortgage became the commonly accepted vehicle of home finance. In the 60 years that followed, home ownership rates stabilized between 60% and 65% through good economic times and recessions and interest rates ranging from below 6% to above 18%. Subprime lending demonstrated that increasing the home ownership rate through the widespread use of lending programs with high default rates is inherently unstable. Managing the home ownership rate is not a subject of governmental policy. Any legislative initiative to specifically limit home ownership rates would be politically unpalatable; however, either a market-based initiative or a legislative initiative that prevents the widespread use of loan programs subject to high rates of default rates would effectively manage the home ownership rate and prevent painful declines in that rate. Home ownership rates decline as homeowners become renters, a painful process known as foreclosure.

What did not cause the bubble?

There are a wide variety of ideas for preventing future housing bubbles, and all the ideas in the public forum are not discussed here. Some of the more popular are examined to demonstrate why they would not be successful. Most of the ideas that will not work are some form of direct regulation of interest rates, secondary mortgage market activities, price-to-income ratios or investment of equity capital. All regulatory initiatives carry a common problem: there is little enforcement once a bubble starts inflating. When times are good, there is immense political pressure for regulators to look the other way. When there is no apparent, immediate harm from a given practice, there is only a vague memory of a time long ago when circumstances were quite different and some restrictive law was passed. The law may seem quaint and old-fashioned or simply an obstruction to the wheels of progress. The rationalizations and justifications for ignoring laws are many, and the pressure to do so is intense when powerful lobbying interests are pressuring Congressmen who subsequently pressure government regulators.

Many believe that lower interest rates created the Great Housing Bubble, and the regulation of interest rates would prevent future bubbles. This is wrong on both counts. The lowering of interest rates did help precipitate the bubble by reducing borrowing costs and increasing home prices; however, once house prices started to rise, prices went much higher than the lower interest rates alone can account for. At most, one-third to one-half of the national price increase was due to lower interest rates, and less than 10% of the increase in coastal areas can be attributed to these lower rates. The direct regulation of mortgage interest rates would disrupt the free flow of capital in the mortgage market. If the regulated rate was too low, no money would be made available, and if the rate was too high, excess money would flow into real estate working to create another bubble. No form of mortgage interest rate regulation would prevent a future bubble because interest rates were not responsible for the Great Housing Bubble.

Much of the responsibility for the bubble can be attributed to the flow of funds into the market from hedge funds through collateralized debt obligations. There have also been calls for greater regulation of hedge funds and the secondary mortgage market. Any kind of regulation would likely restrict the flow of money to all mortgages and disrupt the secondary market. Also, regulating hedge funds themselves will prove problematic, if for no other reason, it is difficult to define exactly what a hedge fund is. Also, hedge funds are simply investment vehicles, and it is unclear exactly what they do that other investment entities do not do that causes problems resulting in financial bubbles. Much of the demonization of hedge funds is demagoguery and looking for someone to blame. Many of the problems with the secondary markets will correct themselves as investors stop investing in products that lose money. In fact, one of the greatest challenges in the aftermath of the Great Housing Bubble is going to be getting investors back into the secondary market. One of the market-based solutions proposed herein addresses these issues. Direct legislative intervention to hedge funds and collateralized debt obligations would be more disruptive than productive.

Another proposed solution is to regulate the loan-to-income ratio of the borrower. When 30-year fixed-rate mortgages first came out, mortgage debt was limited to two and one-half times a borrower's yearly income. It was an artificial limit that made sense when interest rates were higher and people were accustomed to putting less money toward housing payments. A legislative cap on the loan-to-income ratio would prevent future housing bubbles, if it was enforced. This would not work for the same reason lenders went away from the two-and-one-half-times-income standard years ago: it does not reflect changes in borrowing power due to changes in interest rates. This idea of regulating loan-to-income ratios is actually an evolution of the idea of regulating interest rates. If the total loan-to-income ratio is limited, very low interest rates do not cause dramatic price increases, but since low interest rates were not really the cause of the bubble, limiting the loan-to-income ratio is not addressing the real cause of the bubble. Plus, there are ways to get around a cap on home loan borrowing by obtaining other loans not secured by real estate. It would be relatively easy for a borrower to obtain bridge financing to acquire a property and then obtain a HELOC to pay off the bridge financing. In the end, the borrower would have borrowed more than the cap amount thus rendering any cap meaningless. To close the various loopholes, more regulations would be required, and a regulatory nightmare would ensue. A better and more effective method of limiting borrowing is to regulate the debt-to-income ratio. This idea is explored in the next section.

What did cause the bubble?

The Great Housing Bubble was caused by an expansion of credit that enabled irrational exuberance and wild speculation. The expansion of credit came in the form of relaxed loan underwriting terms including high debt-to-income ratios, lower FICO scores, high combined-loan-to-value lending including 100% financing, and loan terms permitting negative amortization. Addressing the conditions of expanding credit is a legitimate focus for intervention in the credit markets. Another major lending problem is unrelated to the terms: low documentation standards. The credit crunch that gripped the markets in late 2007 was exacerbated by the rampant fraud and misrepresentation in the loan documents underwriting the loans packaged and sold in the secondary mortgage market. It is essential to an evaluation of the viability of a mortgage note to know if the borrower actually has the income necessary to make the payments. When investors lost confidence in the underlying documents, the whole system seized up, and it was not going to work properly until the documentation improved to reflect the reality of the borrower's financial situation. Any remedy for the housing bubble must address the issue of poor documentation in order to facilitate the smooth operation of the secondary market.

There are some factors that created the Great Housing Bubble that cannot be directly regulated. One of these is the lax enforcement of existing regulations as described previously. Even though lenders and investors lost a great deal of money during the price crash, their behavior during the bubble was still predatory. Lenders peddled unstable loan programs to borrowers who could not afford the payments. They did not do this to obtain the property as is ordinarily the case with predatory lending; they did it to obtain a fee through loan origination. Since they felt insulated from the losses to these loans being packaged and sold to investors, they were in a position to profit at the expense of borrowers–the definition of predatory lending. Another factor that cannot be regulated is the crazy behavior of borrowers caught up in a speculative mania. It is not possible to stop people from overpaying for real estate, but it is possible from preventing them from doing so with borrowed money. If people wish to risk their own equity in property speculation, it is their money to lose, but when lender money is part of the equation, the entire financial system can be put at risk, which it was during the Great Housing Bubble. The fickle nature of borrowers became apparent during the decline of the bubble when many borrowers behaved in a predatory manner refusing to make payments on loans they could have afforded to make because the property had declined in value. Borrowers who were grateful to receive 100% financing and what was perceived at the time to be favorable loan terms were not hesitant to betray the lenders when their speculative investment did not go as planned.

The 30-year fixed-rate conventionally-amortizing mortgage with a reasonable downpayment is the only loan program proven to provide stability in the housing market. Many of the "affordability" products used during the Great Housing Bubble and many of the deviations from traditional underwriting standards created the bubble. Mortgage debt-to-income ratios greater than 28% and total indebtedness greater than 36% have a proven history of default. Despite this fact, debt-to-income ratios greater than 50% were common in the most extreme bubble markets. [143] Limiting debt-to-income ratios is critical to stopping loan defaults and foreclosures. Lower FICO scores was the hallmark of subprime lending. FICO scores provide a fairly accurate profile of a borrower's willingness and ability to pay their debts as planned. Low FICO scores are synonymous with high default rates. Limiting availability of credit to those with low FICO scores was a historic barrier to home ownership because these people default too much. The free market solved this problem. Subprime was dead. High combined-loan-to-value (CLTV) lending including 100% financing is also prone to high default rates. In fact, it is more important than FICO score. FICO scores are very good at predicting who will default when downpayments are large, but when borrowers have very little of their own money in the transactions, both prime and subprime borrowers defaulted at high rates. Many prime borrowers are more sophisticated financially, and the unscrupulous recognized 100% financing as a perfect tool for speculating in the real estate market and passing the risk off to a lender. The primary culprits that inflated the housing bubble were the negative amortization loan and interest-only loans where lenders qualified buyers on their ability to make only the initial payment. As the Great Housing Bubble began to deflate, Minnesota and some other states passed laws restricting the use of negative amortization loans and required lenders to qualify borrowers based on their ability to make a fully amortized payment. The Minnesota law is a good template for the rest of the nation.

Any proposal to prevent bubbles from reoccurring in the residential real estate market must properly identify the cause, provide a solution that is enforceable, and allow for the unhindered working of the secondary mortgage market. The solutions outlined below are both market-based, meaning it does not require government regulation, and regulatory based, meaning it entails some form of civil or criminal penalties to prevent certain forms of behavior leading to market bubbles. All changes are difficult to implement and the solutions presented here would be no exception. Any policies which prevent future bubbles will be opposed by those who profit from these activities and homeowners who are in need of the next bubble to get out of the bad deals they entered during the Great Housing Bubble. Despite these difficulties, it is imperative that reform take place, or the country may experience another housing bubble with all the pain and financial hardship it entails.

Market Solutions

The secondary mortgage market was created in the 1970s by the government sponsored entities, Freddie Mac, Fannie Mae, and Ginnie Mae. This market was expanded by the creation of asset-backed securities where mortgage loans are packed together into collateralized debt obligations (CDOs). This flow of capital into the mortgage market is a necessary and efficient tool for delivering money to borrowers for home mortgages. This market must remain viable for the continued health of residential real estate markets. The problem during the Great Housing Bubble was that the buyers of CDOs did not properly evaluate the risk of loss through default on the underlying mortgage notes that were pooled. The reason these risks were not evaluated properly is due to the appraisal methods used to value real estate serving as collateral backing up these loans.

There is one potential market-based solution that would require no government regulation or intervention that would prevent future bubbles from being created with borrowed capital: change the method of appraisal for residential real estate from valuations based exclusively on the comparative-sales approach to a valuation derived from the lesser of the income approach and the comparative-sales approach. Both approaches are already part of a standard appraisal, so little additional work is necessary–other than appraisers will have to focus on doing the income approach properly. In the current lending system, the income approach is widely ignored. This change of emphasis in valuation methods could come from the investors in CDOs themselves. When the fallout from the Great Housing Bubble is evaluated, it is clear that the comparative-sales approach simply enables irrational exuberance because the past foolish behavior of buyers becomes the basis for future valuations allowing other buyers to continue bidding up prices with lender and investor money. Prices collapsed in the Great Housing Bubble because prices became greatly detached from their fundamental valuation of income and rent. This occurred because the comparative-sales approach enables prices to rise based on the irrational exuberance of buyers. If lenders would have limited their lending based on the income approach, and if they would not have loaned money beyond what the rental cashflow from the property could have produced, any price bubble would have to have been built with buyer equity, and lender and

187

investor funds would not have been put at risk. There is no way to prevent future bubbles, and the commensurate imperilment of our financial system, as long as the comparative-sales approach is the exclusive basis of appraisals for residential real estate.

Investor confidence in the market for CDOs and all mortgages was shaken during the decline of the Great Housing Bubble–and rightly so. Investors were losing huge sums, and nobody clearly understood why. There was a widespread belief these losses were caused by some outside factor rather than a systemic problem enabled by the lenders and investors themselves. [144] For investor confidence to return to this market, investors must first ascertain a more accurate evaluation of potential losses due to mortgage default. This requires an accurate appraisal of the fundamental value of the residential real estate serving as collateral for the mortgage loans that comprise the CDOs. Since the fundamental value of residential real estate, the value to which prices ultimately fall during a price decline, is determined by the potential for rental income from the property, revaluing properties using the income approach would provide a more accurate measure of the value of the mortgage note and thereby the CDO.

The ratings agencies who rate the various tranches of CDOs must adopt the method of valuation utilizing the lesser value of the income approach and the comparative-sales approach. The ratings agency's recommendations and ratings carry significant weight with investors, and the ratings agencies clearly made a tragic error in their ratings of CDOs during the Great Housing Bubble. If the ratings agencies properly evaluate the underlying collateral backing up the mortgages that are pooled together in a CDO, investors will regain confidence in the ratings, and money will return to the secondary market. If investors in CDOs recognize the chain of valuation as described, they would be unwilling to purchase CDOs valued by other methods. If investors are unwilling to purchase CDOs where the underlying collateral value is measured using the comparative-sales approach and instead demand a valuation based on the income approach, the syndicators of CDOs will be forced to respond to investor demands or they will not be able to sell their syndications. Investors and the ratings agencies can mandate a new valuation method for residential home mortgages.

In September of 2008, the Federal Government took "conservatorship" of the GSEs responsible for maintaining the secondary mortgage market. With the collapse of the asset-backed securities markets and CDOs, the GSE swaps were the only viable market for mortgage paper. This provides a unique opportunity for changing the market dynamics with limited government intervention. If the government in its role as conservator were to decide to mandate a change in appraisal methods, the secondary market would be forced to accept this change. Like any sweeping change in methodology, it could be phased in over time to properly train appraisers and work out the details of implementation. If the GSEs lead, the rest of the market will follow.

The main objection with the income approach is the difficulty of evaluating market rents, particularly in markets where there may not be many (or any) comparative properties for rent in the market. This is an old problem, one that has been studied in great detail by the Department of Labor Bureau of Labor Statistics. [145] Comparative rents have been collected by the DOL since the early 1980s as part of their calculation of the Consumer Price Index. The problem of irrational exuberance in the late 1970s in coastal markets, particularly California, caused the consumer price index to rise rapidly. Since the CPI is widely used as an index for cost-of-living adjustments, volatility in this measure caused by the resale housing market needed to be urgently addressed. After over a decade of study, the DOL decided to value the change in housing costs by a comparative rental approach rather than a change in sales price approach used previously. This smoothed the index and reduced volatility because the consumptive aspect of housing services were tethered to rents and incomes rather than being subject to the volatility caused by irrational exuberance in the housing market.

The Department of Labor Bureau of Labor Statistics measures the market rental rate in markets across the United States. It breaks down the market into subcategories based on the number of bedrooms, and it does a good job of estimating market rents in the various subcategories. These numbers are updated each year. The figures from the DOL would serve as a basis for evaluation of market rents, and it may be the only basis in areas where there are few rentals. In submarkets where there is sufficient rental activity, the income approach can use real comparables to make a more accurate evaluation. Appraisers will decry the lack of available data on rentals as many rentals, particularly for single-family detached homes are done by private landlords who do not report these transactions; however, if this method of appraisal were the standard, private companies would spring up to track these transactions and maintain an up-to-date database. Valuing properties based on the income approach may be more difficult than the comparative-sales approach, but when the latter method is fundamentally flawed, ease-of-use is not a compelling reason to continue to rely on it.

There is also the objection that the income approach method of valuing residential real estate has the same problems as the comparative-sales approach because both approaches rely on finding similar properties and making an estimation of market value by adjusting the values of comparative properties. In both approaches the appraiser must explain their reasons for the adjustments to justify the appraised value of the subject property, and this is a potential source of abuse of the system. No system is perfect, but the potential to inflate prices though manipulating appraisals based on the income approach is far less than the potential problems emanating from the comparative-sales approach because the basis of adjustment in the income approach is a property's fundamental value whereas the basis of adjustment in the comparative-sales approach is the prices paid by buyers subject to bouts with irrational exuberance. If lenders start accepting appraisals where the income approach contains adjustments to value that increase the appraised amount 100%–something that would have been required to justify pricing seen during the Great Housing bubble–then the system is hopelessly broken. The main argument for using the income approach is that its basis is the fundamental value whereas the basis for the comparative-sales approach is whatever price the market will currently bear. Prices are not likely to decline below a properties fundamental value where as a property may decline significantly from a point-in-time estimate of market value. Using the income approach lessens the risk to lenders and investors and ensures the smooth operation of the secondary mortgage market. Using the comparative-sales approach exclusively results in the turmoil witnessed during the price decline of the Great Housing Bubble.

Regulatory Solutions

The regulatory solution proposed herein is simple, yet far reaching. It comes in two parts, the first is to limit the amount lenders can loan to borrowers with a rather unique enforcement mechanism, and the second is to increase the penalties for borrowers who commit mortgage fraud. The following is not in legalese, but it contains the conceptual framework of potential legislation that could be enacted on the state and/or federal level. A detailed discussion of the text follows:

Loans for the purchase or refinance of residential real estate secured by a mortgage and recorded in the public record are limited by the following parameters based on the borrower's documented income and general indebtedness and the appraised value of the property at the time of sale or refinance:

1. *All payments must be calculated based on a 30-year fixed-rate conventionally-amortizing mortgage regardless of the loan program used. Negative amortization is not permitted.*
2. *The total debt-to-income ratio for the mortgage loan payment, taxes and insurance cannot exceed 28% of a borrower's gross income.*
3. *The total debt-to-income of all debt obligations cannot exceed 36% of a borrower's gross income.*
4. *The combined-loan-to-value of mortgage indebtedness cannot exceed 90% of the appraised value of the property or the purchase price, whichever value is smaller except in specially sanctioned government programs.*

Any sums loaned in excess of these parameters do not need to be repaid by the borrower and no contractual provision is permitted that can be interpreted as limiting the borrower's right to exercise this right, make the loan callable or otherwise abridge the mortgage agreement.

This last statement is the most critical. This is how the enforcement problem can be overcome. Regulators are pressured not to enforce laws when times are good, and decried for their lack of oversight when times are bad. If the oversight function becomes a potential civil matter policed by the borrowers themselves, the lenders know exactly what their risks and potential damages are. Any lender foolish enough to make a loan outside of the parameters would not need to fear the wrath of regulators, they would need to fear the civil lawsuits brought by borrowers eager to get out of their contractual obligations. If any borrower could obtain debt forgiveness by simply proving their lender exceeded these guidelines based on the loan documents, no lender would do this, and regulatory oversight would be practically unnecessary. One key to making this work is to prohibit lenders from introducing a "poison pill" to the loan documents that would make borrowers hesitant to bring suit, otherwise lenders would make their loan callable in the event of a legal challenge forcing the borrower to refinance or sell the property. Basically, if the borrower brought suit and won, they would see principal reduction equal to the deviation from the standards, if they brought suit and lost, they would have no penalty. Most of these cases would be decided by summary judgment based on a review of the loan documents thus minimizing court costs.

Another pillar to the system is the documentation of income as part of the loan document package–the *"borrower's documented income"* from the proposed legislation. One of the most egregious practices of the Great Housing Bubble was the fabrication of income by borrowers that was facilitated and promoted by originating lenders. Stated-income loan programs were widespread, and they were the cause of much of the uncertainty in the secondary mortgage market during the initial stages of the credit crunch in the deflation of the bubble. Basically, investors had no idea if the borrowers to whom they had lent billions of dollars were capable of paying them back. Without proper documentation of income, investors lost all confidence in the secondary mortgage market. Stated-income loan programs were one of the first casualties of the credit crunch. These programs should be eliminated totally due to the inherent potential for fraud and the undermining of confidence in the secondary mortgage market stated-income loans create. If lenders can be sued based on the content of the loan documents, and if borrowers can be fined or go to jail for committing fraud or misrepresentation on loan documents, both parties have strong incentive to prepare these documents completely and correctly. Originating lenders will argue this adds to their costs and will result in higher application fees. The amount in question is very small, particularly relative to the dollar amount of the transaction. A small amount of additional expense here will provide huge benefits by assuring investors the borrowers to whom they are loaning money really have the income to pay them back. The benefit far outweighs the cost.

If such a law were passed, agency interpretation and court case precedents will end up defining adequacy in loan documentation. A single W2 does not establish a work history, but 2 years worth is probably excessive documentation. One of the most contentious areas will likely be documenting the income of the self-employed. In theory, the self employed must document their incomes to the US government either through Schedule C reports or corporate K-1s. The argument the self-employed have traditionally made is that these documents understate their income. Since many self employed take questionable tax deductions, there is probably some truth to the claim that tax records understate their income; however, why should the self-employed get to have both benefits? If the self-employed had to use their tax returns as loan documentation, they probably would not be quite so aggressive in taking deductions. A new business without a tax return or with only one year of taxable receipts probably is not stable enough to meet standards of income necessary to assume a long-term debt.

The poor quality of loan documentation during the bubble was a mistake of originating lenders; therefore, in this proposal much of the burden of paperwork and liability for mistakes falls on the lenders. During the deflation of the bubble, lenders paid an enormous price for some of their lax paperwork standards, but much of the problem was also due to borrowers misrepresenting themselves in the loan documents. There were instances where lenders encouraged this behavior, but in the majority of cases, the document fraud was perpetrated by the borrowers. The only recourse available to a lender is a civil suit as there are few criminal penalties associated with loan documentation and almost no enforcement. It can be very difficult and costly for lenders to pursue civil damages, and few lenders attempt it even when they have a strong case. To create a more balanced set of responsibilities, the borrowers must face criminal penalties for fraud and misrepresentation on loan documents. If borrowers know the lender can turn documents over to a prosecutor who will charge the borrower with a crime if they make false material statements, borrowers will be much less likely to commit these acts.

The parameters of the forming limitations on the debt-to-income ratio and combined-loan-to-value are essential to prevent bubbles in the housing market and to prevent the banking system from becoming imperiled in the future. People will commit large percentages of their income to house payments when prices are rising quickly; however, they do this out of fear of being "priced out" and greed to make a windfall from appreciation. These are the beliefs that inflate a bubble. Borrowers cannot sustain payments above the traditional parameters for debt service without either defaulting or causing a severe decline in discretionary spending. The former is bad for the banks, and the latter is bad for the entire economy. This must be prevented in the future. There are a number of reasons why high combined-loan-to-value lending is a bad idea: it promotes speculation by shifting the risk to the lender, it encourages predatory borrowing where borrowers "put" the property to a lender, it promotes a high default rate because borrowers are not personally invested in the property, it discourages saving as it becomes unnecessary, and it artificially inflates prices as it eliminates a barrier to market entry. This last reason is one of the arguments used to get rid of downpayment requirements. The consequences of this folly became readily apparent once prices started to fall.

The payment must be measured against "*30-year fixed-rate conventionally-amortizing mortgage regardless of the loan program used.*" One of the worst loan programs of the Great Housing Bubble was the 2/28 ARM sold to large numbers of subprime borrowers. These borrowers were often qualified only on their ability to make the initial payment, and these borrowers were generally not capable of making the fully amortized payment when the loan reset after 2 years. Regulations like this would prevent a recurrence of the foreclosure tsunami triggered by the use of this loan program. It is also important to ban negative amortization because it would allow the loan balance to grow beyond the parameters of qualification, and it invites property speculation. Perhaps borrowers would not be concerned because they would receive debt forgiveness of the expanding balance. Lenders should be wary of these loans after their dismal performance in the deflation of the bubble, but institutional memory is short, and these loan programs could make a comeback if they are not specifically outlawed. This provision is careful to allow interest-only loans. They are still a high-risk product, but an argument can be made that these loans have a place, and there is no need to completely ban them. They will not have a future as an affordability product capable of driving up prices if the borrower must still qualify for the fully amortized payment.

For the lending provisions to have real impact, they must apply to both purchases and to refinances, thus the clause, *"Loans for the purchase or refinance of residential real estate."* If the rules only applied to purchases, there would be a tremendous volume in refinances to circumvent the regulations. The caps on debt-to-income ratios, mortgage terms and combined-loan-to-value only have meaning if they are universally applied. The combined-loan-to-value standard is based on the *"appraised value of the property at the time of sale or refinance."* The new appraisal methods will have impact here. It is important that the records need only be accurate as of the time of the transaction. If a borrower experiences a decline in their income or if the property declines in value to where they no longer meet the loan standard, it does not mean they can go petition for debt relief.

The regulations would only need to apply to loans *"secured by a mortgage and recorded in the public record."* People can still borrow money from any source they wished as long as the lender knows they will not have any claim on residential real estate. If a lender wanted to issue a loan secured by real estate outside of the outlined standards, the borrower would not have to pay back that money. If a borrower has non-recorded debts which create a total indebtedness requiring more than 36% of their gross income, they would not be eligible for a home equity loan even if they met the other qualifications. In such circumstances, it is better to limit borrowing than increase the probability of foreclosure.

Many states have non-recourse laws on their books. These laws serve to protect the borrower from predatory lending because the lender cannot go after other assets of the borrower in the event of default. In theory this should make lenders more conservative in their underwriting; however, the behavior of lenders in California, a non-recourse state, during the Great Housing Bubble was not conservative. These laws do serve to protect borrowers, and they should be enacted for purchase-money mortgages in all 50 states.

Since one of the goals of regulatory reform is to inhibit the behavior of irrational exuberance, the sales tactics of the National Association of Realtors should be examined and potentially come under the same restrictions as securities brokers through the Securities and Exchange Commission. After the stock market crash which helped precipitate the Great Depression, Congress created the Securities and Exchange Commission to regulate the sales activities of securities brokers. There are strict regulations in place governing the representations made concerning the future performance of investment opportunities. These protections were put in place to protect the general public from the false promises made by stockbrokers in the 1920s which many naïve investors believed. The same analogy holds true for Realtors. The National Association of Realtors has launched numerous advertising campaigns suggesting erroneously that residential real estate is a great investment and appreciation will make home buyers wealthy. [146] The mantra of all realtors is that house prices always go up. There are currently no limits to the distortions and outright lies realtors can tell prospective buyers with regards to the investment potential of residential real estate. Buyers are already prone to believe the fallacies of unlimited riches in real estate, and these fallacious beliefs lead to housing bubbles. Realtors should be prevented from making representations concerning the investment potential of real estate. Since the regulatory framework for this kind of regulation and oversight is already in place under the auspices of the Securities and Exchange Commission, Congress would merely need to make Realtors subject to these regulations in order to solve the problem.

The result of these restrictions will be that all homeowners will have at least 10% equity in their properties unless they have borrowed from a government program like the FHA where the combined-loan-to-value can exceed the limits. This equity cushion would buffer lenders from predatory borrowing and a huge increase in foreclosures if prices were to decline. Home equity in the United States has been declining since the mid 1980s, and it actually declined while prices rose during the Great Housing Bubble due to the rampant equity extraction. The lack of an equity cushion exacerbated the foreclosure problem as many homeowners who owed more on their mortgage than the house was worth simply stopped making payments and allowed the house to fall into foreclosure.

Summary

A future bubble in the housing market must be prevented. The economic and personal problems resulting from the deflation of the Great Housing Bubble must not be inflicted on another generation. Just as those who endured the Great Depression struggled to understand what went wrong and prevent its reoccurrence, we must prevent another bubble in the housing market. There are both market-based alternatives and regulatory-based policies that could serve to prevent the next housing bubble. The market based solution proposed herein is to expand the use of the income approach to property appraisal to tether prices to fundamental values. The regulatory solution proposed herein is a multifaceted approach that limits lending to within certain standards. The policing mechanism is a shift to civil enforcement through allowing borrowers to obtain debt forgiveness for amounts lent outside of the approved parameters.

The Great Housing Bubble was an epic event impacting the lives of nearly every household in the United States and around the world. At first it was a giant house party fueled by excessive borrowing and spending by homeowners.

The hangover was not pleasant. As of the time of this writing the full history of the fallout is not yet recorded. The decline in prices to this point has been breathtaking and unprecedented. When the full history is written, and the final impact of the bubble is measured, many will remember the Great Housing Bubble as one of the most important historical events of their lifetime.

Bibliography

Anderson, R. G., & Gascon, C. S. (2008). *Offshoring, Economic Insecurity, and the Demand for Social Insurance.* St, Louis, MO: Federal Reserve Bank of St. Louis.

Ashcraft, A. B., & Schuermann, T. (2008). *Understanding the Securitization of Subprime Mortgage Credit.* New York, NY: Federal Reserve Bank of New York.

Baker, D. (2002). The Run-up in Home Prices: a Bubble. *Challenge* , 93+.

Baker, K., & Kaul, B. (2002). Using Multiperiod Variables in the Analysis of Home Improvement Decisions by Homeowners. *Real Estate Economics* , 551+.

Balen, M. (2003). *The Secret History of the South Sea Bubble.* New York, NY: HarperCollins Publishers Inc.

Bernanke, B. S. (1999). *Japanese Monetary Policy: A Case of Self-Induced Paralysis.* Washington, DC: Institute for International Economics.

Bernanke, B. S. (2008). Reducing Preventable Mortgage Foreclosures. *Independent Community Bankers of America Annual Convention* (p. 1). Orlando, FL: Board of Governors of the Federal Reserve System.

Bernanke, B. S., & Boivin, J. (2002). *Monetary Policy in a Data-Rich Environment.* Princeton, NJ: Princeton University.

Bernanke, B. S., & Gertler, M. (2000). *Should Central Banks Respond to Movements in Asset Prices?* Princeton, NJ : Princeton University.

Bernanke, B. (2007). The Economic Outlook. *Before the Joint Economic Committee, U.S. Congress* (p. 1). Washington, D.C.: Board of Governers of the Federal Reserve.

Bikhchandani, S., Hirshleifer, D., & Welch, I. (1998). Learning from the Behavior of Others: Conformity, Fads, and Informational Cascades. *The Journal of Economic Perspectives* , 26.

Black, A., Fraser, P., & Hoesli, M. (2006). House Prices, Fuindamentals and Bubbles. *Journal of Business Finance & Accounting* , 1535+.

Boucher, M. (1999). *The Hedge Fund Edge.* New York, NY: John Wiley & Sons, Inc.

Boykin, J. H., & Haney, R. L. (1997). *Financing Real Estate.* Prentice Hall College Division.

Brown, S. J. (2006). How Critical Is the Housing Market? *ABA Banking Journal* , 64.

Buffet, W. (2002). *Berkshire Hathaway annual report for 2002.* Omaha, NE: Berkshire Hathaway.

Burdekin, R. C., & Siklos, P. L. (2004). *Deflation: Current and Historical Perspectives (Studies in Macroeconomic History) .* New York, NY: Cambridge University Press.

BusinessWeek Magazine . (2006, September 11). Nightmare Mortgages. *BusinessWeek* , p. 1.

Campbell, S. D., Davis, M. A., Gallin, J., & Martin, R. F. (2005). *A Trend and Variance Decomposition of the Rent-Price Ratio in Housing Markets.* Washington, DC: Board of Governors of the Federal Reserve System.

Cannon, S., Miller, N. G., & Pandher, G. S. (2006). Risk and Return in the U.S. Housing Market: A Cross-Sectional Asset-Pricing Approach. *Real Estate Economics* , 519+.

Capell, P. (2004). Eight Tips for Buyers Making Competitive Bids. *Real Estate Journal.com* , p. 1.

Capra, F. (Director). (1946). *It's a Wonderful Life* [Motion Picture].

Carter, J. (2006). *Mastering the Trade.* New York, NY: McGraw-Hill, Inc.

Case, K. E., & Shiller, R. J. (2004). *Is There a Bubble in the Housing Market.* New Haven, CT: Cowles Foundation for Research in Economics, Yale University.

Case, K. E., & Shiller, R. J. (1988). *The Behavior of Home Buyers in Boom and Post-Boom Markets.* New Haven, CT: Cowles Foundation for Research in Economics, Yale University.

Chambers, M. S., Garriga, C., & Schlagenhauf, D. (2007). *Mortgage Contracts and Housing Tenure Decisions.* St. Louis, MO: Federal Reserve Bank of St. Louis.

Chambers, M., Garriga, C., & Schlagenhauf, D. E. (2007). *Accounting for Changes in the Homeownership Rate.* St. Louis, MO: Federal Reserve Bank of St. Louis.

Chomsisengphet, S., & Pennington-Cross, A. (2006). *Subprime Refinancing: Equity Extraction and Mortgage Termination.* St. Louis, MO: Federal Reserve Bank of St. Louis.

Credit Suisse. (2007). *Mortgage Liquidity du Jour: Underestimated No More.* Credit Suisse Equity Research.

Crone, T. M., & Nakamura, L. I. (2004). *Hedonic Estimates of the Cost of Housing Services -- Rental and Owner-Occupied Units.* Philadelphia, PA: Federal Reserve Bank of Philadelphia.

Dalton, J. F., Jones, E. T., & Dalton, R. B. (1999). *Mind over Markets.* Greenville, SC: Traders Press, Inc.

Daniel, K., Hirshleifer, D., & Subrahmanyam, A. (1998). Ivestor Psychology and Security Market Under- and Overreactions. 58.

Das, S. (2005). *Credit Derivatives: CDOs and Structured Credit Products.* New York, NY: John Wiley & Sons, Inc.

Davis, M. A., & Palumbo, M. G. (2006). *The Price of Residential Land in Large U.S. Cities.* Washington, D.C.: Federal Reserve Board.

Davis, M., & Heathcote, J. (2003). *Housing and the Business Cycle.* Washington, DC: Board of Governors of the Federal Reserve System.

Deming, W. E. (2000). *The New Economics for Industry, Government, Education - 2nd Edition.* Boston, MA: The MIT Press.

Deng, Y., & Gabriel, S. (2006). Risk-Based Pricing and the Enhancement of Mortgage Credit Availability among Underserved and Higher Credit-Risk Populations. *Journal of Money* , 1431+.

Dent, H. S. (2006). *The Next Great Bubble Boom.* New York, NY: Free Press.

Doms, M., & Krainer, J. (2007). *Innovations in Mortgage Markets and Increased Spending on Housing.* San Francisco, CA: Federal Reserve Bank of San Francisco.

Doms, M., Furlong, F., & Krainer, J. (2007). *Subprime Mortgage Delinquency Rates.* San Francisco, CA: Federal Reserve Bank of San Francisco.

Douglas, M. (1990). *The Disciplined Trader, Developing Winning Attitudes.* New York, NY: New York Institute of Finance.

Douglas, M. (2000). *Trading in the Zone.* New York, NY: New York Institute of Finance.

Engen, E. M., Gale, W. G., & Uccello, C. E. (2004). *Lifetime Earnings, Social Security Benefits, and the Adequacy of Retirement Wealth Accumulation.* Washington, D.C.: Federal Reserve Board.

Fabozzi, F. J., Davis, H. A., & Choudhry, M. (2006). *Introduction to Structured Finance.* New York, NY: John Wiley & Sons, Inc.

Fishbein, A. J. (2008). *Piggyback Loans at the Trough: California Subprime Home Purchase and Refinance Lending in 2006.* Washington, D.C.: Consumer Federation of America.

Fishbein, A. J., & Woodall, P. (2006). *Exotic or Toxic? An Examination of the Non-Traditional Mortgage Market for Consumers and Lenders.* Washington, D.C.: Consumer Federation of America.

Fisher, J. D., & Quayyum, S. (2005). *The great turn-of-the-century housing boom.* Chicago, IL: Federal Reserve Bank of Chicago.

Fletcher, J. (2005). *House Poor, Pumped-Up Prices, Rising Rates, and Mortgages on Steroids.* New York, NY: HarperCollins Publishers Inc.

Frame, W. S., & White, L. J. (2005). Fussing and Fuming over Fannie and Freddie: How Much Smoke, How Much Fire? *The Journal of Economic Perspectives* , 28.

Gallin, J. (2006). The Long-Run Relationship between House Prices and Income: Evidence from Local Housing Markets. *Real Estate Economics* , 417+.

Gallin, J. (2003). *The Long-Run Relationship between House Prices and Income: Evidence from Local Housing Markets.* Washington, DC: Federal Reserve Board.

Gallin, J. (2004). *The Long-Run Relationship between House Prices and Rents.* Washington, D.C.: Federal Reserve Board.

Ganguin, B., & Bilardello, J. (2004). *Standard & Poor's Fundamentals of Corporate Credit Analysis.* New York, NY: McGraw-Hill.

Garber, P. M. (1989). Tulipmania. *The Journal of Political Economy* , 26.

Geary, L. H. (2002, May 21). Riches to Rags: Millionairs who go Bust. *CNN/Money* , p. 1.

Gerardi, K., Shapiro, A. H., & Willen, P. S. (2007). *Subprime Outcomes: Risky Mortgages, Homeownership Experience, and Forclosures.* Boston, MA: Federal Reserve Bank of Boston.

Gibbon, E. (1999). *Decline & Fall of the Roman Empire, New Ed edition.* Hertfordshire, United Kingdom: Wordsworth Editions Ltd.

Green, R. K., & Wachter, S. M. (2007). Praveen Kujal1 and Vernon L. Smith. *Housing, Housing Finance & Monetary Policy* (p. 64). Jackson Hole, Wyoming: Federal Reserve Bank of Kansas City.

Greenspan, A. (1996). The Challenge of Central Banking in a Democratic Society. *Annual Dinner and Francis Boyer Lecture of The American Enterprise Institute for Public Policy Research.* Washington, D.C.: Federal Reserve Board.

Greenspan, A. (2004). Understanding Household Debt Obligations. *Credit Union National Association 2004 Governmental Affairs Conference.* Washington, DC: Federal Reserve Board.

Grigg, W. N. (2004, May). Will the Housing Bubble Burst? Our Socialist Mortgage System and Easy Money Policy Have Created a Dangerously Inflated Housing Bubble That, If Pricked, Could Take the Economy Down with It. *The New American* , p. 20+.

Gross, D. (2004, February 27). Alan Greenspan: ARMed and Dangerous. *Slate Magazine: Moneybox* , p. 1.

Gross, D. (2007, July 26). The Real Morons of Orange County. *Moneybox* , p. 1.

Haines, C. L., & Rosen, R. J. (2006). Bubble, bubble, toil, and trouble. *Economic Perspectives* , 35.

Hall, C. (2004). *Timing the Real Estate Market.* New York, NY: McGraw-Hill.

Haney, R. L., Berens, G., & Miles, M. E. (1995). *Real Estate Development: Principles and Process.* Washington, D.C.: Urban Land Institute.

Haubrich, J. G., & Lucas, D. (2006). *Who holds the toxic waste? An investigation of CMO holdings.* Cleveland, OH: Federal Reserve Bank of Cleveland.

Heffernan, S. (2005). *Modern Banking.* New York, NY: John Wiley & Sons, Inc.

Helbling, T., Conover, E., & Terrones, M. (2003). Chapter II: When Bubbles Burst. *World Economic Outlook* , 61+.

Himmelberg, C., Mayer, C., & Sinai, T. (2005). *Assessing High House Prices: Bubbles, Fundamentals, and Misperceptions.* New York, NY: Federal Reserve Bank of New York.

Hockley, C. A. (2005, June 7). Are CAP Rates Still a Valid Indicator of Value? *RealtyTimes* , p. 1.

Jaeger, W. (2006). The Effects of Land-Use Regulations on Property Values. *Environmental Law* , 105+.

Johnson, D., & Halliburton, M. (2007). The Subprime Credit Crunch. *ABA Banking Journal* , 64+.

Kahneman, D., & Tversky, A. (1979). Prospect Theory: An Analysis of Decision under Risk. *Econometrica* , 33.

Kahneman, D., Knetsch, J. L., & Thaler, R. H. (1991). The Endowment Effect, Loss Aversion, and Status Quo Bias. *The Journal of Economic Perspectives* , 15.

Kiyosaki, R. T., & Lechter, S. L. (2000). *Rich Dad, Poor Dad: What the Rich Teach Their Kids About Money--That the Poor and Middle Class Do Not!* Lebanon, IN: Business Plus.

Kolbe, P. T. (2007, Summer). Affordability in the Single-Family Housing Market. *Business Perspectives* , p. 8+.

Kornfield, J. (1993). *A Path with Heart: A Guide Through the Perils and Promises of Spiritual Life.* New York, NY: Bantam Books.

Kornfield, J. (2000). *After the Ecstasy, the Laundry: How the Heart Grows Wise on the Spiritual Path.* New York, NY: Bantam Books.

Kornfield, J. (1993). *The Inner Art of Meditation.* Louisville, CO: Sounds True.

Kornfield, J. (1996). *The Roots of Buddhist Psychology.* Louisville, CO: Sounds True.

Krainer, J. (2003). House Price Bubbles. *FRBSF Economic Letter* , 4.

Krainer, J. (2006). Residential Investment over the Real Estate Cycle. *FRBSF Economic Letter* , 4.

Krainer, J., & Wei, C. (2004). House Prices and Fundamental Value. *FRBSF Economic Letter* , 4.

Kruger, J., & Dunning, D. (1999). Unskilled and Unaware of It: How Difficulties in Recognizing One's Own Incompetence Lead to Inflated Self-Assessments. *Journal of Personality and Social Psychology* , 14.

Kujal, P., & Smith, V. L. (2003). *Fairness and Short Run Price Adjustment in Posted Offer Markets.* Madrid, Spain: University of Carlos III De Madrid.

Kujal, P., & Smith, V. L. (1991). *The Endowment Effect.* Madrid, Spain: Universidad Carlos III De Madrid.

Kuttner, K. N., & Posen, A. S. (2001). *Passive Savers and Fiscal Policy Effectiveness in Japan.* Washington, DC: Institute for International Economics.

Lacour-Little, M. (2004, March). Equity Dilution: An Alternative Perspective on Mortgage Default. *Real Estate Economics* , p. 359+.

Leamer, E. E. (2007). Housing Is the Business Cycle. *Housing, Housing Finance and Monetary Policy* (p. 74). Jackson Hole, WY: Federal Reserve Bank of Kansas City.

Leamer, E. E. (2007). Housing Is the Business Cycle. *Housing, Housing Finance, and Monetary Policy* (p. 73). Jackson Hole, Wyoming: Federal Reserve Bank of Kansas City.

Lefevre, E. (1994). *Reminiscences of a Stock Operator.* New York, NY: John Wiley & Sons, Inc.

Leventis, A. (2007). *A Note on the Differences between the OFHEO and S&P/Case-Shiller House Price Indexes.* Washington, D.C.: Office of Federal Housing Enterprise Oversight.

Libby, R., Libby, P., & Short, D. (2004). *Financial Accounting, 4th Edition.* Columbus, OH: McGraw-Hill.

Lindsey, L. B. (2007, Spring). Fear and Greed: Why the American Housing Credit Crisis Is Worse Than You Think. *The International Economy* , p. 22+.

Lowy, M. (1991). *High Rollers: Inside the Savings and Loan Debacle.* Westport, CT: Praeger Publishers.

Lucas, D. J., Goodman, L. S., & Fabozzi, F. J. (2006). *Collateralized Debt Obligations: Structures and Analysis, 2nd Edition.* New York, NY: John Wiley & Sons Inc.

Mackay, C., Vega, J. d., & Fridson, M. S. (1996). *Extraordinary Popular Delusions and the Madness of Crowds & Confusion de Confusiones.* New York, NY: John Wiley & Sons, Inc.

Magee, R. D. (1998). *Technical Analysis of Stock Trends, 7th Edition.* Boca Raton, FL: St. Lucie Press.

Mankiw, N. G. (2006). *Principles of Macroeconomics.* South-Western College Pub; 4 edition.

Mankiw, N. G., & Weil, D. N. (1989). The Baby Boom, the Baby Bust and the Housing Market. *Regional Science and Urban Economics* , 24.

Martin, R. F. (2005). *The Baby Boom: Predictability in House Prices and Interest Rates.* Washington, DC: Federal Reserve Board of Governors.

McCarthy, J., & Peach, R. W. (2004). *Are Home Prices the Next Bubble.* New York, NY: Federal Reserve Bank of New York.

McElroy, K. (2004). *Rich Dad's Advisors®: The ABC's of Real Estate Investing: The Secrets of Finding Hidden Profits Most Investors Miss.* Lebanon, IN: Business Plus.

McMillan, L. G. (2004). *McMillan on Options, Second Edition.* Hoboken, NJ: John Wiley & Sons, Inc.

McMillan, L. G. (2002). *Options as a Strategic Investment, Fourth Edition.* New York, NY: New York Institute of Finance.

Miles, R. P. (2004). *Warren Buffett Wealth: Principles and Practical Methods Used by the World's Greatest Investor.* New York, NY: John Wiley & Sons, Inc.

Minsky, H. P. (1982). *Can "It" Happen Again? Essays on Instability and Finance.* Unknown: M.E. Sharpe.

Minsky, H. P. (2008). *Stablizing an Unstable Economy.* New York, NY: McGraw-Hill.

Mints, V. (2006). *THe Mortgage Rate and Housing Bubbles.* Moscow, Russia: Housing Finance International.

BIBLIOGRAPHY

Mortgage Bankers Association. (2007). *National Delinquency Survey.* Mortgage Bankers Association.

Muellbauer, J. (2007). Housing, Credit and Consumer Expeditures. *Housing, Housing Finance, and Monetary Policy* (p. 63). Jackson Hole, WY: Federal Reserve Bank of Kansas City .

Myers, D., & Ryu, S. (2008). Aging Baby Boomers and the Generational Housing Bubble: Foresight and Mitigation of an Epic Transition. *Journal of the American Planning* , 1-17.

Natenberg, S. (1988). *Options Volatility and Pricing Strategies.* Chicago, IL: Probus Publishing Company.

National Multi Housing Council, National Apartment Association. (2004). *Renting Can Be a Smart Investment.* Washington, DC & Alexandria, VA: National Multi Housing Council, National Apartment Association.

Orman, S. (2006). *The 9 Steps to Financial Freedom: Practical and Spiritual Steps So You Can Stop Worrying, 3rd edition.* New York, NY: Three Rivers Press.

Orwell, G. (1950). *1984.* New York, NY: Signet Classics.

Paulson, H. M. (2007). Current Housing and Mortgage Market Developments. *Georgetown University Law Center* (p. 1). Washington, D.C.: US Department of Treasury.

Peterson, J. R. (2005). Designer Mortgages: The Boom in Nontraditional Mortgage Loans May Be a Double-Edged Sword. So Far, Most Banks Have Moved Cautiously. *ABA Banking Journal* , 30+.

Poole, R., Ptacek, F., & Verbrugge, R. (2005). *Treatment of Owner-Occupied Housing in the CPI.* Washington, DC: Federal Economic Statistics Advisory Committee.

Porter, D., & Smith, V. (1992). *Price Expectations in Experimental Asset Markets with Futures Contracting.* Pasadena, CA: California Institute of Technology.

Posen, A. S. (2003). *It Takes more than a Bubble to Become Japan.* Washington, DC: Institute for International Economics.

Posen, A. (2006). *Why Central Banks Should Not Burst Bubbles.* Washington, DC: Institute for International Economics.

Rappaport, J. (2006). *A Guide to Aggregate House Price Measures.* Kansas City, MO: Federal Reserve Bank of Kansas City.

Rubino, J. (2003). *How to Profit from the Coming Real Estate Bust.* Rodale.

Schiller, T. (2007, Fall). Housing: Boom or Bubble. *Business Review* , p. 10.

Schwager, J. D. (2003). *Stock Market Wizards.* New York, NY: Harper Collins.

Shakespeare, W. (1603). *Macbeth.* Stratford-upon-Avon.

Shiller, R. J. (2001). *Bubbles, Human Judgment, and Expert Opinion.* New Haven, CT: Cowles Foundation for Research in Economics, Yale University.

Shiller, R. J. (2002). *From Efficient Market Theory to Behavioral Finance.* New Haven, CT: Cowles Foundation for Research in Economics, Yale University.

Shiller, R. J. (2007). *Historic Turning Points in Real Estate.* New Haven, CT: Cowles Foundation for Research in Economics, Yale University.

Shiller, R. J. (2004). *Household Reaction to Changes in Housing Wealth.* New Haven, CT: Cowles Foundation for Research in Economics, Yale University.

Shiller, R. J. (2005). *Irrational Exuberance.* Doubleday.

Shiller, R. J. (2007). *Understanding Recent Trends in House Prices and Home Ownership.* New Haven, CT: Cowles Foundation for Research in Economics, Yale University.

Shiller, R. J., & N.Weiss, A. (1998). Moral Hazard in Home Equity Conversion. *AREUEA–ASSA session* (p. 29). Chicago Illinois: AREUEA–ASSA session.

Shiratsuka, S. (2003). *Asset Price Bubble in Japan in the 1980s: Lessons for Financial and Macroeconomic Stability.* Tokyo, Japan: Institute for Monetary and Economic Studies -- Bank of Japan.

Shleifer, A. (2000). *Inefficient Markets: An Introduction to Behavioral Finance.* Oxford University Press, USA.

Sinai, T. (2008). *The Inequity of Subprime Mortgage Relief Programs.* Washington, DC: FreedomWorks Foundation.

Smith, V. L. (2000). Exchange, Economic Theory, and the Hayek Critique. *Encyclopedia of Cognitive Science* , 42.

Smith, V. L. (2004). Human Nature: An Economic Perspective. *Daedalus* , 67+.

Smith, V. L., & Porter, D. (1992). *Price Expectations in Experimental Asset Markets with Futures Contracting.* Pasadena, CA: California Institute of Technology.

Smith, V. L., Suchanek, G. L., & Williams, A. W. (1988). Bubbles, Crashes, and Endogenous Expectations in Experimental Spot Asset Markets. *Econometrica* , 56.

Soros, G. (1994). *The Alchemy of Finance: Reading the Mind of the Market.* New York, NY: John Wiley & Sons, Inc.

Soto, J. H. (2006). *Money, Bank Credit, and Economic Cycles.* Ludwig von Mises Institute.

Sullivan, P. (2006, January 20). William 'Bud' Post III; Unhappy Lottery Winner. *Washington Post* , p. 1.

Susanne Cannon, N. G. (2003). *Risk and Return in the U.S. Housing Market: A Cross-Sectional Asset-Pricing Approach.*

Talbott, J. R. (2006). *Sell Now! The End of the Housing Bubble.* New York, NY: St. Martins Press.

Talbott, J. R. (2003). *The Coming Crash in the Housing Market.* New York, NY: McGraw-Hill, Inc.

Taleb, N. N. (2007). *The Black Swan: The Impact of the Highly Improbable.* New York, NY: Random House.

Thompson, E. A., Treussard, J., & Hickson, C. R. (2004). *Predicting Bubbles and Bubble-Substitutes.* Los Angeles, CA: Department of Economics UCLA.

Tversky, A., & Kahneman, D. (1991). Loss Aversion in Riskless Choice: A Reference-Dependent Model. *The Quarterly Journal of Economics* , 27.

BIBLIOGRAPHY

Vitale, J. (1998). *There's a Customer Born Every Minute: P.T. Barnum's Secrets to Business Success*. AMACOM.

Wallace, G., Elliehausen, G., & Staten, M. (2005). *Are Legislative Solutions to Abusive Mortgage Lending Practices Throwing Out the Baby with The Bath? Guidance From Empirical Research*. Washington, D.C.: Georgetown University.

Wallace-Wells, B. (2004, April). There Goes the Neighborhood: Why Home Prices Are about to Plummet-And Take the Recovery with Them. *Washington Monthly* , p. 30+.

Wolff, M. (1998). *Burn Rate: How I Survived the Gold Rush Years on the Internet* . New York, NY: Simon & Schuster.

Zuckoff, M. (2005). *Ponzi's Scheme: The True Story of a Financial Legend.* New York, NY: Random House.

Index

C

call option, 111
capitulation stage, 120, 121
Case-Shiller index, 78, 141, *See*
    S&P/Case-Shiller
Cashflow investors, 41
Cashflow Investors, 106, 107, 162
CDO, 60, 61, 62, 64, 67, 68, 69, 70, 188
Charles Ponzi, 124, *See* Ponzi Scheme
CLTV, 66, 111, 186
collateral, 24, 33, 63, 64, 68, 91, 98,
    100, 148, 187, 188
collateralized debt obligation. *See* CDO
combined-loan-to-value, 65, 66, 185,
    186, 190, 192, 193, 194, *See* CLTV
commodities, 41, 57, 103, 110, 111,
    133
commodities exchange, 110
Community Facilities District, 34
comparative-sales approach, 68, 69, 70,
    187, 188, 189
conspicuous consumption, 96, 123
Consumer Price Index. *See* CPI
consumptive value, 26, 32, 39
Conventional mortgage, 12, 13, 87
cost approach, 68
cost of ownership, 4, 21, 23, 31, 32, 34,
    35, 36, 37, 38, 39, 42, 46, 48, 49, 84,
    107, 108, 109, 142, 144, 145, 167
counter-offer, 177
covenants, conditions, and restrictions,
    34
CPI, 31, 148, 189
credit crunch, 19, 29, 37, 63, 75, 93, 97,
    98, 118, 119, 185, 191
credit cycle, 29, 92, 102, 117
credit default swaps, 61
Credit ratings, 63
Credit Suisse, 93
cultural pathology, 121, 123, 133

D

debtor's prisons, 166
debt-to-income, 9, 28, 65, 67, 73, 75,
    82, 83, 84, 86, 87, 91, 92, 98, 135,
    137, 140, 153, 154, 155, 158, 167,
    181, 185, 186, 190, 192, 193, *See*
    DTI

debt-to-income ratio, 9, 65, 67, 75, 84,
    135, 153, 154, 155, 158, 185, 190,
    192
default rates, 9, 16, 17, 23, 27, 28, 64,
    65, 66, 67, 75, 83, 92, 93, 95, 99, 101,
    159, 181, 183, 186
deflation, xix, 13, 25, 63, 98, 102, 133,
    137, 148, 164, 167, 179, 180, 191,
    192, 193, 194, *See* Monetary
    Deflation
demand curve, 85, 88
denial stage, 117, 118, 119
Department of Labor, 31, 39, 189
Department of Treasury, 129
despair stage, 120, 121
Developers, 54
discount rate, 40, 41, 42, 43, 47
discounted cashflow analysis, 40, 46,
    104
document stamps and taxes, 42
DOL, 189, *See* Department of Labor
downpayments, 19, 29, 66, 91, 96, 99,
    111, 112, 120, 186
downward spiral, 91, 107, 120
DTI, 67, 84, 87, 154, 155, 158

E

Economic Stimulus Act of 2008, 128
efficient markets theory, 113, 114, 115,
    136
Emergency Economic Stabilization Act
    of 2008, 129
emotional cycle, 133
enthusiasm stage, 116, 117, 118, 119
entitlement process, 3, 88
entry-level buyers, 89, 90, 99
Equifax, 12
equity, 5, 6, 20, 21, 23, 24, 25, 26, 27,
    29, 35, 60, 61, 62, 67, 72, 89, 91, 96,
    105, 107, 111, 119, 122, 123, 125,
    131, 160, 161, 165, 167, 171, 173,
    181, 184, 186, 187, 193, 194
equity tranche, 61, 62
equivalent rents, 31, 49
exotic financing, 5, 9, 75, 80, 81, 87,
    101, 124, 132, 144, 145, 146, 159,
    160, 167, 170
Experian, 12

INDEX

End Notes

[1] "Out, out, brief candle! Life's but a walking shadow, a poor player that struts and frets his hour upon the stage and then is heard no more: it is a tale told by an idiot, full of sound and fury, signifying nothing." Macbeth Quote (Act V, Scene V). (Shakespeare, 1603)

[2] Partial list of prominent real estate bubble and related blogs:

The Irvine Housing Blog – http://www.irvinehousingblog.com/
Patrick.net – http://patrick.net/housing/crash.html
The Real Estate Bubble Blog – http://www.thehousingbubbleblog.com/index.html
The House Bubble – http://housebubble.com/
Implode-o-meter – http://ml-implode.com/
Bubble Markets Inventory Tracking – http://bubbletracking.blogspot.com/
Housing Doom – http://housingdoom.com/
Southern California Real Estate Bubble Crash – http://www.socalbubble.com/
Calculated Risk – http://calculatedrisk.blogspot.com/
Housing Panic – http://housingpanic.blogspot.com/
Professor Piggington – http://piggington.com/
Dr. Housing Bubble – http://drhousingbubble.blogspot.com/
Bubble Meter – http://bubblemeter.blogspot.com/
The Real Estate Bloggers – http://www.therealestatebloggers.com/
Housing Bubble Casualty – http://www.housingbubblecasualty.com/
Housing Bubble Bust – http://www.housingbubblebust.com/
Real Estate Realist – http://www.realestaterealist.com/
Housing Wire – http://www.housingwire.com/
Sacramento Area Flippers In Trouble – http://flippersintrouble.blogspot.com/
Seattle Bubble – http://seattlebubble.com/blog/
Westside Bubble Blog – http://westside-bubble.blogspot.com/
Marin Real Estate Bubble – http://marinrealestatebubble.blogspot.com/
Sonoma Housing Bubble – http://sonomahousingbubble.blogspot.com/
New Jersey Real Estate Report – http://njrereport.com/
New York City Housing Bubble – http://nychousingbubble.blogspot.com/

[3] Much of the author's personal study of Buddhism comes from the writings and recordings of the author Jack Kornfield (Kornfield, The Roots of Buddhist Psychology, 1996), (Kornfield, The Inner Art of Meditation, 1993), (Kornfield, A Path with Heart: A Guide Through the Perils and Promises of Spiritual Life, 1993), (Kornfield, After the Ecstasy, the Laundry: How the Heart Grows Wise on the Spiritual Path, 2000). The audio recordings of the Roots of Buddhist Psychology have been particularly influential.

[4] The stock market experienced a 500% gain in a five year period before its infamous crash. Much of the reason for the wild increase in pricing was very low margin requirements. People were allowed to buy 10 times as much stock as they had money due to 10:1 margin trading. This expansion of credit through the broker's margin is what drove prices up, and when prices started to fall, margin calls cascaded through the market and resulted in a crash.

[5] Robert Shiller in his book Irrational Exuberance (Shiller, Irrational Exuberance, 2005) discusses precipitating factors at length from pages 31 -54. Most of the factors he mentions are macro-factors or more specifically related to the stock market.

[6] According to data from the US Census Bureau and The US Department of Labor, wage growth since 1976 has averaged 4.62% and inflation has averaged 4.42%.

[7] From 2002-2006 in Irvine, California, the median house price increased by an amount *each year* equal to the median income.

[8] Karl Case and Robert Shiller noted that a buyer's willingness to pay high prices depended in part on their perception of risk of price decline (Case & Shiller, The Behavior of Home Buyers in Boom and Post-Boom Markets, 1988). Very few buyers in the markets they surveyed during the coastal boom of the late 1980s though prices could go down.

[9] Psychologists have noted narrative-based thinking is extremely important in human decision making (Shiller, Historic Turning Points in Real Estate, 2007). When realtors or anyone working in sales creates a compelling narrative, it is very effective in motivating buyers.

[10] The author could not find the source for the widely cited quote from Irving Fisher where he said, "Stock prices have reached what looks like a permanently high plateau." It is held as the standard for incorrect market prognostications.

[11] Robert Shiller has noted there is a tendency among investors to overestimate how unique an investment they favor is. These investors fail to take into account the supply response to higher prices (Shiller, Understanding Recent Trends in House Prices and Home Ownership, 2007). Supply shortages are never permanent. The ends of booms are almost always associated with an unexpected glut of supply. Also, the idea of there being "not enough land" was cited in surveys going back to 1988 (Case & Shiller, The Behavior of Home Buyers in Boom and Post-Boom Markets, 1988).

[12] William Jaeger studied the issue of land use control limiting local housing supply in his paper The Effects of Land-Use Regulations on Property Values (Jaeger, 2006). His conclusions are as follows: "Land-use regulations can affect property values in a variety of complex ways. In the context of laws like Oregon's Measure 37, requiring that landowners be compensated if regulations reduce property values, the economic effects of land use regulations on property values have been widely misinterpreted because two very different economic concepts are being confused and used interchangeably. The first concept is "the effect of a land use regulation on property values" which measures the change in value when a regulation is added to many parcels. The second concept is "the effect of an individual exemption, or variance, to an existing land use regulation," which measures the change in value when a regulation is removed from only one parcel. The effect of a land-use regulation on property values can be positive or negative, whereas removing a land-use regulation from one property can be expected to have a positive effect. Indeed, many land-use regulations actually increase property values by creating positive "amenity effects" and "scarcity effects. "As a result of these differences, a positive estimate for removing a land-use regulation cannot be interpreted as proof that the other concept was negative. Despite this, a positive value for an individual exemption to a land-use regulation continues to be interpreted as proof that compensation is due under Oregon's Measure 37. Indeed, this mistaken interpretation may be partly responsible for public sentiment that land-use regulations tend to reduce property values."

[13] In the paper, Asset Price Bubble in Japan in the 1980s: Lessons for Financial and Macroeconomic Stability (Shiratsuka, 2003), the author reached the following conclusion, "Japan's experience of asset price bubble is characterized by euphoria, that is, excessively optimistic expectations with respect to future economic fundamentals, which lasted for several years and then burst. Under such circumstances, policymakers are unlikely to take an appropriate policy response without evaluating whether asset price hikes are euphoric or not, and forecast a correct path for the potential growth rate. In so doing, it is deemed important to assess the sustainability of financial and macroeconomic stability." The paper is more history than analysis, but it provides a good background understanding of the Japanese housing and stock market bubble.

[14] Karl Case and Robert Shiller mentioned a report in the Harvard Business Review that spoke of businesses in boom regions were unable to attract labor due to the high cost of housing. (Case & Shiller, The Behavior of Home Buyers in Boom and Post-Boom Markets, 1988)

[15] Karl Case and Robert Shiller noted (Case & Shiller, Is There a Bubble in the Housing Market, 2004) overwhelming agreement with the statement "Housing prices have boomed in [city] because lots of people want to live here." Another recurring idea in the "everyone wants to live here" meme is the "rich Asians are buying." This fallacy is promoted in every real estate bubble. (Case & Shiller, The Behavior of Home Buyers in Boom and Post-Boom Markets, 1988)

---

[16] Michael Wolff wrote the book Burn Rate: How I Survived the Gold Rush Years on the Internet (Wolff, 1998) describing the strange investor behavior of the internet startup era.

[17] Robert Shiller's surveys have demonstrated most home purchasers have little real knowledge or agreement about the underlying causes of price rallies. Most would cite clichés, images or popular fallacies rather than hard evidence or analysis of data with correspondence to prices. (Case & Shiller, The Behavior of Home Buyers in Boom and Post-Boom Markets, 1988)

[18] Stated-Income Loans also known as "liar loans" were widespread during the bubble. People frequently fabricated their income.

[19] One of the more interesting phenomenon observed in the scholarly literature during a financial bubble is the number of analysts who look at the data and are unable to form an objective opinion about what the data shows them. In the paper Bubbles, Human Judgment, and Expert Opinion (Shiller, Bubbles, Human Judgment, and Expert Opinion, 2001), Robert Shiller examines this phenomenon. In his introduction he noted, "There are many who have been arguing in effect that the market (or major components of it) has been undergoing a bubble. It would seem that it is essential to their notion of a bubble that investors' actions are, in one way or another, foolish. Others sharply disagree with these bubble stories, and it is precisely this intimation of foolishness that seems to bother them. It seems to them just implausible that investors at large have been foolish." The tone of many of the journal articles seems rather defensive and dismissive of the idea of a bubble even when the evidence is clear. One can surmise this tone is the result of the "foolishness" Dr. Shiller describes. In his conclusion he writes, "human patterns of less-than-perfectly rational behavior are central to financial market behavior, even among investment profession-als, while at the same time there is little outright foolishness among investors. It is hard for writers in the news media, who describe financial markets, to convey the nature of any essential irrationality, since they cannot all review the relevant social science literature in their news article. They are left with punchy references to pop psychology that may serve to discredit them in many eyes. That is part of the reason why we have been left with a sense of strong public disagreement about the nature of speculative bubbles." It is amazing to this author how so many academics along with the general public can completely miss financial bubbles and deny their existence past the point where it is obvious to everyone. Ben Stein was the poster child for this behavior during the Great Housing Bubble. One of the scholarly references showing this dismissal of the obvious is The great turn-of-the-century housing boom (Fisher & Quayyum, 2005) by Jonas D. M. Fisher and Saad Quayyum. In it they reach the following completely erroneous conclusion right at the peak of the bubble, "To the extent that the quantities can be understood by considering the underlying economic fundamentals, such as productivity growth and the evolution of the mortgage market, then the recent growth in house prices is probably not due to excessive speculation in the housing market, such as occurs in a bubble. We argue that our findings point toward the high prices being driven by fundamentals." Even at the very peak of the insanity, there are well-educated market observers that miss the signs or believe the fallacies which serve to inflate the bubble.

[20] Alan Greenspan made the following statements at the Credit Union National Association 2004 Governmental Affairs Conference, "Indeed, recent research within the Federal Reserve suggests that many homeowners might have saved tens of thousands of dollars had they held adjustable-rate mortgages rather than fixed-rate mortgages during the past decade, though this would not have been the case, of course, had interest rates trended sharply upward. American homeowners clearly like the certainty of fixed mortgage payments. This preference is in striking contrast to the situation in some other countries, where adjustable-rate mortgages are far more common and where efforts to introduce American-type fixed-rate mortgages generally have not been successful. Fixed-rate mortgages seem unduly expensive to households in other countries. One possible reason is that these mortgages effectively charge homeowners high fees for protection against rising interest rates and for the right to refinance. American consumers might benefit if lenders provided greater mortgage product alternatives to the traditional fixed-rate mortgage. To the degree that households are driven by fears of payment shocks but are willing to manage their own interest rate risks, the traditional fixed-rate mortgage may be an expensive method of financing a home." It is a good thing Alan Greenspan was our central banker and not a financial adviser. Many people who "benefited" from the mortgage product alternatives lost their homes in foreclosure. There is a reason homeowners like fixed-rate mortgages. How exactly are borrowers supposed to "manage their own interest rate risks" without using fixed-rate mortgages? Perhaps if Alan Greenspan had thought that statement through, his advice might have been different. Daniel Gross wrote about the folly of this speech in his weekly column on the internet magazine Slate (Gross, Alan Greenspan: ARMed and Dangerous, 2004). Mr. Gross noted the following, "Greenspan also conspicuously ignored the non-monetary benefits associated with fixed-rate mortgages. Homebuyers pay a premium for the ability to lock in a fixed interest rate – and hence have utter certainty on the size of

their payment for up to three decades. But in return, they receive peace of mind, security, and the ability to plan."

[21] According to Credit Suisse, the average credit score for Alt-A borrowers was 717 and for subprime borrowers it was 646.

[22] There was a steep rise in prices in California and selected large metropolitan areas of the East Coast during 1987, 1988 and 1989. This was followed by a 7 year period of slowly declining prices as fundamentals caught up. This is considered by some to be a bubble because prices showed a detachment from fundamentals and a later return to the former relationship. This "bubble" did not see capitulatory selling, so it did not show the behavior of classic asset bubbles.

[23] A study by Consumer Federation of America's Allen J. Fishbein Piggyback Loans at the Trough: California Subprime Home Purchase and Refinance Lending in 2006 (Fishbein, Piggyback Loans at the Trough: California Subprime Home Purchase and Refinance Lending in 2006, 2008), reveals the following "1.26 million home purchase and refinance loans in California metropolitan areas in 2006 and found about one sixth of California home purchase borrowers taking out single, first lien mortgages and one quarter of refinance borrowers received subprime loans in 2006. The subprime mortgage market provides loans to borrowers who do not meet the credit standard for prime loans. To compensate for the increased risk of offering loans to borrowers with weaker credit, lenders charge subprime borrowers higher interest rates – and thus higher monthly payments – than prime borrowers. California has historically had lower rates of subprime lending than the national average, but the rates of subprime lending crept up in 2006. Additionally, more than a third of California home purchase borrowers also utilized a second "piggyback" loan on top of a primary, first lien mortgage. Piggyback loans combine a primary mortgage with a second lien home equity loan, allowing borrowers to finance more than 80 percent of the home's value without private mortgage insurance. These borrowers took out loans on as much as 100 percent of the value of the home in 2006. More than half these piggyback borrowers received subprime loans on their primary mortgages. Many subprime loans are adjustable rate mortgages (ARMs) that reset to higher interest rates after the first two years, meaning that homeowners that received subprime purchase or refinance mortgages in 2006 are likely to see their interest rates and monthly payments increase – in many cases significantly – in 2008. Moreover, as real estate markets cool and decline, borrowers that utilized piggyback financing could find themselves owing more on their mortgage than their homes are worth." An earlier related study, Exotic or Toxic? An Examination of the Non-Traditional Mortgage Market for Consumers and Lenders (Fishbein & Woodall, Exotic or Toxic? An Examination of the Non-Traditional Mortgage Market for Consumers and Lenders, 2006) by Allen J. Fishbein and Patrick Woodall also sounded the alarm concerning exotic financing.

[24] This data comes from the Credit Suisse Report (Credit Suisse, 2007). The source of their data was Loan Performance.

[25] The impact of exotic mortgage terms was explored by Matthew S. Chambers, Carlos Garriga and Don Schlagenhauf in the paper Mortgage Contracts and Housing Tenure Decisions (Chambers, Garriga, & Schlagenhauf, 2007). Their abstract reads as follows, "We find that different types of mortgage contracts influence these decisions through three dimensions: the downpayment constraint, the payment schedule, and the amortization schedule. Contracts with lower downpayment requirements allow younger and lower income households to enter the housing market earlier. Mortgage contracts with increasing payment schedules increase the participation of first-time buyers, but can generate lower homeownership later in the life cycle. We find that adjusting the amortization schedule of a contract can be important. Mortgage contracts which allow the quick accumulation of home equity increase homeownership across the entire life cycle." The cold reality of negative amortization loans is summed up in the observation that increasing payment schedules decrease home ownership over time. People default when their payments go up. It is the fatal flaw of all these loan programs. One of the more amusing papers from the bubble was written by James Peterson (Peterson, 2005) "Designer Mortgages: The Boom in Nontraditional Mortgage Loans May Be a Double-Edged Sword. So Far, Most Banks Have Moved Cautiously." The lenders during the Great Housing Bubble were anything but cautious.

[26] This data comes from the Credit Suisse Report (Credit Suisse, 2007). The source of their data was Loan Performance.

[27] This data comes from the Credit Suisse Report (Credit Suisse, 2007). The source of their data was Mortgage Asset Research Institute.

[28] Anecdotal evidence indicates the practice of fabricating loan application income was common. There were a few high-profile arrests, as is always the case with this kind of phenomenon. As of the early 2008, no

definitive studies have been undertaken to assess how widespread was the practice of intentionally fabricating loan application data by mortgage brokers.

[29] Payments to investors from collateralized debt obligations were actually made by the servicer. If the borrower failed to make payments, the servicer would make them to the investor. When the loan was discharged through sale, the servicer would then recoup the money, plus interest, on any payments made on behalf of the borrower.

[30] (Libby, Libby, & Short, 2004)

[31] Numerous reports have been compiled on the savings adequacy of Americans. In the report Lifetime Earnings, Social Security Benefits, and the Adequacy of Retirement Wealth Accumulation by Eric M. Engen, William G. Gale, Cori E. Uccello (Engen, Gale, & Uccello, 2004), the authors detail the savings patters on various generations preparing for retirement.

[32] Robert Shiller constructed a graph of housing prices from 1890-2005 for the book Irrational Exuberance (Shiller, Irrational Exuberance, 2005). The rate of appreciation during this 115 year time period is 0.7% over the rate of inflation. The data from the US Census Bureau shows a 2.0% increase over inflation since 1940, however much of this increase was during the baby boom right after WWII and it does not reflect the improvement in house quality during this time. The 0.7% statistic is referenced a number of times in this work.

[33] Robert Shiller titled his groundbreaking book Irrational Exuberance (Shiller, Irrational Exuberance, 2005) after a phrase in a speech given by Alan Greenspan, FED chairman from 1986-2006, in a speech at the Annual Dinner and Francis Boyer Lecture of The American Enterprise Institute for Public Policy Research, Washington, D.C., December 5, 1996 (Greenspan, The Challenge of Central Banking in a Democratic Society, 1996). The term "irrational exuberance" is used synonymously in this writing to describe the behavior of buyers in creating an asset price bubble.

[34] Human nature being what it is, another real estate bubble will form unless measures are taken to prevent one. The projections of how long it will take markets to recover vary depending on the variables analyzed. Later chapters explore this question in detail.

[35] Joe Vitale in his book There's a Customer Born Every Minute: P.T. Barnum's Secrets to Business Success (Vitale, 1998) disputes the contention that PT Barnum ever uttered the phrase with which he is credited.

[36] The conclusion of the paper Subprime Refinancing: Equity Extraction and Mortgage Termination (Chomsisengphet & Pennington-Cross, 2006) is as follows, "Consistent with survey evidence the propensity to extract equity while refinancing is sensitive to interest rates on other forms of consumer debt. After the loan is originated, our results indicate that cash-out refinances perform differently from non-cash-out refinances. For example, cash-outs are less likely to default or prepay, and the termination of cash-outs is more sensitive to changing interest rates and house prices." The sensitivity to changes in interest rates is not surprising as borrowers will take the money if it is a good deal, and they will repay it when the deal is less favorable. The observation that these loans have lower default rates and are less likely to be paid back early is quite surprising. This may have been an artifact of the bubble rally, and future data may show these loans do not perform as well as in previous years.

[37] Robert Shiller wrote a paper on Household Reactions to Changes in Housing Wealth (Shiller, Household Reaction to Changes in Housing Wealth, 2004). He reached no definitive conclusions concerning the reactions to households to increasing home prices. At the time of his writing, the bubble was inflated enough to be obvious to him, and he does mention the bubble and its potential problems. The impact of mortgage equity withdrawal had not reached absurd height in early 2004, but by 2006, the pattern of household spending had become fairly obvious. In 2007 Oxford professor John Muellbauer wrote Housing, Credit and Consumer Expenditures (Muellbauer, 2007). His conclusion is that the spending "wealth effect" was insignificant in the past due to more restrictive credit policies which limited access to home equity (financial prudence on the part of lenders.) After the "liberalization" of credit markets and the dramatic increase in prices of the housing bubble, the consumer spending brought about by the wealth effect became pronounced. The wealth effect observed in the Great Housing Bubble was much larger than the wealth effect of the stock market bubble which preceded, and the effect was twice as large in the United States as it was in Great Britain.

[38] There is a lack of scholarly studies on the financial results of home improvement projects (Baker & Kaul, 2002). Builder behavior is often revelatory of the state of the market. In most markets new home builders do not put in rear yard landscaping because they are not able to obtain a return on the investment. Also, the fact that builders have multitudes of upgrade options from a base package indicates the premium finishes do not provide a market return unless specifically requested by a purchaser. Builders can profit in that circumstance.

217

[39] The evidence of consistent refinancing is anecdotal, but it is reinforced by national statistical trends from the US Governments Flow of Funds accounting.

[40] In the paper (Leamer, Housing Is the Business Cycle, 2007), the author has graphs showing the loss of manufacturing jobs after the recession of 2001.

[41] (Gibbon, 1999)

[42] In the paper Innovations in Mortgage Markets and Increased Spending on Housing (Doms & Krainer, Innovations in Mortgage Markets and Increased Spending on Housing, 2007), Mark Doms and John Krainer document how financial innovation helped facilitate the housing bubble. Their abstract is as follows: "Innovations in the mortgage market since the mid-1990s have effectively reduced a number of financing constraints. Coinciding with these innovations, we document a significant change in the propensity for households to own their homes, as well as substantial increases in the share of household income devoted to housing. These changes in housing expenditures are especially large for those groups that faced the greatest financial constraints, and are robust across the changing composition of households and their geographic location. We present evidence that young, constrained households may have used newly designed mortgages to finance their increased expenditures on housing." Notice the "innovation" reduced financing constraints. This is the definition of loose credit. They also note the increase in home ownership and the increase in debt-to-income ratios. The latter is a telltale sign of a housing market bubble. The exotic loans tended to be concentrated in younger households who used to be excluded from the housing market due to lack of downpayments and insufficient income. Basically, exotic loans were given to persons who were not ready for home ownership, and the high default rates among this group should not have been a surprise.

[43] In response to the dramatic increase in subprime delinquencies in 2007, the Federal Reserve Bank of San Francisco commissioned a report on Subprime Mortgage Delinquency Rates (Doms, Furlong, & Krainer, Subprime Mortgage Delinquency Rates, 2007). The report's conclusions were as follows: "First, the riskiness of the subprime borrowing pool may have increased. Second, pockets of regional economic weakness may have helped push a larger proportion of subprime borrowers into delinquency. Third, for a variety of reasons, the recent history of local house price appreciation and the degree of house price deceleration may have affected delinquency rates on subprime mortgages. While we find a role for all three candidate explanations, patterns in recent house price appreciation are far and away the best single predictor of delinquency levels and changes in delinquencies. Importantly, after controlling for the current level of house price appreciation, measures of house price deceleration remain significant predictors of changes in subprime delinquencies. The results point to a possible role for changes in house price expectations for explaining changes in delinquencies." In later sections the relationship between default rates and default losses is explored. When prices decline, default losses increase because lenders get less money from the collateral in a foreclosure. This report from the FRBSF demonstrates that lenders also face higher default rates, probably due to borrowers "giving up" when they owe more on their mortgage than their house is worth. These two phenomenon have a negative synergy. In a related report by Kristopher Gerardi, Adam Hale Shapiro, and Paul S. Willen titled Subprime Outcomes: Risky Mortgages, Homeownership Experiences, and Foreclosures (Gerardi, Shapiro, & Willen, 2007), the authors make the following observations, "First, homeownerships that begin with a subprime purchase mortgage end up in foreclosure almost 20 percent of the time, or more than 6 times as often as experiences that begin with prime purchase mortgages. Second, house price appreciation plays a dominant role in generating foreclosures. In fact, we attribute most of the dramatic rise in Massachusetts foreclosures during 2006 and 2007 to the decline in house prices that began in the summer of 2005."

[44] In the paper Unskilled and Unaware of It: How Difficulties in Recognizing One's Own Incompetence Lead to Inflated Self-Assessments (Kruger & Dunning, 1999), the authors noted the tendency of individuals to overestimate their own competence and abilities. Their primary conclusion is as follows "People tend to hold overly favorable views of their abilities in many social and intellectual domains. The authors suggest that this overestimation occurs, in part, because people who are unskilled in these domains suffer a dual burden: Not only do these people reach erroneous conclusions and make unfortunate choices, but their incompetence robs them of the metacognitive ability to realize it." It is a perfect description of the general public and their relationship to complex financial agreements like Option ARMs.

[45] The author is a believer in the Austrian School of Economics. Two of the sources of research and understanding on the credit cycle are The Hedge Fund Edge: Maximum Profit / Minimum Risk Global Trend Trading Strategies (Boucher, 1999), and Money, Bank Credit, and Economic Cycles (Soto, 2006).

[46] There are a number of research papers discussing the pros and cons of various methodologies for calculating equivalent rent. Hedonic Estimates of the Cost of Housing Services: Rental and Owner-

Occupied Units (Crone & Nakamura, 2004) Treatment of Owner-Occupied Housing in the CPI (Poole, Ptacek, & Verbrugge, 2005).

47 Robert Shiller noted "that real owners' equivalent rent and real building costs track each other fairly well, as one might expect. But neither of them tracks real home prices at all, suggesting that some other factor – I will argue market psychology – plays an important role in determining home prices."

48 Depending on the market, rental rates grow at a rate around 1% over the rate of inflation. Rental rates are closely aligned with income growth, and in markets where income growth is strong, rental rates increase at approximately the same rate.

49 John Krainer, chief economist for the Federal Reserve Bank of San Francisco, pointed out in 2004 "The price-rent ratio for the U.S. and many regional markets is now much higher than its historical average value." (Krainer & Wei, House Prices and Fundamental Value, 2004) This is one of the first papers (other than those by Robert Shiller) to recognize the data was pointing to a housing bubble.

50 The full text of the Proposition 13 law can be found at http://www.leginfo.ca.gov/.const/.article_13A

51 In California, the first half of regular secured property tax bills are due November 1st, and delinquent after December 10th; the second half are due February 1st, and delinquent after April 10th each year. If the delinquent date falls on a Saturday, Sunday, or government holiday, then the due date is the following business day.

52 All information regarding tax rates comes from the Internal Revenue Service. http://www.irs.gov/

53 There are many studies that have mentioned the use of price-to-rent ratios as being similar to price-to-earnings ratios of stocks. Some of the studies are good, and some are not. Bubble, bubble, toil and trouble is of the latter variety (Haines & Rosen, 2006). Typical of these studies is that they will look at the data, see the obvious signs of a bubble, and proceed to dismiss the obvious as something else. Even though the national data for price-to-rent clearly shows a bubble, even in their own graphs, the authors dismiss the idea because "all real estate is local." The paper was written for the Federal Reserve, but it could have been written for the National Association of Realtors. Another silly statement they make is "Thus, what appears to be a bubble in some markets might just be a reflection of normally high volatility in those markets." This is like saying "what appears to be a bubble isn't a bubble because bubbles are normal in these markets." When the authors can look right at the data and not understand what they are seeing, there is little hope the paper will draw the right conclusions.

54 The study A Trend and Variance Decomposition of the Rent-Price Ratio in Housing Markets by Sean D. Campbell, Morris A. Davis, Joshua Gallin, and Robert F. Martin (Campbell, Davis, Gallin, & Martin, 2005) uses method of estimating the investment premium people pay for homes in bubble markets based on the expectation of future rental growth. This entire approach is flawed as it assumes people are investing based on cash flows. This would be a rational approach, but most people who buy in financial manias know little or nothing about cashflow or how to value it. The real reason they are "investing" is to capture speculative price changes. Trying to determine a fundamental valuation based on cashflow is an interesting exercise in math and statistics, but it completely fails to capture the real motivation behind buyers in the marketplace.

55 In the article "Are CAP Rates Still a Valid Indicator of Value?" (Hockley, 2005), the author noted "On the West Coast, California investors have driven the price of investments to levels never before seen. California CAP rates are hovering between 4 percent and 7 percent, even with no or low increases in rent. Investors are betting on appreciation gains."

56 Robert Shiller has been studying homebuyer behavior since the late 1980s. His surveys have consistently show the general public believes houses will appreciate in value at more than double their recorded historical rate.

57 The 1.4% rate of house price appreciation over the rate of inflation is based on the US Census Bureau measurement of house price and the US Department of Labor's Consumer Price Index.

58 In their paper Loss Aversion in Riskless Choice: A Reference-Dependent Model (Tversky & Kahneman, 1991), the authors discuss the premise that losses and disadvantages have greater impact on preferences than gains and advantages. This explains much of the unusual behavior of sellers in price declines.

59 Many in the academic community do not seem to understand the true nature of land prices. In their paper The Price of Residential Land in Large U.S. Cities (Davis & Palumbo, 2006) Morris A. Davis; Michael G. Palumbo talk about residential land prices as being a determinant of house prices rather than the other way around. This mistake concerning the valuation of land is prevalent in the general public, but it is surprising to see academics continue to respond to this fallacy.

[60] The author has worked with many builders in Southern California. At one time, the author shared an office with the former Division President of Taylor Woodrow Homes who at the time was the President of the Orange County Building Industry Association. The $85 SF is anecdotal, but it is a reliable number from multiple sources.

[61] There were numerous news stories in 2007 of impairment charges from various national builders.

[62] The Village of Woodbury information can be found on the Irvine Company website: http://www.villagesofirvine.com/VILLAGES-AND-RESIDENCES/Woodbury-Overview.aspx

[63] The author was involved with the analysis of a project that was purchased as raw land for $10,000,000 in 2001 in Riverside County, California. The owner sold the project to a major homebuilder in three phases in 2004 and 2005 for a total of $95,000,000.

[64] Most participants in the housing market believe changes in interest rates are responsible for changes in housing prices (Case & Shiller, The Behavior of Home Buyers in Boom and Post-Boom Markets, 1988). There is actually very little correlation between interest rates and house prices. Interest rates are very important for determining the amount a borrower can obtain in a loan, but other factors are more critical to determining the actual price of real estate.

[65] Most of the technical data on the secondary market found in this section comes from the paper Fussing and Fuming over Fannie and Freddie: How Much Smoke, How Much Fire? (Frame & White, 2005). Another paper with excellent historical background on the evolution of the secondary mortgage market is The Housing Finance Revolution (Green & Wachter, 2007) by Richard Green and Susan Wachter. Perhaps the finest overview of the functioning of the secondary mortgage market with respect to subprime is Understanding the Securitization of Subprime Mortgage Credit by Adam B. Ashcraft and Til Schuermann (Ashcraft & Schuermann, 2008).

[66] In the paper Who Holds the Toxic Waste? An Investigation of CMO Holdings (Haubrich & Lucas, 2006), the authors provide a good background on the CMO (CDO by another name) market. Their analysis of who holds the bad paper is suspect due to lack of data. Also, many "insurers" were not insurance companies. These were private, unregulated firms who often had little financial ability to make good on their obligations.

[67] (Soros, 1994)

[68] (Burdekin & Siklos, 2004)

[69] Even if a homeowner's house is worth less than the mortgage, there is still option value in the property. If the homeowners is not far underwater, it may not take much time for values to return and provide them with equity in the property.

[70] Robert Shiller's surveys of market attitudes in 1989 showed 95% of respondents in the bubble markets of San Francisco and Orange County said they thought of their purchase as an investment at least in part. Also, the tendency to view housing as an investment is a defining characteristic of a housing bubble (Case & Shiller, Is There a Bubble in the Housing Market, 2004). Since housing bubbles portend of disastrous declines, the investment motive as a risk to CDOs is very real.

[71] FHA Guidelines for appraisals only require the use of the income approach for income producing properties.

[72] Real Estate prices in California have bubbled 3 times since the 1970s. After prices peaked in the late 70s and then again in the late 80s, prices declined until they came back into alignment with historic fundamental valuations. This is strong confirmation of the theory of buyers waiting for rental equivalence before purchasing when prices drop.

[73] The Dutch tulip bulb mania was documented in the book Extraordinarily Popular Delusions and the Madness of Crowds (Mackay, Vega, & Fridson, 1996). The activities associated with the tulip mania have long been held as the archetype of a speculative bubble. Peter Garber in his paper Tulipmania (Garber, 1989) lays out the case that speculation in the Dutch tulip market in 1634-1637 was not necessarily irrational exuberance. He draws these conclusions based on the similar behavior of modern agricultural markets for rare flowers. The assumption behind his conclusions is that modern markets do not display symptoms of irrational exuberance which is highly suspect. Markets dealing with very rare commodities are always subject to wild price swings due to irrational exuberance because the commodity in question truly is rare. This plays to one of the central fallacies of irrational exuberance that the market is experiencing a severe shortage. Of course, like any market, even if the commodity is rare, if the demand is fickle and prone to irrational exuberance, there is a strong detachment from fundamental valuations due to excessive speculation.

[74] There are circumstances where FICO scores of responsible citizens may characterize them as subprime. Some people do not use credit or maintain credit lines. They are very responsible, but their credit scores would make them subprime. Also, people who go through divorce, illness, a job loss or some other financial problem may temporarily become subprime. Responsible citizens who become subprime can generally recover their FICO scores in a short period of time. In fact, the original business plan for subprime was based on this idea.

[75] There were some valiant attempts during the bubble to determine if the price increases really were a bubble. The literature of the time almost universally missed it despite the obvious signs in the data. In the paper Assessing High House Prices: Bubbles, Fundamentals, and Misperceptions (Himmelberg, Mayer, & Sinai, 2005) the authors used almost the same approach to the analysis presented in this writing and reached the opposite conclusion, "As of the end of 2004, our analysis reveals little evidence of a housing bubble. In high appreciation markets like San Francisco, Boston, and New York, current housing prices are not cheap, but our calculations do not reveal large price increases in excess of fundamentals." By the end of 2004, the data was unambiguously in support of a financial bubble. One of the few authors who recognized the problems early on was John Krainer an economist with the Federal Reserve Board of San Francisco (Krainer, House Price Bubbles, 2003).

[76] Jordan Rappaport provides an overview of the various methods of house price measurement in A Guide to Aggregate House Price Measures (Rappaport, 2006).

[77] In the paper A Note on the Differences between the OFHEO and S&P/Case-Shiller House Price Indexes by Andrew Leventis (Leventis, 2007), the author makes the following observation: "OFHEO's House Price Indexes (the "HPI") and home price indexes produced by S&P/Case-Shiller are constructed using the same basic methodology. Both use the repeat-valuations framework initially proposed in the 1960s and later enhanced by Karl Case and Robert Shiller. Important differences between the indexes remain, however. The two models use different data sources and implement the mechanics of the basic algorithm in distinct ways."

[78] Praveen Kujal and Vernon L. Smith noticed an interesting phenomenon in the studies of perceptions of fairness in their paper (Kujal & Smith, Fairness and Short Run Price Adjustment in Posted Offer Markets, 2003), "perceptions of fairness cause people to resist price increases following abrupt changes in conditions with no cost justification. Fairness is thus interpreted as being a result of expectations that are not sustainable." This implies that people have an intuitive sense that nothing is justifying the dramatic increase in prices during a bubble rally. There is no perception of fairness because houses are not any better, nor are houses any more expensive to build. The increase in prices has no justification in cost. Carl Case and Robert Shiller also noticed the same behavior among sellers in financial manias who felt guilty that the buyer paid so much (Case & Shiller, The Behavior of Home Buyers in Boom and Post-Boom Markets, 1988).

[79] In the paper Are House Prices the Next "Bubble?" (McCarthy & Peach, 2004) the authors completely missed the implications of the rising price-to-income ratio. Some amount of the increase in price (less than 50%) nationally can be attributed to lower interest rates. The authors make the statement, "The marked upturn in home prices is largely attributable to strong market fundamentals: Home prices have essentially moved in line with increases in family income and declines in nominal mortgage interest rates." An analysis of the impact on lower interest rates on actual payments and debt-to-income ratios would have revealed their conclusion erroneous, but no such analysis was undertaken. In the paper (Gallin, The Long-Run Relationship between House Prices and Income: Evidence from Local Housing Markets, 2003) Joshua Gallin reaches the following, completely erroneous conclusion, "More formally, many in the housing literature argue that house prices and income are cointegrated. In this paper, I show that the data do not support this view. Standard tests using 27 years of national-level data do not find evidence of cointegration."

[80] The paper for the Federal Reserve Board by Joshua Gallin, (Gallin, The Long-Run Relationship between House Prices and Rents, 2004) demonstrates there is a relationship between these variables long term. What is interesting is the Mr. Gallin did not reach the same conclusion with respects to the relationship between house prices and income (Gallin, The Long-Run Relationship between House Prices and Income: Evidence from Local Housing Markets., 2006) despite the fact that rents and income track each other very closely.

[81] In the paper Housing: Boom or Bubble (Schiller, 2007), author Tim Schiller shows a chart on page 17 that looks very similar to the one in this work (He used a different data source, but the results were almost the same.) The chart shows the obvious sign of a massive housing bubble with prices showing a deviation in the price-to-rent relationship 5 times the previous high of the coastal bubble of the early 1990s. Despite the visual appearance of the chart, he goes on to say the rally in prices was supported by fundamentals.

221

Obviously, he was proven wrong. There is a history of scholarly papers on the price-to-income ratio that completely missed the housing bubble.

[82] Praveen Kujal and Vernon L. Smith noted in The Endowment Effect (Kujal & Smith, The Endowment Effect, 1991) that even small changes in the bid/ask spread results in a large decline in transaction volume.

[83] Robert Shiller noted that the causes of a major turning point signifying the popping of a real estate bubble are "fuzzy." (Shiller, Historic Turning Points in Real Estate, 2007) Any events associated with the end of a speculative bubble may be simply coincidental.

[84] Federal Reserve Chairman Ben Bernanke gave a speech (Bernanke B. , 2007) in front of the Joint Economic Committee of the U.S. Congress on March 28, 2007 when he claimed, "Although the turmoil in the subprime mortgage market has created severe financial problems for many individuals and families, the implications of these developments for the housing market as a whole are less clear. The ongoing tightening of lending standards, although an appropriate market response, will reduce somewhat the effective demand for housing, and foreclosed properties will add to the inventories of unsold homes. At this juncture, however, the impact on the broader economy and financial markets of the problems in the subprime market seems likely to be contained. In particular, mortgages to prime borrowers and fixed-rate mortgages to all classes of borrowers continue to perform well, with low rates of delinquency." In short, the FED Chairman completely missed the scale and scope of the problem. Either that, or he knew how bad the problem was and chose to lie for public relations impact.

[85] According to Credit Suisse, 80% of subprime loans were the 2/28 variety.

[86] The information on New Century Financial comes from their website.

[87] Studies have shown people feel less need to save when house prices are increasing in value (Baker D. , 2002).

[88] Social psychology is an important factor in the transmission of booms and speculative mania; however, the perception of this fact by market participants is not common. Most individuals attribute price increases to some fundamental factor whereas the actual price movements are driven mostly by mass psychology. (Case & Shiller, The Behavior of Home Buyers in Boom and Post-Boom Markets, 1988)

[89] Karl Case and Robert Shiller noted (Case & Shiller, Is There a Bubble in the Housing Market, 2004) 90% or more of households expected house prices to increase in the following year during price rallies. It is the expectation of 10-year appreciation that is most striking. Market participants in the coastal bubble markets expected a 10-year average annual increase of near 15%. This would mean a tripling of prices over a 10-year period.

[90] (Miles, 2004)

[91] In the paper Investor Psychology and Security Market Under- and Overreactions (Daniel, Hirshleifer, & Subrahmanyam, 1998), the authors document that investors have two biases which negatively impact their financial decisions: first, they have an overreliance on private information and analysis with regards to asset prices, and they have a biased self-attribution or belief in themselves that causes them to be overconfident in their investment outcomes. In short, people go into denial because they are overconfident about the direction of the trade.

[92] The best books for understanding the mindset of a professional trader are the books by author Mark Douglas (Douglas, The Disciplined Trader, Developing Winning Attitudes, 1990) and (Douglas, Trading in the Zone, 2000). He lays out the emotional issues of trading in great detail.

[93] (Mints, 2006) According to Victor Mints in his study of the Moscow housing market, the number of vacant houses held for sale by speculators showed the same pattern as the United States.

[94] In their paper Prospect Theory: an Analysis of Decision under Risk (Kahneman & Tversky, Prospect Theory: An Analysis of Decision under Risk, 1979), the authors note a tendency of people to overweight low probability events which contributes to the attractiveness of insurance and gambling. Toward the end of the rally of the Great Housing Bubble when prices stopped rising, it became apparent that a resurgent rally was not very likely; however, many still bought in anticipation of this rally because 100% financing was available and they tended to overweight the probability of a rally.

[95] In the paper Moral Hazard in Home Equity Conversion (Shiller & N.Weiss, Moral Hazard in Home Equity Conversion, 1998), Robert J. Shiller and Allan N.Weiss document the moral hazard issues in cash-out refinancing as follows "Home equity conversion as presently constituted or proposed usually does not deal well with the potential problem of moral hazard. Once homeowners know that the risk of poor market performance of their homes is borne by investors, they have an incentive to neglect to take steps to maintain the homes' values. They may thus create serious future losses for the investors." They miss

the most serious problem resulting in lender losses, the predatory "put" exercised by borrowers. There are clearly moral hazards in cash-out refinancing; they are even more severe than the ones documented in this paper.

96 The author has a difficult time believing that a God would intervene in a financial market based on the purchase of an idol. It is not surprising a superstition like this one would spring up once houses started to be traded more frequently. There are myths about the practice going back hundreds of years, but references to the practice only go back to the early 1980s – a time corresponding to the slump after the first California real estate bubble. http://www.snopes.com/luck/stjoseph.asp

97 Much of the history of the Efficient Markets theory is outlined in Robert Shiller's paper (Shiller, From Efficient Market Theory to Behavioral Finance, 2002), "The efficient markets theory reached the height of its dominance in academic circles around the 1970s. Faith in this theory was eroded by a succession of discoveries of anomalies, many in the 1980s, and of evidence of excess volatility of returns. Finance literature in this decade and after suggests a more nuanced view of the value of the efficient markets theory, and, starting in the 1990s, a blossoming of research on behavioral finance. Some important developments in the 1990s and recently include feedback theories, models of the interaction of smart money with ordinary investors, and evidence on obstacles to smart money." One of the groundbreaking papers of the early 1990s that influenced the change in economics thinking from efficient markets to behavioral finance was the work by David Porter and Vernon Smith (Porter & Smith, 1992) on Price Expectations in Experimental Asset Markets with Futures Contracting. In this paper, the authors demonstrated the volatility of returns was excessive as prices detached greatly from fundamental values and stayed detached for extended periods of time.

98 In the paper Anomalies: The Endowment Effect, Loss Aversion, and Status Quo Bias (Kahneman, Knetsch, & Thaler, The Endowment Effect, Loss Aversion, and Status Quo Bias, 1991), the authors, Daniel Kahneman, Jack L. Knetsch, and Richard H. Thaler, begin to lay the foundations for behavioral finance theory by documenting the many anomalies the efficient markets theory could not explain, "Economics can be distinguished from other social sciences by the belief that most (all?) behavior can be explained by assuming that agents have stable, well-defined preferences and make rational choices consistent with those preferences in markets that (eventually) clear. An empirical result qualifies as an anomaly if it is difficult to "rationalize," or if implausible assumptions are necessary to explain it within the paradigm."

99 In the paper Learning from the Behavior of Others: Conformity, Fads, and Informational Cascades (Bikhchandani, Hirshleifer, & Welch, 1998), the authors, Sushil Bikhchandani, David Hirshleifer and Ivo Welch, describe the phenomenon of herd behavior and observational learning. Much of human learning is accomplished through observation and imitation of others. This valuable survival skill results in the herd behavior observed in financial markets. It is the driving force behind the price-to-price feedback loop responsible for irrational exuberance.

100 In House Prices, Fundamentals and Bubbles (Black, Fraser, & Hoesli, 2006), the behavior of momentum investors is characterized as evidence against rationality in the marketplace. For the typical amateur speculator this is certainly true, but for momentum traders who have learned how to buy and sell to profit from the momentum, it is a rational and profitable method of speculation.

101 In Risk and Return in the U.S. Housing Market: A Cross-Sectional Asset-Pricing Approach (Cannon, Miller, & Pandher, 2006), the authors noted a 10% increase in volatility with each 2.48% increase in annual returns. This strongly suggests bubble volatility occurs just because prices are rising.

102 An article in Real Estate Journal.com
(http://www.realestatejournal.com/buysell/markettrends/20050106-capell.html) from the Greed stage in the bubble anecdotally documents properties selling for over list and realtors telling clients to write emotional letters to sellers (Capell, 2004).

103 Karl Case and Robert Shiller noted (Case & Shiller, The Behavior of Home Buyers in Boom and Post-Boom Markets, 1988) that prices in the early 80s leveled off, but they did not decline at the conclusion of the first California housing bubble of the late 1970s. This convinced people that prices could not decline and that if they just waited long enough prices would come back. This belief caused people to bid up prices even higher in the coastal bubble of the late 1980s. When the decline of that bubble (25%) was forgotten, market participants inflated the Great Housing Bubble.

104 In Robert Shiller's studies, very few market participants said they would lower their prices until they found a buyer (Case & Shiller, The Behavior of Home Buyers in Boom and Post-Boom Markets, 1988).

105 (Orwell, 1950)

---

[106] Vernon L. Smith noted in Human Nature: An Economic Perspective that "We should all love rich people, because they consume such a small percentage of their accumulation, leaving almost all of it to work in the economy and make the rest of us better off." (Smith, Human Nature: An Economic Perspective, 2004)

[107] Newspapers frequently print stories of lottery winners who spent all their winnings or were unhappy after the windfall (Geary, 2002) (Sullivan, 2006).

[108] Karl Case and Robert Shiller noted (Case & Shiller, Is There a Bubble in the Housing Market, 2004) that Wisconsin had almost no volatility in the ratio of house price to income whereas the coastal bubble markets have price volatility where income only explains about half of the movement in price seen over longer terms.

[109] Median income information is available from the US Census Bureau: http://www.census.gov/hhes/www/income/income.html

[110] Median home sales price from US Census Bureau.

[111] Data for the California market is from DataQuick Information Systems and the California Association of Realtors.

[112] BusinessWeek wrote one of the finest articles on the mortgage problem in 2006. In it they reference the now infamous Map of Misery showing the distribution of Option ARMs throughout the United States. The source of their data is not given. The data presented in this work on the loans in Minnetonka, MN and Orange County, California, come from this map. Two of the most moronic lender statements of the housing bubble are in the article's final paragraph, "Analyst Frederick Cannon of Keefe Bruyette & Woods says most banks don't apologize for their option ARM businesses. 'Almost without exception everyone says [the option ARM] is a great loan, it's plenty regulated, and don't bug us,' he says. In an April letter to regulators, Cindy Manzettie, chief credit officer for Fifth Third Bank in Cincinnati, said it's not the 'lender's responsibility to help the consumer determine the appropriate payment option each month.... Paternalistic regulations that underestimate the intelligence of the American public do not work.'" Those statements are wrong on every point, but they do serve to illustrate the mindset of lenders during the bubble.

[113] Charles Ponzi was an Italian immigrant who arrived in the United States in 1903. He was a consummate schemer and tried numerous get-rich-quick schemes. He hit the con-man's jackpot in 1920 with a scheme involving international postal reply coupons. When the structure collapsed, Ponzi paid out all his gains and ended up penniless. He was sentenced to prison in 1921 for mail fraud. (Zuckoff, 2005)

[114] Hyman Minsky was a controversial economist of the late 20th century. He wrote extensively as a professor of economics at Washington University in St. Louis. (Minsky, Can "It" Happen Again? Essays on Instability and Finance, 1982) (Minsky, Stablizing an Unstable Economy, 2008) As the Great Housing Bubble began to deflate, the causes were readily identified in Minsky's work from decades earlier. His writings rose from obscurity and attained a new prominence due to his prescience.

[115] Todd Sinai in his paper, The Inequity of Subprime Mortgage Relief Programs (Sinai, 2008), documented the moral hazards involved with the various programs in the public forum of the time. He accurately characterized the problem as follows, "These programs may help some borrowers, but they do not bestow these benefits equitably. Some reward those who made riskier decisions over those who made prudent decisions, exclude those who live in states that experienced an early economic downturn, benefit those with high incomes at the expense of others, and spread the costs of the program among all taxpayers or future borrowers – regardless of whether they benefit from the proposals."

[116] The Hope Now Alliance website address is http://www.hopenow.com/.

[117] The Hope for Homeowners Act of 2008 was built on 5 principals: 1. Long-term affordability. The program is built on the idea, expressed by Federal Reserve Chairman Bernanke, that creating new equity for troubled homeowners is likely to be a more effective way to avoid foreclosures. New loans will be based on a family's ability to repay the loan, ensuring affordability and sustainable homeownership. 2. No investor or lender bailout. Investors and/or lenders will have to take significant losses in order to benefit from the proceeds of the loans refinanced with government insurance. However, these losses would be less than the losses associated with foreclosure. 3. No windfall for borrowers. Borrowers will share their new equity and future appreciation equally with FHA. Borrowers will pay for the FHA insurance. 4. Voluntary participation. This will be a voluntary program. No lenders, servicers, or investors will be compelled to participate. 5. Restore confidence, liquidity, and transparency. Credit markets are fearful and frozen in part because banks and other financial institutions do not know what their subprime mortgages and related securities are worth. The uncertainty is forcing lenders to hoard capital and stop

the lending necessary for economic growth. This program will help restore confidence and get markets flowing again.

[118] (Capra, 1946)

[119] Since real estate is associated with high transaction costs, heterogeneity and illiquidity, there is little opportunity for arbitrage (Black, Fraser, & Hoesli, 2006) (An investor cannot sell a house short.) These factors cause house prices to correct slowly without large numbers of foreclosures.

[120] Large variations in regional markets suggests the markets will deteriorate at different rates and at different times. (Baker D. , 2002) The extreme bubble markets of the coasts will deteriorate the most, and they may deteriorate the fastest due to the profusion of exotic financing.

[121] Rental data is from U.S. Department of Labor Bureau of Labor Statistics.

[122] Adam Posen wrote Why Central Banks Should Not Burst Bubbles. (Posen A. , 2006) His conclusions are as follows, "Central banks should not be in the business of trying to prick asset price bubbles. Bubbles generally arise out of some combination of irrational exuberance, technological jumps, and financial deregulation (with more of the second in equity price bubbles and more of the third in real estate booms). Accordingly, the connection between monetary conditions and the rise of bubbles is rather tenuous, and anything short of inducing a recession by tightening credit conditions prohibitively is unlikely to stem their rise. Even if a central bank were willing to take that one-in-three or less shot at cutting off a bubble, the cost-benefit analysis hardly justifies such preemptive action. The macroeconomic harm from a bubble bursting is generally a function of the financial system's structure and stability – in modern economies with satisfactory bank supervision, the transmission of a negative shock from an asset price bust is relatively limited, as was seen in the United States in 2002. However, where financial fragility does exist, as in Japan in the 1990s, the costs of inducing a recession go up significantly, so the relative disadvantages of monetary preemption over letting the bubble run its course mount. In the end, there is no monetary substitute for financial stability, and no market substitute for monetary ease during severe credit crunch. These two realities imply that the central bank should not take asset prices directly into account in monetary policymaking but should be anything but laissez-faire in responding to sharp movements in inflation and output, even if asset price swings are their source." His argument is sound, but he does point out that if bubbles get too large, the fallout can be even more disastrous than attempts to restrain them. This argues against his central point, and the Japanese example does show what can happen if bubbles are allowed to get too large. Ben Bernanke also wrote a paper titled Should Central Banks Respond to Movements in Asset Prices? (Bernanke & Gertler, Should Central Banks Respond to Movements in Asset Prices?, 2000). He professes a belief that the activities of the Central Bank should not target asset prices, although his behavior as FED chairman has been interpreted as an attempt to bolster market prices. In a later paper (Bernanke & Boivin, Monetary Policy in a Data-Rich Environment, 2002) Bernanke also explored the uses and aggregation of data by the Federal Reserve. He seemed to be preparing himself for the job of FED Chairman. The focus of policy debate and academic research in the wake of the Great Housing Bubble is likely to be the issue of asset bubbles in general. Central Banks around the world learned how to control inflation in the 1980s and 1990s, but their policies have tended to create excess liquidity which has resulted in financial bubbles.

[123] (Bernanke B. S., Japanese Monetary Policy: A Case of Self-Induced Paralysis, 1999)

[124] Adam Posen in his paper It Takes more than a Bubble to Become Japan (Posen A. S., 2003), outlines the causes of the prolonged recession after the bursting of the stock and real estate bubbles in Japan. He agrees with Ben Bernanke's conclusion that aggressive monetary easing is the solution to the problem, "Central bankers should learn from Japan's bubble the benefits of a more thoughtful approach to assessing potential growth and of easing rapidly in the face of asset price declines and not be concerned with targeting asset prices or pricking bubbles per se." In a related paper Passive Savers and Fiscal Policy Effectiveness in Japan (Kuttner & Posen, 2001) by Kenneth N. Kuttner; Adam S. Posen, the authors reaffirm their conclusions on the mistakes of the Japanese Central Bank in handling their asset bubbles. The authors note that despite excessive borrowing of the central government, Japanese citizens continue to by government debt at very low cost and in effect subsidize their own borrowing.

[125] In the paper Offshoring, Economic Insecurity, and the Demand for Social Insurance (Anderson & Gascon, 2008), Richard G. Anderson and Charles S. Gascon describe the problems associated with offshoring, in particular the increased demand of social services caused by the fear of offshoring.

[126] The inflation adjusted chart for the S&P/Case-Shiller index was drawn by the following method. The index value was then divided by the consumer price index date from the U.S. Department of Labor Bureau of Labor Statistics. The resulting number was converted to a baseline value of 1 so the data could be represented as a percentage change.

[127] One of the factors not included on the list of those that may negatively impact the housing market during the decline of the Great Housing Bubble was the potential problems created by the aging of baby boomers. In the study Aging Baby Boomers and the Generational Housing Bubble (Myers & Ryu, 2008), the authors explore the potential impacts of baby boomers selling their homes and downsizing from their McMansions. The impact of this group, though potentially significant, is very difficult to model and understand. There is no way to know what this generation will do and when they will do it. To speculate that this group would undergo a massive change in their habitation during the collapse of a major housing bubble does not seem plausible, although it is possible. It seems more likely that the baby boomers will not start retiring and potentially downsizing until the crash is past, and any changes in their housing situation will be spread out over many years rather than being concentrated in a short timeframe. The retirement of the baby boomers could serve to depress appreciation in those areas the baby boomers move out of, but it may also stimulate another construction boom in the areas they move in to.

[128] The Federal Reserve has very little control over long-term interest rates. In an unpublished paper from the University of Washington, the authors examined the correlation between the 10-year Treasury Note and long term mortgage rates. They found the correlation to be greater than 95%. However, when they checked for correlation between the Federal Funds Rate and long-term mortgage rates, the correlation dropped to 35%. The most recent example occurred when the Federal Funds Rate when from 2% in June 2004 to 6.25% in October 2006, and the contract mortgage rate barely budged moving from 6.29% to 6.36%.

[129] Karl Case and Robert Shiller concluded price declines could only come through an economic downturn (Case & Shiller, The Behavior of Home Buyers in Boom and Post-Boom Markets, 1988). This theory was disproven by the Great Housing Bubble. There has also been research suggesting that housing downturns are actually the cause of economic downturns (Leamer, Housing Is the Business Cycle, 2007).

[130] A paper by Edward Leamer (Leamer, Housing Is the Business Cycle, 2007) draws strong parallels between residential construction spending and the beginning and ending of economic recessions.

[131] The foreclosure chart was drawn by taking the notices of trustee sales and the notices of default and dividing these figures by the monthly sales rate. Since there is considerable variability in these numbers from month to month, the figures have been averaged to smooth out the noise in the data and reveal the underlying trends.

[132] In the paper Accounting for Changes in the Homeownership Rate (Chambers, Garriga, & Schlagenhauf, 2007), the authors concluded 56% to 70% of the increase in home ownership rates was due to "innovations" in the lending industry, in particular the lowering of downpayment requirements. Much of the remainder they attributed to demographic factors. The increase in home ownership among younger households was almost entirely driven by new financing terms, while changes among older households were much more to do with increasing income.

[133] One of the issues not discussed in this writing is the potential impact of generational shifts in housing. A model for generational changes presented in The Baby Boom: Predictability in House Prices and Interest Rates (Martin, 2005) resurrects the early theories of Mankiw and Weil (Mankiw & Weil, The Baby Boom, the Baby Bust and the Housing Market, 1989)in which they predicted the collapse of housing prices in Japan in 1990 and the ongoing disruption in their housing market caused by the decline in population from the Baby Boom demographic bubble. In their 1988 paper Mankiw and Weil famously and incorrectly predicted the same phenomenon would occur in the United States. Instead, the United States witnessed the Great Housing Bubble. It is the author's opinion that the differing impacts in the Japanese market and the United States market has far more to do with the degree of asset inflation and other macroeconomic impacts than it does with generational demographic factors. While it is certainly possible that the aging of baby boomers will have a negative impact on the United States housing market, it is not clear what impact baby boomers will have. It is assumed they will downsize their accommodations, but this may not be the case. Many may chose to retire and live out their lives in the houses where they lived pre-retirement. If this occurs there will be no mass selloff of homes depressing housing prices.

[134] In the paper Housing and the Business Cycle (Davis & Heathcote, 2003), the authors document the strong relationship between residential investment and the general economy. Residential investment is much more volatile than the swings in the general economy, but it moves in the same direction. In a later paper obviously drawing for this paper's title (Leamer, Housing Is the Business Cycle, 2007) the author goes a step further and postulates that the housing market is a driving force in the economy. Previously, conventional wisdom was that housing followed economic cycles and did not drive them. These findings are also bolstered by a report for the Federal Reserve Bank of San Francisco (Krainer, Residential Investment over the Real Estate Cycle, 2006). All the reports reach the same conclusion: residential investment is closely linked to the economic cycle. In another related study on the fallout of financial

bubbles, (Helbling, Conover, & Terrones, 2003) Chapter II: When Bubbles Burst. The authors note the financial drag caused by the decline in asset prices.

135 By mid-2008 lenders were so overwhelmed with foreclosures that many began bidding less than the loan amount in hopes auction bidders would limit their losses and they would not acquire even more residential real estate.

136 Homeowners who owe more on their mortgage than their house is worth in the resale market are by definition homedebtors. The fact that they cannot leave the place they live means they are effectively in prison.

137 Japan endured 15 years of slow deflation from the combined stock market and real estate bubbles of the late 1980s. The 1990s are known in Japan as "the lost decade" due to the problems from the slow deflation of their asset bubble.

138 In July of 2008, the Fed made changes to Reg Z which would have been helpful in reducing the size of the housing bubble, the amount of fraud during the bubble, and the resulting pain of the bust. Unfortunately, they were at least five years too late. The changes to Reg Z were: The rule, for "higher-priced loans: 1. Prohibits a lender from making a loan without regard to borrowers' ability to repay the loan from income and assets other than the home's value. A lender complies, in part, by assessing repayment ability based on the highest scheduled payment in the first seven years of the loan. To show that a lender violated this prohibition, a borrower does not need to demonstrate that it is part of a "pattern or practice. 2. Prohibits a lender from relying on income or assets that it does not verify to determine repayment ability. 3. Bans any prepayment penalty if the payment can change during the initial four years. For other higher-priced loans, a prepayment penalty period cannot last for more than two years. 4.Requires that the lender establish an escrow account for the payment of property taxes and homeowners' insurance for first-lien loans. The lender may offer the borrower the opportunity to cancel the escrow account after one year. The rule, for all closed-end mortgages secured by a consumer's principal dwelling: 1. Prohibits certain servicing practices: failing to credit a payment to a consumer's account as of the date the payment is received, failing to provide a payoff statement within a reasonable period of time, and "pyramiding" late fees. 2. Prohibits a creditor or broker from coercing or encouraging an appraiser to misrepresent the value of a home. 3. Creditors must provide a good faith estimate of the loan costs, including a schedule of payments, within three days after a consumer applies for any mortgage loan secured by a consumer's principal dwelling, such as a home improvement loan or a loan to refinance an existing loan. The rule, for all mortgages: Requires advertising to contain additional information about rates, monthly payments, and other loan features. The rule also bans seven deceptive or misleading advertising practices, including representing that a rate or payment is "fixed" when it can change. "

139 In their paper Predicting Bubbles and Bubble Substitutes (Thompson, Treussard, & Hickson, 2004), the authors contend that certain kinds of bubble intentionally created by government authorities can have positive long-term effects.

140 The subprime mortgage industry may mount a comeback in the aftermath of the Great Housing Bubble. The original business plan was to take borrowers who had good incomes and savings to put toward a downpayment, but they had low FICO scores which prevented them from getting a Prime loan. These borrowers used subprime as bridge financing until their FICO scores improved and they could refinance into Prime loans. The subprime business plan relied on capacity (income) and collateral (downpayment) to make up for the lack of good credit. Those who go through foreclosure in the bubble will end up with bad credit, but they may have good income and savings. They will be an underserved borrower class that will likely prompt resurgence in subprime lending. The problem with subprime was not that the borrowers had poor credit scores; it was that lenders ignored capacity and collateral on the loans. This is why Alt-A and Prime loans also performed poorly when prices deflated. Subprime will likely resurface, whereas Alt-A is permanently defunct.

141 Much of California's lingering economic troubles of the early 90s can be linked to diminished consumer spending due to excessive mortgage obligations. Many people inaccurately point to job losses in the aerospace industry as the cause of California's economic weakness, but this sector was small, and the contraction only lasted a couple of years, whereas the economic slump persisted almost 6 years.

142 This is the primary argument against any kind of legislative reform (Wallace, Elliehausen, & Staten, 2005).

143 When credit first began to tighten in 2007, the government sponsored entities who insure mortgage loans for sale in the secondary market issued a series of guidelines on the loans they would insure. In the first version, debt-to-income ratios were limited to 50%. In a subsequent revision in late 2007, the debt-to-income ratio was limited to 45%. The tightening of credit was slow enough to keep some transactions

occurring in the market, but fast enough to stop underwriters from originating bad loans. As of the time of this writing it is anticipated that the ratio will continue to fall.

[144] In his groundbreaking work The Black Swan: The Impact of the Highly Improbable (Taleb, 2007), the author describes how unpredictable and dramatic events shape our history.

[145] There is a great synopsis of the history and calculation of the rental components of the consumer price index contained in the report Treatment of Owner-Occupied Housing in the CPI (Poole, Ptacek, & Verbrugge, 2005).

[146] In 2008 the National Association of Realtors launched a commercial advertising campaign claiming that residential real estate doubles in value every 10 years. Besides the obvious inaccuracy of the claim, it is the kind of claim no stockbroker would be allowed to make.

19548430R00133

Made in the USA
Lexington, KY
23 December 2012